JOURNAL FOR THE STUDY OF THE OLD TESTAMENT SUPPLEMENT SERIES
374

Sheffield Academic Press
A Continuum imprint

JOURNAL FOR THE STUDY OF THE OLD TESTAMENT
SUPPLEMENT SERIES

374

Editors
David J.A. Clines
Philip R. Davies

Executive Editor
Andrew Mein

Editorial Board
Richard J. Coggins, Alan Cooper, J. Cheryl Exum, John Goldingay,
Robert P. Gordon, Norman K. Gottwald, John Jarick,
Andrew D.H. Mayes, Carol Meyers, Patrick D. Miller

Sheffield Academic Press
A Continuum imprint

Feminist Interpretation of the Bible and the Hermeneutics of Liberation

edited by

Silvia Schroer &
Sophia Bietenhard

Journal for the Study of the Old Testament
Supplement Series 374

Copyright © 2003 Sheffield Academic Press
A Continuum imprint

Published by Sheffield Academic Press Ltd
The Tower Building, 11 York Road, London SE1 7NX
15 East 26th Street, Suite 1703, New York, NY 10010

www.continuumbooks.com

British Library Cataloguing-in-Publication Data
A catalogue record for this book is available from the British Library

Typeset by Sheffield Academic Press
Printed on acid-free paper in Great Britain by Bookcraft Ltd, Midsomer Norton, Bath

ISBN 0-8264-6689-3 (hardback)
ISBN 0-5670-8372-1 (paperback)

In memory of
Choon-Ho You-Martin
(†20 March 2002)

CONTENTS

FOREWORD

The Prehistory of the International Symposium
in Ticino, Switzerland, 2-7 July 2000

The idea of organizing an international conference about 'feminist exegesis and the hermeneutics of liberation' grew from many years of contact between Swiss women theologians and Elisabeth Schüssler Fiorenza, New Testament scholar and Harvard Professor. Schüssler Fiorenza's work in the field of feminist exegesis and hermeneutics has earned worldwide recognition since the 1980s, becoming a standard reference not only in the feminist academic world but also for all movements that participate in the 'ecclesia of women'. The symposium was conceived on this basis in order to make possible direct, personal communication between women biblical scholars from throughout the world possible. The discussions were to have centered around the question of the liberative nature (for women) of feminist hermeneutics and exegesis. The speakers were given the task of explaining and elucidating their hermeneutic approach to the Bible and illustrating it utilizing a biblical text. They were requested to take a critical position with regard to concepts such as 'woman', 'gender', 'feminist' and 'liberation' and to consider to what extent, for whom and in what sense their feminist hermeneutics is liberative.

The symposium took place at the historical Monte Verità center above Ascona in Ticino, the southern-most canton in Switzerland. Fourty-two women from 20 different countries from all five continents came. In addition to Christians from all the major denominations, two Jewish scholars also participated. This was the first opportunity for such a diverse international group of feminist biblical scholars to work together intensely over the course of several days. And it was the aim of the Swiss hosts to do everything within their power to make this event possible. They arranged the financing of the travel and lodging expenses for the majority of the participants. Without intensive fundraising and the financial support of numerous non-university organizations the conference would not have taken place or would have developed merely into a neo-colonial event that reflected current international structures of power and wealth.

At Monte Verità near Ascona

Switzerland is not traditionally well known as a home to feminist exegesis, but our country's longstanding tradition of democracy, plurality, ecumenism and its multi-lingual constitution have created a natural atmosphere for international encounters. The European Society of Women in Theological Research (ESWTR) was founded in Ticino in 1986 for this reason. And it was the Swiss section within this organization that took the lead in promoting international contact, working with Greek women theologians to prepare an international conference in Crete in 1999. And as hosts to the symposium in Ascona it was particularly important to the organizers that women from all contexts would have the opportunity not only to participate in the discussions planned but also alternately to have the opportunity to lead the discussions.

The fact that this 'synagogue' or 'ecclesia' of women met at Monte Verità, the 'mountain of truth', is not without a touch of humor or irony. But mention of the history of this village is also important. The region around Locarno has been a haven for outcasts and intellectuals from across Europe since about 1870. Ascona and Monte Verità became the center of a utopian society based on visions of early Christian communism, of freedom and common ownership of property. Ascona and Monte Verità gave birth to revolutionary ideas about health, nature, love and psychology. Women played key roles in this community throughout its history— famous, special women. It is perhaps also symbolic that the four founders of Monte Verità, one of whom was pianist and feminist Ida Hofmann, left Monte Verità for Brazil via Spain in 1920.

In Retrospect

The multi-cultural diversity of the participants made the symposium a very colorful event in every aspect from the beginning. In addition to the main presentation of the day and various workshops in smaller groups, the tone and direction of the conference were determined to great extent by the extremely lively, at times even heated plenary discussions. The contents of these discussions were both scholarly and down-to-earth, and their open, collective spirit corresponded more to international religious gatherings than typically Western academic congresses.

The symposium did not provide any answers at its conclusion; rather, it formulated more precise questions, numerous observations and new challenges. The contributions to this publication revolve around these themes and questions; the various aspects presented here offer a sort of profile of the symposium and hint at its significance for the 42 participants. The goal of this publication is to present something of this immense spectrum to academic audiences as well as to provide impulses for continued work with regard to the questions of the hermeneutics of liberation and feminist exegesis.

The participants (organizers, interpreters and speakers included) at the conference were:

Elżbieta Adamiak, Poznan, Poland
Margit Balog, Debrecen, Hungary
Stella Baltazar, Sathyamangalam, Erode Dt, India
Sophia Bietenhard, Zurich, Switzerland
Nancy Cardoso Pereira, São Paulo, Brazil
Pauline Chakkalakal, Richmond Town, Bangalore, India
Musa W. Dube, Botswana
Irene Foulkes, San José, Costa Rica
Elisabeta Geréb, Cluj-Napoca, Romania
Éva Geröfi, Budapest, Hungary
Regula Grünenfelder, Luzerne, Switzerland
Tal Ilan, Jerusalem, Israel
Christine Janowski, Tübingen, Germany
Eleni Kasselouri, Thessaloniki, Greece
Esther Kobel, Reinach, Switzerland
Kyung-Sook Lee, Seoul, Korea
Christl Maier, Berlin, Germany
Elisabeth Miescher, Riehen, Switzerland
Verena Mühletaler, Berne, Switzerland
Julia Müller-Clemm, Berne, Switzerland
Ruth Muthei, Nairobi, Kenya
Edit Nagy, Budapest, Hungary
Minda Peranginangin-Tampubolon, Medan, Indonesia
Anna Britta Perkins, Wellesley MA, USA
Sarolta Püsök, Cluj-Napoca, Romania
Viola Raheb, Bethlehem, Palestine
Adele Reinhartz, Hamilton, Canada
Franziska Schär, Basel, Switzerland
Silvia Schroer, Berne, Switzerland
Susanne Schüepp, Luzerne, Switzerland
Elisabeth Schüssler Fiorenza, Cambridge MA, USA
Irène Schwyn, Berne, Switzerland

Regula Strobel, Fribourg, Switzerland
Marianne Strub, Basel, Switzerland
Yak-Hwee Tan, Singapore
Marie-Theres Wacker, Münster, Germany
Elaine Wainwright, Banyo, Australia
Heike Walz, Basel, Switzerland
Renita J. Weems, Nashville TN, USA
Marguerite Wieser, Geneva, Switzerland
Choon-Ho You-Martin, Korea and Munich, Germany
Edith Zingg, Luzerne, Switzerland

About the Selection and Organization of the Contributions

The editors were guided primarily by three principles with regard to the selection and organization of the contributions in this publication. First, we wanted to make the revised versions of the main speakers' presentations available for further contemplation and discussion. Second, the lively discussions in the plenary session that followed these presentations are represented here in two forms: a thematically organized series of highlights in the middle of the book offer insight into the main points of these oral discussions; narrative texts supplement the academic presentations and reflect the diversity of the international discussions about the Bible. Third, the international character of these discussions are reflected in eight contributions, post-symposium reflections more precisely, that have not been organized thematically but in correspondence with the geographical regions represented by the main speakers: North and South America, Africa, Western and Eastern Europe, the Near East and Asia. We thereby hope to avoid lending the inter-contextual discussions any sort of thematic hierarchy or any hint of judgment with regard to their content; at the same time we thereby would like to point out that many questions proved to be relevant throughout the spectrum of geographical and cultural contexts. Unfortunately, a contribution from a Greek-Orthodox perspective is wanting. And we also were forced to do without a contribution from Elisabeth Schüssler Fiorenza, whose writings and whose presence at the symposium often find echo in the contributions to this publication.[1] We are especially grateful for her participation.

---

1.   For E. Schüssler Fiorenza's work, cf. the references to her publications in Silvia Schroer's contribution ' "We Will Know Each Other by Our Fruits": Feminist Exegesis and the Hermeneutics of Liberation' in this book.

Thanks

As is customary in such undertakings, the pleasant task of expressing thanks remains for the end. Professor Philip Davies, the publisher of Sheffield Academic Press, reacted spontaneously and openly to our idea of publishing this book in the Anglo-American realm. Just as the symposium was made possible by the financial support of numerous organizations, this publication likewise has been subsidized substantially by contributions from: the Swiss Federal Institute of Technology Zurich; the Swiss Academy of Humanities and Social Sciences; the Emil Brunner Foundation Zurich; the Synod Council of the Protestant Church Bern-Jura; the Catholic Interaid Organization Fastenopfer Lucerne; the Bethlehem Mission of Immensee; the Foundation for Women's Projects, the Protestant Women's Federation of Switzerland. Mark Manion and Daniel Dubach were responsible for the competent English translations and editing, and Duncan Burns guided the manuscript through production. Dorothee Bertschmann, Irène Schwyn, Julia Müller-Clemm, Jürg Baumgartner, Moisés Mayordomo and Henriette Guthauser assisted us with such very necessary and tedious work as the transcription of the symposium tapes, proofreading, computer assistance and additional translations. We thank all of these persons and organizations for helping to make this publication about feminist exegesis and the hermeneutics of liberation available to a broad international audience for discussion. We are sorry for the delay in publication, caused on the one hand by the enormous difficulties of trying to create a formally homogenous book from the heterogeneity of academic standards, theological thinking and different priorities of feminist scholars concerning living, fighting and writing, and on the other hand by the difficulties of trying to convince academic institutions to finance such an unusual book.

Silvia Schroer, Sophia Bietenhard
Berne, May 2003

Elżbieta Adamiak (*1964)
Elżbieta Adamiak studied theology in Lublin (Poland), Regensburg (Germany) and Nijmegen (Holland). She earned her doctorate with a dissertation on the image of Mary in the feminist theology of C. Halkes. She is an assistant in the Department for Fundamental Theology and Dogma at Adam Mickiewicz University in Poznan (Poland). She has been a committee member of the European Society of Women in Theological Research since 1999.

Stella Baltazar (*1952)
Stella Baltazar is a sister of the Franciscan Missionaries of Mary. She earned Masters degrees in Christianity and in Sociology from the University of Mysore, India. She is currently a consultant/resource person for Caritas Switzerland, monitoring their projects in India. She also is an EATWOT (Ecumenical Association of Third World Theologians) National Coordinator. Stella Baltazar is involved in organizing women at the grassroots level, training animators for the empowerment of marginalized women and evolving a feminist spirituality and theology in the Indian context.

Sophia Bietenhard (*1960)
Sophia Bietenhard was born in Switzerland. She completed studies as a pedagogue and as a Protestant theologian/pastor. She earned her doctorate with a dissertation on the figure of Joab in 2 Samuel and has worked on various publications on feminist exegesis and Old Testament hermeneutics. Sophia Bietenhard works as a pedagogue and in adult education.

Nancy Cardoso Pereira (*1959)
Nancy Cardoso Pereira is a Methodist pastor. She has been working with the aged and with reflection groups on topics such as the Bible, the women's movement and the land reform movement in Brazil. Presently

she is working at the Pastoral Land Commission and teaching philosophy and anthropology at Castelo University in São Paulo. Her research interests are in the prophecies of Elijah and, above all, folk religion in the Hebrew Bible. She also writes poetry and is the co-editor of the feminist theological journal *Mandroga*.

Musa W. Dube (*1964)

Musa W. Dube was born and lives in Botswana. She is a lecturer at the University of Botswana, teaching New Testament studies. She has authored several publications on postcolonial feminist biblical interpretation, including *Postcolonial Feminist Interpretation of the Bible* (2000).

Tal Ilan (*1956)

Tal Ilan was born in Kibbutz Lahav in Israel. She attended schools in Israel and England and served in the Israeli Defense Forces from 1975 to 1977. She then studied at Hebrew University in Jerusalem from 1978 to 1990, writing her dissertation on Jewish women in the Greco-Roman period. She is a freelance scholar, teaching at academic institutions in the United States, Europe and Israel. She lives in Jerusalem.

Kyung-Sook Lee (*1948)

Kyung-Sook Lee studied at Ewha Women's University in Seoul, Korea, and completed her doctoral studies at Göttingen University in Germany. From 1981 to 1988 she taught at Mokwon University in Daejon, Korea, and has taught at Ewha Women's University in Seoul since 1989. Her research interests are in Old Testament studies and feminist theology.

Philomena Njeri Mwaura (*1957)

Philomena Njeri Mwaura is a lecturer in the Department of Religious Studies at Kenyatta University in Kenya, where she recently completed her doctoral studies.

Viola Raheb (*1969)

Viola Raheb was born in Bethlehem. She studied educational science and Protestant theology in Heidelberg. From 1998 until 2002 she was a school inspector for the Protestant Lutheran Schools in Jordan and Palestine. She is an active member of various national and international human rights groups and regularly lectures about Palestine throughout Europe and the United States.

*Adele Reinhartz (*1953)*
Adele Reinhartz is Professor in the Department of Religious Studies at McMaster University in Hamilton, Ontario, Canada. She teaches in the area of first-century Judaism and Christianity and has worked extensively on the Gospel of John, feminist criticism, biblical narrative and, most recently, the interconnections between the Bible and film.

*Silvia Schroer (*1958)*
Silvia Schroer studied Catholic Theology and Classical Philology in Münster and Munich (Germany) and in Fribourg (Switzerland). She earned her doctorate for research on Old Testament reports about the visual arts in Ancient Israel and earned a position as the first woman lecturer in the Theology Department in Fribourg with her postdoctoral thesis. She is Professor of Old Testament and Related Studies in the Protestant Theology Department at the University of Berne. For a number of years she has applied her research interest in ancient oriental iconography to the service of feminist exegesis.

*Yak-Hwee Tan (*1954)*
Yak-Hwee Tan is an ordained minister with the Presbyterian Church in Singapore. She completed her Masters studies at the Austin Presbyterian Theological Seminary in Texas and at the Union Theological Seminary in Virginia. She is a PhD candidate in religion, major in New Testament Studies, at Vanderbilt University in Tennessee. Her research is on the representation of the Johannine community from a postcolonial perspective.

*Marie-Theres Wacker (*1952)*
Marie-Theres Wacker is Professor of Old Testament and Women's Research at the Catholic Faculty of Münster University in Germany. She is the author of several books on feminist exegesis and, together with Luise Schottroff, co-editor of a feminist Bible commentary, *Kompendium Feministische Bibelauslegung* (1999, American translation in preparation). Her research interests are in feminist-exegetical methods and hermeneutics, the debate on biblical monotheism, Hellenistic Judaism and prophecy.

*Heike Walz (*1966)*
Heike Walz was born in Germany. She studied theology and diaconal sciences in Heidelberg (Germany), Montpellier (France) and Tübingen (Germany), and did pastoral training at the Protestant Church of the

Palatinate in Germany, ecumenical training at the Presbyterian Church of Ghana, assistantship at the Presbyterian Women's Center Abokobi and pastoral ministry in Bad Dürkheim in Germany. Heike Walz is a teaching assistant for mission studies and ecumenism in the Theology Department of the University of Basel, working on her doctoral project 'New Ways of Being Church—Feminist Intercultural Ecclesiology'.

Renita J. Weems (*1954)
Renita J. Weems is Associate Professor of Hebrew Bible at Vanderbilt University in Nashville, Tennessee. She obtained her Masters and PhD degrees from Princeton Theological Seminary in Princeton, New Jersey, and has published, among others, a commentary to the Song of Songs and a study of the marriage metaphors in prophetic literature. Her research interests are in prophetic literature, hermeneutics, biblical theology and feminist/womanist theory. Her teaching duties at Vanderbilt University include a special studies program on 'Black Churches'. Renita J. Weems is also an ordained minister, author of books on women's spirituality and wholeness and a widely acclaimed public speaker.

[Asterisked dates indicate birth year]

Silvia Schroer

Elisabeth Schüssler Fiorenza's pioneering book *In Memory of Her* was published in 1983. It represented the first rigorous hermeneutic approach to feministic exegesis. This hermeneutic approach with a specific feminist character took a position, on the one hand, against the Church's traditional treatment of the biblical texts and, on the other hand, against the premises of traditional biblical scholarship. It explicitly employed historical-critical methodology and was clearly rooted in liberation theology.

In the following years Elisabeth Schüssler Fiorenza developed and refined her feminist critical hermeneutics in diverse publications[1] while women around the world began to work with the biblical texts on the basis of her books, at times even in contradiction of her theories, but in any case stimulated by them. In German-speaking regions feminist exegesis became a vibrant and productive branch of theology.[2] It soon became evident, however, that feminist exegesis had not developed its own methodology but had simply adopted all of the existing methodological tools available, using them in conjunction with a specific feminist aim. It also became clear that feminist exegesis did not bring hidden truths to light on the basis of the biblical texts, that is, it did not launch a new reformation but actually had an ambivalent relationship to the Bible.

The symposium at Monte Verità provided, among other things, an opportunity to re-examine the hermeneutics of liberation in feminist exegesis 17 years after the initial publication of *In Memory of Her*. What assumptions do we make when reading and interpreting biblical texts? What roles do

---

1.   Schüssler Fiorenza 1992, 1998 and 1999. The international dialogue about feminist biblical hermeneutics is documented in Schüssler Fiorenza (ed.) 1993.

2.   Schottroff, Schroer and Wacker 1998; cf. also the comprehensive *Kompendium Feministische Bibelauslegung*, edited by Schottroff and Wacker (1998).

categorical concepts such as woman, gender, feminism and liberation play in the process? We organizers placed the emphasis on the question of liberation in order to open the forum to women from all parts of the world, especially given the fact that the post-modern feminist-exegetic discussion that has developed over the past years has involved the participation of women primarily from Northern and Western Europe and the United States.

The participants did not have any clear answers to the questions posed or even a common agenda to take home with them at the end of the sym- posium, but the intensive discussions and dialogues that characterized the conference and that can only be hinted at in this publication shed light on many issues and provided further direction. I would like to focus on some of these topics, those that I think are significant for the future, without making claim to completeness or comprehensiveness.

An important foundation for this discussion was laid by Elisabeth Schüssler Fiorenza at the beginning of the conference. She questioned the adequacy of the concept of 'gender' for feminist hermeneutics. Although 'gender' names an important factor that shapes our perception of the world and real relationships, this factor never appears alone but always in combi- nation with other factors such as membership in a class or group, in a religious community, and so on. This concept is too simplistic to be an analytical key and thus dangerous when employed alone. Even feminist sociologists have come to recognize its deficiencies and now employ it with much more restraint than some years ago, if at all.[3] Schüssler Fio- renza, who employed the term 'patriarchy' as an analytical category in earlier publications in order to describe different forms of domination in a culture, has changed her terminology for similar reasons and now speaks of 'kyriarchy'.[4]

According to Schüssler Fiorenza, feminism is the radical notion that women are people, that is, full citizens. Feminism strives to expose veiled and open discrimination of women within the kyriarchal pyramid as well as in the intrinsic ideologies that sustain it, and fights for the recognition of the complete rights of half of humanity.

---

3.   Cf., in this regard, Scott 2001 and Opitz 2001.

4.   The preparation of the conference was particularly served by reading Schüssler Fiorenza 1992: 19-50; 1998: 75-104; 1999: 1-14, 31-55.

We Are and Are Not Speaking the Same Language

A responsible treatment of biblical tradition by women cannot be globalized; it cannot be uniformly defined worldwide; it can, however, be discussed globally. Every 'context' involves a different 'history with the Bible' that has shaped this context and that has influenced and will continue to influence the treatment of biblical texts. A North American African American woman reads the Bible with the knowledge that her ancestors found strength and courage in the Bible during the time of slavery. A Christian Indian reads biblical texts in a culture that has not been primarily shaped by Christianity; she reads the Bible as one sacred book among others and thus remains in a continual inter-religious dialogue. A Hungarian or a Romanian woman reads the Bible with the knowledge that smuggling the Bible into her country during the communist dictatorship was just as dangerous as smuggling weapons, and that the precious books were confiscated and shredded in order to extinguish the people's religious roots. A Brazilian woman reads the Bible after 20 years of liberation theology and grass-roots work in the unending battle for the fundamental rights of her people. A secular Jewish woman reads the Bible as a historian with the knowledge that modern Israel would not exist without this religious book. A Christian Palestinian is torn between the liberating message of the biblical texts and the oppression and violence that the Bible and its interpretation set free in the Holy Land, especially for her people. A Swiss woman is confronted in reading the Bible with the legacy of the Reformation and with dialectical theology. The examples are endless; the spectrum in Europe alone is immense.

Listening to Each Other—Obeying Each Other

The need for a 'contextual' hermeneutics of the Bible stands juxtaposed with the call to keep the feminist theological discussion about biblical exegesis alive as a worldwide discussion. Without such a discussion it is not possible to recognize the real differences that exist in a pluralistic environment. Talk of pluralism and contextuality, however, can also veil inequalities; it can conceal indifference or randomness. When feminist exegetes from the United States or Western Europe plead for a 'contextual' hermeneutics of the Bible, then they are also obliged, for example, to critically examine their own role in a discussion marked by inequality and discrepancies of power as well as to examine their theology for a biased orientation toward the Occident.[5]

'Contextual', however, may not signify 'inviolable'. Together we are certainly able to shed light on questions such as whether our respective exegeses fulfill the requirements to be described as liberative for women or what liberation for women in specific contexts concretely signifies. Social, political and religious liberation can play various roles in the words and acts of resistance, in the consciousness of a people, in laws and institutions, in language and in behavior. It is often simpler to find agreement with regard to when the exegesis of a text contributes to the oppression of women, compelling them to silence. We can agree on the usefulness of or the danger involved in concepts such as 'sex', 'gender', 'patriarchy' or 'kyriarchy'.

The worldwide discussion among women, which Schüssler Fiorenza describes in a political and not religious sense as the 'ecclesia' of women, does not serve to create a universally valid approach but in the first place to warn one another about traps and blind alleys. I would like to describe the function of this discussion with an antiquated word that might set alarm bells ringing in the ears of some women. It is important that we listen to each other and obey each other and thus prove ourselves as 'God's daughters', as the coequal daughters of the goddess Sophia (Wisdom), who is vindicated by all of her children.[6] The practice of sisterly obedience signifies: being prepared to be deeply touched and changed by the experiences, views and admonitions of another woman.

A positive example of this from recent years is the controversy about anti-Judaism in feminist biblical interpretations. The heated debate that was set off by the legitimate objections of Jewish women led to a very constructive learning process among Christian women exegetes and set new standards for feminist exegesis.[7] As for the racist, colonial implications of our readings of the Bible, such a learning process has yet fully to take place, at least in Western Europe. One's own perspective can alert to many dangers while making blind to others, so that the exchange in the worldwide 'synagogue' or the 'ecclesia' of women can lead to substantial gains in exegetic, hermeneutic areas of work. For example, with regard to the example of anti-Judaism, it is certainly responsible for women from

---

5.   With regard to the consequences in Bible studies, cf. Schroer 1999a.

6.   With regard to the significance of the children of Wisdom in Mt. 11.16-19, cf. Staubli 2001.

7.   Cf. Schottroff and Wacker (ed.) 1996 and Schroer 1999b.

North America or Western Europe to point out this issue to Christian women from other contexts, for example, Latin America or Greece. It is quite apparent that the Greek-Orthodox tradition has remained very anti-Judaic until this day. But a true dialogue with feminist Orthodox theologians can only take place if the issue of anti-Judaism is not employed in a know-it-all manner against these women or their tradition. We would be much better served to focus on our participation in the dialogue and to ask questions instead of knowing better!

The Main Problem: Hegemony

During the symposium the hegemonic claims of Western feminist exegetes was a frequent topic of discussion. Exegetes from countries outside of the Western Hemisphere complained that given their unique experiences and concepts they did not want to be forced into existing frameworks, for example, that of critical feminist hermeneutics. For similar reasons during the 1990s, Black women's groups employed the term 'womanist' and Hispano-American women's groups the term 'mujerista' in order to differentiate themselves from the white women's 'feminist' movement. Inclusivity can be the guise for any form of domination and oppression. The worldwide discussion among feminist exegetes has been shaped by neo-colonial power structures, favoring those, for example, who have had the opportunity to receive a university education, to do research and to publish (above all, in English). Others who have not enjoyed these opportunities are condemned should they want to participate in the discussion, to react, to respond to something that is not their own, to something that has been determined by others. Of course, they are free to accept, to reject, to modify, but they can never be the first to define the system and the guidelines, they can never lead the discussion. Even in the field of theology the global market is not built upon fair play. And a solution to this profound problem is not in sight. Feminist studies and academics still are bound too closely with the unjust structures of the patriarchal world.

Not Without Enlightenment?

The issue of hegemony became particularly (but not exclusively) evident with regard to the question of whether the principles of the Enlightenment that are so fundamental for exegesis and theology in the Occident can be prescribed *tale quale* to other cultures, in particular, to non-Western feminist exegesis or theology. True, everyone agreed that gender analysis or the historical-critical analysis of biblical texts has encouraged liberation on the whole. But they have also entailed a promulgation of cultural oppression to this day. The textual analysis and the systemization of experiences is something very foreign, for example, to the culture of biblical exegetes from Brazil.

The 'ecclesia' of women may not become a congress whose goal is to provide foreign aid in the form of Western standards of feminist exegesis, nor may it exclude women who, for example, are not familiar with or do not utilize the principles of historical-critical exegesis. But how can we learn to discover liberating, constructive strength from the unfamiliar, for instance, from a feminist exegete whose approach to the biblical stories of miracles is not at all historical-critical? Am I forced as a Western exegete to choose between imposing my principles on others or abandoning the dialogue? Or do I dare perhaps even to learn something relevant from the encounter?

A broad consensus was reached that the historical-critical approach to biblical texts by feminist theologians can be described as liberative insofar that they can provide emancipation from the problematical (patriarchal) glorification of the authority of the biblical texts. We should not forget that the existence of this aspect of emancipation is due in great part to the Jewish philosopher Baruch Spinoza. In a similar manner, other systems of approach such as Jewish biblical interpretation or the interpretation of biblical texts through stories or painting can provide significant liberative impulses even if they are not familiar with or do not employ historical-critical methods.

The question as to how Western women should deal with the heritage of the Enlightenment and its critical position toward religion was hardly touched upon at the symposium. It is time to stop depicting the principles of the Enlightenment as anti-religious and become enlightened about religion, in the same manner as the sexual emancipation of the 1960s. In contemporary Switzerland, for example, it is no longer a taboo to speak about sex in public. We are enlightened. But most Swiss are very embarrassed to speak about religious experiences and beliefs; they do not even have the vocabulary to express such thoughts. Although their knowledge about sex is up to date, their knowledge about religion is prehistoric. Many Western women, feminist theologians included, not only lack religious praxis but also have only the slightest hint (and this from books or second-hand sources) about what religious functions and forms are. This gradual loss or concealment of religion has been spread throughout the world (without explicit declaration) in the form of feminist literature, as the white lady's neocolonial export item. And it is highly doubtful whether this serves the liberation of (all) women. The enlightened, critical approach of 'feminist studies in religion' which utilizes all the scholarly tools available in the areas of history, literature, sociology, psychology, and so on, is indispensable to feminist theology. But feminist theology also must provide orientation for the 'synagogue' or the 'ecclesia' of women, should it serve the living community. Nothing more or less is necessary than complete 'honesty and openness' in the 'global village'. The real question is whether women theologians can find ways and means to utilize the heritage of the Enlightenment for the liberation of religion and spirituality without in the process replicating existing North–South or East–West hierarchical structures of the ruling patriarchal systems.

The Value of Historical Research

'Our heritage is our power' (Judy Chicago) was one of the key mottos of feminist exegesis during the 1980s. The reconstruction of the history of women Christians or of the YHWH followers was understood as going 'back to the roots'. The skepticism with regard to the possibility of coaxing what really happened out of the sources has since grown much greater. Women who adopt historical methods for their research of the past are quickly suspected of scientific positivism. This development has been brought about in part by the fact that for years many biblical scholars have no longer worked with the text itself but expressly only with the events that take place between the text and its readers, that is, they have reduced themselves to the analysis and interpretation of the process of reception itself. Feminist exegetes may not, however, forgo examination of biblical texts for patriarchal-ideological elements and androcentric constructions; their historical work can provide correctives. In my own work I have frequently employed contemporary images of Palestine/Israel as correctives and as 'external evidence' with regard to reconstructing women's lives and the historical development of religion in ancient Israel.[8] Of course, images can also be a vehicle for (possibly androcentric) ideologies; they have to be received and interpreted. Naturally, a reconstruction that is

8.   Cf. my articles in Schottroff, Schroer and Wacker 1998, as well as in Schroer 1994, 1996, 1997 and 1998. With regard to the feminist discussion about Israel's religious history and the theology of the First Testament, cf. also Wacker 1995.

critical of the biblical texts, for example, the worship of goddesses, is nothing more than a reconstruction. There are nevertheless more or less plausible, conclusive or reliable reconstructions. There is both good and bad historical work and criteria exist to make a differentiation. The complete historical picture is never 'objective', but if it is to be credible it must incorporate as many of the pieces of the puzzle as possible, not just a few.[9]

Sacred or Not Sacred?

There were diverging opinions with regard to the question of whether and to what degree the Bible is a 'sacred scripture' for women.[10] As the contribution by Tal Ilan in this publication demonstrates, it is possible, permissible, in some cases liberative and aesthetic to read the biblical texts like any other literary work from a particular language region or epoch or to employ them as a source of historical information. In this case the areas focused on can overlap with those of the exegetes. It should be remembered, however, that the biblical writings, in contrast to Shakespeare, have only been preserved because they were considered something special or even sacred by religious communities. The possibility of a secular approach to the biblical texts exists due to the religious significance of the texts. The growing discrepancy between the world of the biblical texts and the highly technical world of Western societies, especially in connection with the irreversible process of secularization in many European countries, will make it increasingly necessary to refer to and preserve the biblical texts as part of the Occident's cultural heritage. Since even theology students often have only a minimum knowledge of religion, this means that feminist exegetes also will increasingly have to work against growing religious illiteracy. Knowledge of the Bible is one of the indisputably necessary elements of our feminist critical approach.

The 'Word of God' and 'Holy Scripture' are terms that hint at the extraordinary significance of the biblical texts for Jews and Christians. At the symposium we heard how people in Brazil or in African countries take the sacredness of these writings so seriously that they believe the book itself to have protective or magical powers, leading them, for example, to place the Bible in the foundation of a new house, to eat pages from the Bible, to cleanse themselves with water that contains pulverized pages from the Bible, and so in. Feminist exegetes who are closely bound to a religious

9. Cf. also Schroer and Staubli 2000.
10. With regard to this topic, cf. also Pui-Lan and Schüssler Fiorenza (eds.) 1998.

community, who thus approach the Bible from 'within' and not from the 'exterior', are ready in different degrees to accept the special authority of the biblical texts. As the majority agrees, this authority cannot be imposed but must be earned.

The biblical texts can thus represent the 'Word of God' and 'Holy Scripture' only as determined by women themselves. The normative nature of the writings can only be established in a community of God's daughters based on mutual obedience. Catholic theologians have the advantage with respect to the question of the authority of the texts that their tradition does not limit revelation solely to the Bible and thus have more leeway for defining their concept of the 'Word of God'. For Catholic liberation theologians, for example, the Word of God is life in the first place and not a collection of writings. Moreover, not all biblical texts make claim to be the Word of God, and many that make this claim contradict others that are also in the name of God but with opposing views.

Christian women from Eastern Europe in particular have shown reticence with regard to these questions. The Bible as a whole has been such an important symbol of support and liberation in their history that they are very concerned as to how far the deconstruction and criticism of this book, a book that has offered such great resistance to the inhuman dictatorships in their countries, will continue.[11]

Sola scriptura *or Perhaps also Through Story and Visual Images?*

Various articles in this publication plead for a greater narrative treatment of the biblical tradition. The mainstay of exegetic research comes from written cultures while the biblical writings themselves should be located for the most part much closer to 'oral cultures'. What role does feminist exegesis play in contemporary 'oral cultures'? Narrative traditions are still very much alive in many of the contexts mentioned. The confrontation of biblical stories with other biblical stories as well as with stories native to specific cultures can set much in motion hermeneutically, especially with regard to the images and identity of women.

The study of visual images is likewise significant for feminist exegesis. For centuries biblical stories, depictions of God and central questions of belief have been passed on from generation to generation through visual images. Eli-Jah, for example, an artist, healer and priestess from Kingston, Jamaica, brings the biblical stories alive by painting and interpreting them

---

11. Cf. the article by Elżbieta Adamiak in this publication.

as colorful tales on fabric.[12] She has been influenced, on the one hand, by the images in old catechisms and, on the other hand, by the Rastafari culture, its central symbols, the symbolism of its colors and its messianic expectations. She identifies herself with the prophet Elijah or Queen Esther, and Christ appears to her in the image of the majestic, messianic elephant. This kind of treatment of the Bible is filled with a free and autonomous power.

Many Orthodox Christian women are familiar with the stories and characters in the Bible through icons. Visual images are more primary and powerful than texts in this religious tradition. Similarly, for broad circles of our religiously de-socialized Western societies the biblical tradition is more strongly present in visual images than in text (e.g. in art, advertising, film, etc.).

The biblical texts themselves were greatly influenced by contemporary traditions and experiences of visual images. The beliefs of the ancient Israelites and the early followers of Jesus were not only fed with auditory but above all with visual experiences.[13]

The visual character and tradition of religion has been given surprisingly little attention in feminist exegesis, even though it offers the chance for emancipation from androcentric systems based on texts and their canonization as well as from a theological system of interpretation that is based exclusively on word and text. Until now feminist studies of the Bible have been as equally fixated on the text as mainstream exegesis, that is, they have not yet emancipated themselves in this respect from the traditional domination of dialectical, word-oriented, Protestant theology. The elevation of word and text to an absolute status has continued in postmodern exegesis. Renita Weems rightly has pointed out that texts in themselves cannot liberate or oppress, but that it is people who employ texts in one way or the other. A text as such is not a real world. Given this background it is time to open the canon of biblical texts not only to non-canonical texts but also to visual images and women's stories that are derived from images.

The (heated) debate during the symposium about Pasolini's filming of *The Gospel According to Matthew* (*Il Vangelo Secondo Matteo*, Pier Paulo Pasolini, Italy/France 1964), made it clear to the participants that feminist exegetes should not stop merely at the analysis of films made by men but should also honestly ask themselves what their alternatives to more or less

12. Cf. Hufenus and Staubli 1993; Schader and Schader 1997; Morris 1997: 28, 37.
13. Cf. the work of Othmar Keel and his co-workers (overview in Keel 1992); publications that have appeared in English include Keel and Uehlinger 1998.

'Prosperity' by Eli-Jah; © Eira Schader, Zurich. Acrylic on cloth. A white elephant ('elephant power of victory'), a lion ('Elijah conquering lion') and a dove ('Elijah dove') represent a kind of trinity on its way to the Promised Land and to prosperity. The messianic elephant wears the inscription 'INRI' on its forehead.

'Elijah' by Eli-Jah; © Eira Schader, Zurich. Acrylic on cloth. The prophet Elijah in depression beneath the broom (1 Kgs 19.5-7) and rising up again. Note the wings of the biblical prophet with whom Eli-Jah, the artist, identifies.

'Kandanos'; © Silvia Schroer, Berne. The German triumph stele and its Greek trans-lation as a reminding memorial of the brutal violence against innocent people from the village of Kandanos on Crete during the Second World War.

successful films such as the Prince of Egypt would be. We would thereby learn much about ourselves and our theology. The work with the medium of film brought to light in a drastic fashion how every reading of the Bible is bound to a specific culture and to ideologies. Film makes this much more evident than textual interpretations because it must be explicit and concrete where a text can be implicit or leave something out.

De-Constructiveness and Constructiveness

A central theme throughout the conference was the question with regard to the relationship between feminist exegesis and praxis directed at political or pedagogical change. Under what conditions can feminist exegesis have a liberating effect? When can it give speech to those who cannot speak? Do exegetes look for their themes and hermeneutics in the realities, experiences and struggles of the poorest women? What is their task with regard to women's struggle for survival? The question was often raised as to what feminist exegesis can contribute with respect to a system of globalization that excludes women and functions in a patriarchal-totalitarian manner. Feminist exegetes from a Western context often feel troubled rather than challenged or enriched by a reduction or reversal to elementary and practical needs. They may indeed postulate that reconstruction is just as important as deconstruction and analysis in feminist hermeneutics, but they often are not able to take the step beyond to constructiveness. Many Bible specialists from other contexts are directly involved in grass-roots movements, basis communities or Bible work in their churches. Their discontent with regard to the feminist hermeneutics of white academic women is in part based on the fact that these theories do not correspond to the needs of practical grass-roots work. This also holds true with regard to the applicability or translatability of feminist-critical exegesis in community work, for example, in German-speaking countries.

The call for more constructiveness is an urgent appeal to feminist exegetes to transform creatively their important critical analysis so as not to remain merely de-constructive but to introduce orientation and constructiveness to their work, postulates Elisabeth Schüssler Fiorenza.[14] The material of our analysis exists because of people who have lived a story with the Bible, because of their knowledge, their experiences and their

14. Schüssler Fiorenza 1998: 76-80. With regard to the attempt in the field of biblical anthropology to move from genre to a new, contemporary constructive literature in a critical, scholarly form, cf. Schroer and Staubli 2001.

suffering, and because of an unending, living tradition. Merely describing and analyzing these stories is not yet theology. If women theologians want to be understood as part of the worldwide 'synagogue' or 'ecclesia' of women, then they are also responsible for the radical democratic process that extends from the past through the present and into the future.

The Rulers of the House

If we can liberate ourselves from the necessity to view the biblical texts themselves as normative then they can become a treasury, a *thesauros* (Mt. 13.52) of our religion and of our beliefs. We are then the women scribes that bring out something new and something old and confront the new with the old. We will find worthless, worm-eaten and even harmful things, but also delicacies and treasures. As the rulers of the house we have the right (in the tradition of the goddess of Wisdom, Prov. 9.1-6)[15] to use our provisions, to put something fresh in the storeroom, to repair or change things, to trade things or to discard things. In order to neutralize something poisonous or harmful it is often sufficient merely to leave it in daylight. The inhabitants of the village Kandanos in Crete, for example, have kept alive the memory of the villagers killed by German soldiers in an act of revenge during the Second World War as well as their indictment against the perpetrators with a simple act: they erected the Nazis' victory stele (on which this terrible act of 'heroism' was triumphantly described) in the village and placed a stone next to it with merely the Greek translation of the German text (see the image on p. 12). The memory of that horrible act can thus be better integrated into their lives and transform their history of suffering.

And as rulers of the house we can also choose to have other treasures in our house: pictures and icons, apocryphal writings, the classic myths and sagas, the history of the 'indigenas' or slaves stories, poems by Audre Lorde, and so on.

The image of the rulers of the house and the treasury is more appropriate as a guide for feminist hermeneutics than the attempt to find a single key or code with which we can decode all texts from feminist perspective. This requires women exegetes, however, to have the courage to leave the security of the ordinary behind, to assume the complete responsibility for the treasury and to interpret biblical traditions anew with great sovereignty.

15. With regard to the personification of Wisdom, cf. Schroer 2000a and 2000b.

'We Will Know Each Other by Our Fruits'

Feminist exegesis that intends to be liberative is by no means limited to remain like the prophetic biblical writings and Exodus. It is a continuation of (popular and female) wisdom, of Israel's belief in creation. As the recipient of the Torah at Sinai it represents a continuing tradition and provides directives for the co-existence of people and their rights. The First Testament is thus more decisive for the future of feminist exegesis than the Second Testament, and what preceded the First Testament, the hidden history of Canaan at whose expense the identity of ancient Israel was shaped, could possibly be just as influential as the so-called Apocrypha.[16]

The claim to being liberative cannot be tied to exegetical methodology. A hermeneutics of liberation is directed at the praxis of overcoming the social, political and religious injustices under which women suffer. For feminist exegesis this means that a global discussion about the factors involved in liberation and oppression, about methods and hermeneutics, should take place, but it does not strive to find globally valid approaches to a hermeneutics of liberation; the question as to which feminist exegesis has a liberating function, which exegesis strengthens and encourages women in their struggles, is to be defined contextually. Only the interaction between global discussion, on the one hand, and the option for regionalism as well as the primacy of praxis, on the other hand, can do justice to the complexity of women's lives in the kyriarchy. The category of 'gender' alone is not sufficient (see above) in order to make evident the complex relationships of domination in which women are entangled. Whether a particular feminist exegesis really liberates (specific) women without suppressing others is demonstrated and proven in praxis and in the worldwide dialogue of the 'synagogue' or 'ecclesia' of women. We will know each other by our fruits.

Bibliography

Hufenus, Karl, and Thomas Staubli
    1993   'Bibel—Bilder—Befreiung', *Bibel und Kirche* 48: 115-16.
Keel, Othmar
    1992   'Iconography and the Bible', in *ABD*, III: 358-74.
Keel, Othmar, and Silvia Schroer
    1994   'Von den schmerzlichen Beziehungen zwischen Christentum, Judentum und
                kanaanäischer Religion', *Neue Wege* 88: 71-78.

16. Cf. Keel and Schroer 1994.

Keel, Othmar, and Christoph Uehlinger
    1998   *Gods, Goddesses, and Images of God in Ancient Israel* (Minneapolis: Eisenbrauns).
Morris, Randall
    1997   *Redemption Songs: The Self-Taught Artists of Jamaica* (Winston-Salem State University, North Carolina).
Opitz, Claudia
    2001   'Gender—eine unverzichtbare Kategorie der historischen Analyse. Zur Rezeption von Joan W. Scotts Studien in Deutschland, Österreich und der Schweiz', in Claudia Honegger and Caroline Arni (eds.), *Gender. Die Tücken einer Kategorie. Joan W. Scott, Geschichte und Politik. Beiträge zum Symposion anlässlich der Verleihung des Hans-Sigrist-Preises 1999 der Universität Bern an Joan W. Scott* (Zürich: Chronos Verlag): 95-115.
Pui-Lan, Kwok, and Elisabeth Schüssler Fiorenza (eds.)
    1998   *Women's Sacred Scriptures* (London: SCM Press; Maryknoll, NY: Orbis Books) (= *Concilium* 34.3).
Schader, Angela, and Eira Schader
    1997   'Eli-Jah', *L'art brut* 20: 32-41.
Schottroff, Luise, Silvia Schroer and Marie-Theres Wacker
    1998   *Feminist Interpretation: The Bible in Women's Perspective* (Minneapolis: Fortress Press). (First published 1995 in German as *Feministische Exegese. Forschungsbeiträge zur Bibel aus der Perspektive von Frauen* [Darmstadt: Wissenschaftliche Buchgesellschaft, 1995].)
Schottroff, Luise, and Marie-Theres Wacker (eds.)
    1996   *Von der Wurzel getragen. Christlich-feministische Exegese in Auseinandersetzung mit Antijudaismus* (Leiden: E.J. Brill).
    1998   *Kompendium Feministische Bibelauslegung* (Gütersloh: Chr. Kaiser/Gütersloher Verlag).
Schroer, Silvia
    1994   'Die Aschera. Kein abgeschlossenes Kapitel', *Schlangenbrut* 12.44: 17-22.
    1996   'Der israelitische Monotheismus als Synkretismus. Einblicke in die Religionsgeschichte Israels/Palästinas auf der Basis der neueren Forschung', in Anton Peter (ed.), *Christlicher Glaube in multireligiöser Gesellschaft. Erfahrungen—Theologische Reflexionen—Missionarische Perspektiven* (Immensee: Verlag Neue Zeitschrift für Missionswissenschaft): 268-87.
    1997   'Frauenleben im Alten Testament. Auf dem Weg zu einer feministischen Rekonstruktion der Geschichte Israels', *Schlangenbrut* 15.58: 12-15.
    1998   '"Under the Shadow of Your Wings": The Metaphor of God's Wings in the Psalms, Exodus 19.4, Deuteronomy 32.11 and Malachi 3.20, as Seen through the Perspectives of Feminism and the History of Religion', in Athalya Brenner and Caroline Fontaine (eds.), *Wisdom and Psalms* (A Feminist Companion to the Bible, Second Series, 2; Sheffield: Sheffield Academic Press): 264-82.
    1999a   'Bibelauslegung im europäischen Kontext', in Erhard S. Gerstenberger and Ulrich Schoenborn (eds.), *Hermeneutik—sozialgeschichtlich* (Exegese in unserer Zeit, 1; Münster: LIT-Verlag): 126-30.
    1999b   'Feminismus und Antijudaismus. Zur Geschichte eines konstruktiven Streits', in Walter Dietrich *et al.* (eds.), *Antijudaismus—christliche Erblast* (Stuttgart: W. Kohlhammer): 28-39.

2000a   *Wisdom Has Built Her House: Studies on the Figure of Sophia in the Bible* (Collegeville, MN: Liturgical Press).

2000b   'The Justice of Sophia: Biblical Wisdom Traditions and Feminist Discourses', *Concilium* 36: 67-77.

Schroer, Silvia, and Thomas Staubli

2000   'Saul, David and Jonathan—The Story of a Triangle? A Contribution to the Issue of Homosexuality in the First Testament', in Athalya Brenner (ed.), *Samuel and Kings* (A Feminist Companion to the Bible, Second Series, 7; Sheffield: Sheffield Academic Press): 22-36.

2001   *Body Symbolism in the Bible* (Collegeville, MN: Liturgical Press). (First published 1998 in German as *Die Körpersymbolik der Bibel* [Darmstadt: Wissenschaftliche Buchgesellschaft, 1998]).

Schüssler Fiorenza, Elisabeth

1983   *In Memory of Her: A Feminist Theological Reconstruction of Christian Origins* (New York: SCM Press).

1992   *But She Said: Feminist Practices of Biblical Interpretation* (Boston: Beacon Press).

1998   *Sharing Her Word: Feminist Biblical Interpretation in Context* (Boston: Beacon Press).

1999   *Rhetoric and Ethic: The Politics of Biblical Studies* (Minneapolis: Fortress Press).

Schüssler Fiorenza, Elisabeth (ed.)

1993   *Searching the Scriptures*. I. *A Feminist Introduction* (2 vols.; New York: Crossroad).

Scott, Joan

2001   'Millenial Fantasies: The Future of "Gender" in the 21st Century', in Claudia Honegger and Caroline Arni (eds.), *Gender. Die Tücken einer Kategorie. Joan W. Scott, Geschichte und Politik. Beiträge zum Symposion anlässlich der Verleihung des Hans-Sigrist-Preises 1999 der Universität Bern an Joan W. Scott* (Zürich: Chronos Verlag): 19-38.

Staubli, Thomas

2001   'Die Künder-Kinder der Weisheit. Mt 11,16-19 par Lk 7,31-35 im Licht antiker Texte und Terrakotten', *Lectio Difficilior* 3 (European Electronic Journal for Feminist Exegesis [Berne, Switzerland], available online at <www.lectio.unibe.ch>).

Wacker, Marie-Theres

1995   ' "Religionsgeschichte Israels" oder "Theologie des Alten Testaments"— (k)eine Alternative? Anmerkungen aus feministisch-exegetischer Sicht', in Ingo Baldermann *et al.* (eds.), *Religionsgeschichte Israels oder Theologie des Alten Testaments* (Jahrbuch für Biblische Theologie, 10; Neukirchen–Vluyn: Neukirchener Verlag): 129-55.

Proverbs 31 in a New Interpretation
(A Story Told by Renita Weems, USA)

Let me tell you about one of the most scandalous things that I have done to a text, Proverbs 31, 'who can find a virtuous woman?', something that audiences try to resist, but in the end they have to nod and say 'Aha'. Over the last two years I have been kind of 'deconstructing' it. That is, what we would describe in this setting as feminist womanist interpretation, well, I have been doing it without calling it any of that.

I start by saying: 'Let's look at the story of this woman who works all day and all night and who represents her husband's reputation and she cooks and she sows and her children call her blessed. Now, I think this is an exhausted woman, really!' And then I say: 'Who of us would like this but a man?' I say: 'Who wouldn't love to come home and find a woman who has cooked and cleaned for them and guards their reputation and stays away from her girlfriends and does not engage in idle chatter, who else would say it, who else?' And they all say: 'A man, a man, a man…yes!' A man wrote this. And so we are laughing, and I love humor. I continue asking: 'Don't you see that only a man would write this? What woman would write this? Celebrating exhaustion? Celebrating being crazy out of your mind? Who would write this but a man?' And so I charm them with that, and then I ask: 'Is this really the way you want to live? Aren't those of us who live that way exhausted?' And so we talk about that. Then I go on by quoting: 'Charm is deceptive, beauty is vain, but a woman who fears God…' And I say: 'You know, eventually even a man may stumble on an insight every now and then. And maybe this is an insight he stumbled on, that a woman who fears God is to be praised. So one or another men say things that make no sense, but every now and then they come up with something worth listening to'.

On one level I have deconstructed the text, but on another level I have said: 'But you know, from time to time you find a place here that really might be insightful'. So, without calling it all the stuff that I have been trained to do and that I teach my students at seminary to say, I just did it. I'm speaking in terms of the strategy of how you move people from here to there. I respect the text, I help them identify with the text, I help them to know what they all really know, that truly a man would write here like this. And then at the end I say to them: 'But maybe there is an insight here and there. And let's look at this verse: 'but a woman who fears God is to be praised. Give her the rewards of her labor'. Aha. Yes, to fear God, not men. To charm is deceitful. And we have been trained to be charming, and we have been trained to be beautiful, but beauty vanishes and charm can be expose, but to fear God, now, this is theologically worth preserving'. Those are some of my strategies, for moving grass-roots women from where they are to where I would like to try to take them.

RE-READING FOR LIBERATION:
AFRICAN AMERICAN WOMEN AND THE BIBLE

Renita J. Weems

I am grateful to the planners of this conference for the invitation to gather in the beautiful town of Ascona, Switzerland, to deliberate with women from around the globe on the ways in which our hermeneutics intersect with our social and political identities. Gathering with women from as far away as Australia and Palestine and as nearby (to the US) as Costa Rica and Canada has resulted in a heady week of exchanging stories, comparing journeys and learning to view the world through different eyes. Hearing stories about the brave and challenging work many of us are involved in as the first, only, or one of a handful of women in our countries, universities, religious traditions, and always in our families to reflect on the Bible with feminist eyes, to examine our faith and our culture through the experiences of other women has made all of us view our work differently. We return home feeling less lonely and more a part of a movement that is international in scope and certainly larger than ourselves. It was a week of mixed blessings.

Nestled away as we were in a remote, mountainous retreat, deliberating with women from various parts of the world and from vastly different backgrounds pushed all of us (and each of us) to a high level of self-reflection—more self-reflection than some of us were accustomed to, more self-reflection than some of us could stand. Tensions were strained at times. Our differences sometimes kept us from hearing and understanding each other. But we never stopped trying. Even though it was clear to all very early in the week that five days would not be enough for us to shed all the assumptions and all the baggage that come with being women from colonizing countries and women from countries once colonized. But we tried.

That said, I believe many of us left the symposium more committed than ever to our work as interpreters and scholars of scripture. As for myself, I

left convinced of how important it is for African American women scholars to resist the myopisms of Western feminism by building bridges of
dialogue with women from around the globe. Reading and interpreting the
Bible with the help of those from other cultures reminds us of the extent to
which one's context both limits and illumines interpretation. I knew this
before as a biblical scholar and a North American African American
woman, but I knew it differently after interfacing in Ascona with women
from worlds different from my own. I discovered the truth of Kathleen
O'Connor's observation, 'we are drenched in our contexts' (O'Connor
1998: 324). By the close of the conference, we learned through much pain
and effort how our contexts have both inspired and illumined our
liberatory readings of the Bible and at the same time hindered and blinded
us to the manner in which the Bible has been used to silence the marginalized and to justify centuries of oppressive activity.

Drenched in our contexts as we all proved to be that week in July 2000,
most of us left Ascona committed to finding ways to continue the trans-
cultural dialogue we started. Our future as women reading for liberation
depends upon it. What do I mean? The only way most, if not all of us are
apt to act and speak less arrogantly about our claims about the Bible, not
to mention act and speak less arrogantly toward each other, is if we put
ourselves in situations where we must spend days (preferably a lifetime) in
diverse, multi-cultural, trans-cultural, heterogeneous contexts where, if we
are to survive, we *must* learn to talk with and live peaceably and justly
with people who think and see the world differently from ourselves.

Reflecting and Rethinking a Womanist Identity

One of the benefits of the Ascona symposium was that it forced me at least
to bring to consciousness my own self-interests and to probe my assumptions—both the apparent and the hidden ones—in order to do what I could
to make myself understood to those around me. I have always identified
myself as a biblical scholar who not only traffics in the intellectual world-
making enterprise of scholarship and Academy. But I have also been eager
to make my mark as a public intellectual, a woman in the Academy who
tries to make her work accessible and available to the non-specialists and
grass-roots activists working for liberation in ecclesial and non-ecclesial
contexts. The international context of our symposium brought home to me,
as well as to others, the politics of our various identities and forced all of
us to speak less smugly about the praxis of our work.

Reflecting on biblical interpretation within a multi-cultural context forced me throughout the week to be intentional about examining and explicating the context of my work. It also forced me to examine the ways in which as a woman of African heritage born and reared in North America I live a fractured existence as well as the ways in which my shifting identities stir conflicts within me and resist easy solutions. We women of color doing work in the Western Academy are likely to find ourselves constantly dangling between two realities: the diasporic, postcolonial feminist discourses of our Two-Thirds World sisters and the privileged, hegemonic, theorizing discourses of Western feminism. To proceed as though my North American context was self-evident, inconsequential, or, worst yet, universal, was to be guilty of what postcolonial feminists rightly criticize Western feminism of—namely, the universalist, essentialist and globalizing tendency to presume a universal condition of oppression for all women.[1] I had to face the ways in which I belong both to a marginalized group of readers (African American women/womanists) and a privileged class of interpreters (Western/North American feminists), depending upon the context in which I find myself.

Reading the Bible in multicultural spaces makes (or ought to make) one acutely aware of the intellectual heritage, the political baggage, the social assumptions, and the economic worldview one brings to one's reading. It forces one to face and to declare explicitly on whose behalf one interprets. A constant hurdle for us to overcome as we tried throughout the week to create a safe space for critical dialogue was our inability, and sometimes flat out unwillingness, to acknowledge the ways we use language—especially biblical and theological language—to mask or reinforce differences among us. The politics of the symposium were such that we found ourselves having to work against others and our own cultural baggage in our struggle to understand and to be understood. There were moments in the discussion when we succeeded, there were many more when we did not. We could not outwit cultural backgrounds and at difficult moments had to acknowledge the fact that we were First and Two-Thirds World women, Western and non-Western women, Anglo women and women of color, women from colonized parts of the world and women from colonizing nations, feminist, postcolonial, and womanists scholars, conservative readers and radical interpreters of scripture trying to talk across a gulf of

---

1.   For a helpful discussion of postcolonial feminist theory in general, see Jacqui and Mohanty 1996. Also, for a very helpful attempt to bring postcolonial feminist theory to bear upon reading biblical texts, see Dube 2000.

painful history. Nevertheless, we all walked away from the week acutely aware that even the risk of failure is no excuse for not trying to reach out to one another.

Reading with and reading across cultural borders is part of the ongoing work of women of color in the theological Academy. We do not have the luxury of remaining content to analyze texts but must go the step further to analyze readings, readers, culture, and the worlds that frame each. Ultimately, reading the Bible for liberation is grounded in the acknowledgment and respect for the otherness of those whose otherness is silenced and marginalized by those in power. Thinking about my generation of African American female scholars working as academics in the field of religion, I can say that most of us do not view our work as *accountable* to the Academy, even though we are involved in the discourse of the Academy and are dependent upon the Academy for a large part of our living. But we reserve the right to make our work accountable ultimately to grass-roots African American women, women struggling for voice and representation in institutional circles, ecclesial circles especially.

Many of us who are African American women scholars in religion came into the Academy as a second choice. We came to the Academy of scholars of religions when we discovered as seminarians that despite our training there was no place for us as thinking women of faith in the Church. The Church birthed us and then rejected us. We went on for our graduate degrees because it was the next best thing. And now we stand ambivalently before two audiences, belonging to neither but trying to carve out a space in the discourses of both. And why do we not walk away from the Church? Why not reject the Bible? If it were an individual matter, then the choice would be a simple one, perhaps. There are many parts of myself, for example, that are post-Christian. But it is not just about our/my individual predilections. It is about our/my commitments. To leave the Church would be to leave other African American women behind. To reject the Bible altogether would be to cut off my conversation with the women who birthed me and sent me off to the seminary with their blessings.

Finally, on this point, I for one choose to remain within the black Christian tradition, despite my ambivalences toward it, because it keeps me in conversation with women I care deeply about. Despite the ways American Christianity was forced on our ancestors as Africans brought to this country as slaves, and despite the ways in which patriarchal Christianity has wounded women over the centuries, I remain hopelessly Judeo-Christian in my orientation. I cannot escape its influence upon me. Indeed, as a scholar committed to scholarship that serves liberation purposes my very vision of what a just, equitable, humane and righteous world order looks like is deeply influenced by the utopian imagination and impulses of my Judeo-Christian upbringing. The place where religion proves useful in multi-racial, international discussions like the one in Ascona is when it forces us back to the table to re-open the discussion, to re-think our assumptions, to re-read for our collective liberation, and to give dialogue another chance.

Reflections on Womanist Biblical Hermeneutics

Even after its introduction as a term more than 15 years ago, 'womanist scholarship' remains a nascent conversation in religious and theological studies. The reasons for this are many. Many of them have to do with our lack of a critical mass of scholars writing and reflecting on womanist research, as well as the demands and pressures on our attention as black women in the Academy. The challenge over the years for us has been having to write, teach, theorize and practice our hermeneutics amid obstacles designed to keep us as women in the Academy distracted, silent and forever beginning anew. We have only to observe how little attention is given to the traditions, religious worlds, epistemologies and reading habits of non-Anglo, non-European women by mainstream feminist religious discourse to see how and why the work of womanists fills a crucial void in gender and feminist studies.

Womanist biblical reflections arose out of feminist biblical hermeneutics and liberation theology. Womanist reflections upon the Bible underscore that the experiences of white feminist and those of black male liberationist thinkers are not 'the universal experience' of all marginalized persons. While feminist biblical criticism and black liberation scholarship are inextricably linked, they are not the same. Sexism is one form of oppression black women confront. Racism is another. Classism is yet another. A womanist perspective underscores the fact that North American Anglo women's experience is not the 'universal' experience of women in general. Nor is black male liberationist thinking the 'universal' experience of people of color. The universalizing tendencies of North American feminisms have obscured their Eurocentric biases, seeking to homogenize women in general and women of color especially without regard to our differences of race, religion, nationalities, sexual orientation, and socio-economic backgrounds. Likewise, while black liberation thinking and womanist criticism are inextricably related, the experience of African American women has not always been fully appreciated by black male colleagues involved in liberation discourse. Black liberation work often focuses on race oppression in society, but fails to see oppression based on gender as equally unacceptable. Black theology emerged out of the Black Power movement. It was unifocal in its critique, focusing exclusively on white racism. It failed to address the sexism and the classism experienced by black women. Kelly Brown Douglas notes that 'affected both by the feminist movement in Church and society and their own experience of sexism, black women began to note the exclusion of black women's experience in black theology' as well as the feminist movement (Brown Douglas 1993: 292). Womanist criticism within the theological Academy emerged as a way to correct the myopism of both feminist and black liberation scholarship, believing that every marginalized group has a right and duty to name its own reality and to find a language for mapping out its own vision of liberation.

Like feminist biblical hermeneutics, womanist biblical hermeneutical reflections do not begin with the Bible. Rather, womanist hermeneutics of liberation begin with African American women's will to survive and thrive as human beings and as the female half of a race of people who live a threatened existence within North American borders. The interests of real flesh-and-blood black women are privileged over theory and over the interests of ancient texts, even 'sacred' ancient texts. Even a cursory look at the literature and autobiographical writings of African American women will show that what is celebrated most in our writings is our determination to survive, to nourish, and to protect those things dear to us, and to assert our will to thrive in what often is a hostile and dangerous world. The Bible cannot go unchallenged in so far as the role it has played in legitimating the dehumanization of people of African ancestry in general and the sexual exploitation of women of African ancestry in particular. It cannot be understood as some universal, transcendent, timeless force to which world readers—in the name of being pious and faithful followers—must meekly submit. It must be understood as a politically and socially drenched text invested in ordering relations between people, legitimating some viewpoints and delegitimizing other viewpoints.

Almost from the beginning of our engagement with the Bible as African Americans we have interpreted it differently from those who introduced this book to us. Instead of reading the passages our slaveholders drew our attention to as theologically rationalizing slavery and oppression, we in-sisted upon reading and interpreting the same passages differently or ignoring them altogether. That the Bible was not transmitted to American slaves as a fixed, written text that had to be accepted as is proved to be fortuitous. It freed us from rather rigid notions about the infallibility of its contents. As an aural text in the slave community, one passed down to black people through sermons, song, and public instruction, slaves were free to interact with its contents according to their own interests and cul-tural (re)imaginings. For black women that meant that we could elect either to reject totally those portions of the Bible we considered misogy-nistic, to elevate some portions over others depending upon one's interests, to offer alternative readings in order to counter the dominant discourse, or to supplant biblical teachings altogether with extra-biblical (i.e. cultural) traditions that (in their thinking) offered a fuller, more just vision of the way things ought to be. Because of their fundamental belief in their rights as human beings created in the image of God they rejected antagonistic readings that denied them any subjectivity.[2]

Any attempt, then, to describe African American women's relationship to the Bible and to adduce our strategies for reading the Bible has to take seriously the ways in which the Bible has been (and continues to be) used to rationalize the subjugation of African people of the diaspora living in North America in general and the sexual and gender subjugation of African women of the diaspora living in America in particular.[3] Placing our work in a stream of discussion with other women from different contexts as the Ascona conference did forces one to look at the ways in which our readings have been shaped by the unique circumstances of our North American context. It also reminds us of the ways in which our reading strategies both stand in solidarity with and differ from readings by other women from marginalized communities from around the globe.

A womanist hermeneutics of liberation shares with feminist hermeneu-tics of liberation the goal of changing consciousness and transforming reality. But the main point of our work as womanist scholars, I think, is to empower African American women as readers, as agents, and as shapers of discourse by uncovering the program and agenda of both biblical texts

---

2.   For a fuller treatment of the ways nineteenth-century African American women in particular rejected the dominant antagonistic readings of their day and held to their own 'choice passages' as a way of defining their own subjectivity, see Haywood 2000.

3.   For my fuller discussion of African American women's history of reading and interacting with the Bible, see Weems 1991.

and dominant cultural readings. Real flesh-and-blood people with real vested interests were behind the production and transmission of the Bible's contents; and real flesh-and-blood readers are behind all modes of interpretations and readings with positions and agendas that prompt them to be more invested in one reading over another. The point here clearly is to decenter for marginalized readers the privileged status of the dominant readings and the dominant community of readers. A womanist biblical hermeneutics takes as its starting point the fundamental notion that people have power, not texts. Meaning takes place in the charged encounter between socially and politically conditioned text and socially and politically conditioned real reader. Women have to reclaim their right to read and interpret sacred texts for themselves and should not have to be subject to the misogynistic, patriarchal interests of powerful male readers; and women of color have to insist upon their right to read and interpret sacred texts for themselves and should not have to defend or apologize for their interpretations to privileged women in the culture who remain ignorant to how class, race, and colonialism shape and divide us as women. It should come as no surprise, then, that in womanist criticism no one reading and no one methodology is privileged over another, instead, a creative use of multiple readings and the helpful insights offered by a variety of disciplinary approaches are employed to shed light on the question of how and why readers read as they do.

Because the Bible has been used in North America not only as a source of liberation, but paradoxically and curiously also as a source of inspiration in African American women's struggle for survival, it remains a continuing task of liberation interpreters, as far as I am concerned, to shed light on one of the more intractable questions facing us in our ongoing efforts to rationalize the fact that it continues to occupy an important place in the hearts and minds of many African American women: despite all that we know about its antagonistic role in our oppression as women, how does reading admittedly sexually violent and misogynistic texts continue to have the power to fill many of us with passion and a vision for liberation?

Readers' Love Affair for Stories

To see African American Protestant women's devotions to the stories of the Bible as a continuing example of a naive attachment to the principle of *sola scriptura* or as a slavish belief in these texts as the divinely revealed word of God, the sole authority in all matters religious, is to traffic in partial truths and to be overly determined about a far more complex and subtle aspect of gender, reading and culture. After all, women readers have been reading and identifying with secular texts written by men that romanticize their second class status for centuries.

My argument is that part of African American women's fascination with the Bible—despite all that they may come to know about the hopelessly patriarchal character of the world they inhabit—has to do in great part (though not exclusively, of course) with the insatiable appetite readers have for stories. Through stories grass-roots African Americans communicated their understanding of life, love, suffering, god(s) and their vision of freedom and liberation.

Let me state emphatically that I am not saying that our need or love for stories is the only or even the primary reason for women's devotion to the Bible. I am only asserting that it is one reason that has not been given sufficient (constructive) attention by feminist biblical interpreters. Of course, there are undeniably larger political, economic, historical and ideological forces at work that help to reinforce the illusion of biblical stories as truth/true, divinely inspired, sacred and 'the way things are and have been always'.

People, when making moral choices and decisions in their lives, represent their choices and decisions by turning to stories. To facilitate those moral choices and decisions people look to stories to guide them. It is important to see readers' devotion to biblical stories in general and religious texts in particular as part of their broader fascination within society for narratives, stories and testimonies. The possibility that the Bible alleges to offer its reader the earliest glimpses into human tragedy and triumph is immeasurably comforting to many of its readers. Gender studies may help shed light on how texts shape women's realities. Literary theory can help us understand how narratives are written and how they construct narrative universes for readers to inhabit. But the question of why readers choose this book over that book, why some books bear reading again and again lies not in theory but in cultural history. As one writer put it, 'It has to do with where we look when we try to understand our own lives, how we read texts and what largely unexamined cultural assumptions we bring to interpreting them' (Conway 1998: 4). This is particularly true for African American female readers who turn to the Bible to regain their hope of a world where the first is last and the last is first, where justice eventually dethrones injustice, and the despised are welcomed at the hospitality table and are given the seat of honor there at the table. Regardless of whether the protagonist is male or female, justice and liberation have to be (or perceived to be) at the heart of the story. That the protagonist is female, as in the story of the woman caught in adultery in John 4 or the story of Esther, only sweetens the tale of political, economic, and social reversal at the hands of the divine.

There is no denying that a significant part of our work as womanist interpreters is to radically rethink what it means to continue to read certain kinds of obnoxious, oppressive stories in the Bible where women's rape, abuse, and marginalization is romanticized, subjugated, and excused for the sake of some alleged larger purpose in the story. Stories like those of the rape of Tamar in Genesis 34, the butchering of the Levite's concubine in Judges 19, or the prostitute who anoints Jesus' feet with her tears and hair in Luke 7 are ones we cannot afford to continue reading without serious rethinking. Their story of women's abuse and subjugation may be too costly to hold on to and too hopelessly misogynistic to try saving. We have to find ways to break the hold that these and other androcentric biblical texts have on us as women by rereading these texts in ways in which they were not meant to be read. Part of rereading androcentric texts can entail choosing not to read them at all. Breaking the hold these texts have involves breaking the cycle of uncritically retelling and passing down from one generation to the next violent, androcentric, culturally chauvinistic texts and resisting where necessary the moral vision of such texts. We may find that we have to follow the path of black Christian women readers in the past who in their struggle for freedom and dignity ignored outright certain biblical accounts altogether. I am reminded here of the story of the grandmother of theologian Howard Thurman who after slavery refused to hear passages written by the apostle Paul because she had been made to hear sermons about slaves obeying their master all her life when she was a girl growing up in slavery. Only the Psalms and other parts of the New Testament qualified as worthy words of daily inspiration for Thurman's grandmother. The fact that women like Thurman's grandmother had 'choice passages' demonstrates a perception on the part of even so-called uneducated readers of how the Bible can and has been used against them to promote a vision of a world that silences and further overlooks the oppressed. Its multiple ideological layers and the multiple roles it has played in both silencing and liberating generations of readers forces readers to read the Bible with different eyes, from multiple positions, and with a multi-layered approach. No one way of reading, thinking and talking about biblical stories can be privileged over another.

Feminist scholars have noted for some time now that we have moved beyond the simple recovering and recounting of individual stories about exceptionally prominent or obscured women in the Bible. That was the work of first-wave biblical feminist and womanist scholarship. It was involved not only in exposing the strongly patriarchal environment from which the Bible arose (and hence its misogynistic biases) but also in exposing how women's presence has been further obscured by the biases of male scholars and interpreters. In addition to attempts to understand the social world of women by drawing on discussions from the social sciences, psychoanalysis, archaeology, and so on, works from this period aided us in trying to understand the social patterns, social roles and how societies silence women, obscure the contributions of women, even how these societies seek to construct identity through narratives and legal materials.

The work of the second-wave of biblical feminist and womanist scholarship, namely, recovering and reclaiming women's contributions and presence in the Bible, continues. It continues as long as there remain grassroots women who refuse to leave the Churches that have both, they say, wounded them and blessed them. Recovering the contributions of women such as Hagar, Huldah, Judith, Deborah, Lydia and the Canaanite woman is important for those eager for role models, images, stories and examples from the Bible to help them struggle and survive the hardships of gender oppression.

But we have witnessed a shift to what both feminists and womanists agree is a third phase of biblical liberation criticism which involves rethinking the very act of reading biblical stories. Intrinsic to this movement is an interest in looking closely at stories and their construction, to see how identity is shaped and reinforced and how real readers negotiate identity and meaning when reading. That is: How do real readers read stories? How do stories shape identity? How do stories change identities? Why do some stories become more important to some readers than others? It is here in this third phase of biblical liberation criticism that womanist criticism situates itself best. Womanist biblical criticism is interested in the ways in which African Americans read the Bible, the strategies they use in negotiating meaning and identity from stories, and those they use when resisting the meaning(s) and identities attached to certain stories. Part of what it means to break the hold that texts have over the imagination is for us as readers to be able to decode the strategies and conventions that went into making texts in a way that sheds light on how texts mean and why they mean the way they mean.

I agree with the Australian feminist historian Jill Kerr Conway when she argues that readers turn to stories, even biblical and religious stories, for a variety of reasons (Conway 1998):

1. To learn about how the world looks from inside another person's experience.

2. Because stories satisfy our craving for coherence and our fear of chaos and unpredictability; they offer us the fictive illusion that life flows along a clear, logical line of causation, that it has a beginning, middle and a tidy end.

3. Stories give readers an inner script by which they might live their lives, compare their lives, conform their lives, reshape their lives and test out their lives.

Stories offer readers an inner script to live by, glimpses into the way things are, and more importantly reason and a way to talk about how things ought not to be. Stories can lure readers into seeing the world in different ways, shock them into a critique of the world in which they live and help them imagine the ways things ought to be. In the symbolic, non-threatening way in which stories are passed down, they have the power to galvanize readers into re-imagining the world in ways that previously were unthinkable and impossible. That the Bible purports to describe ancient peoples and ancient times is part of its seduction. For even if it does not in fact describe *the* beginning of human tragedy and human triumph, it does convey to the reader the possibility that *from* the beginning of time there has been human tragedy and human triumph. As a womanist biblical interpreter and teacher my role is to respect readers' needs to view the Bible as a collection of sacred stories while at the same time challenging them to understand their role as agents in the sacred act of preserving stories and passing them down to the next generation. As an agent in the task of preserving and transmitting stories from one generation of women to the next, readers must be empowered (1) to become a part of a story's audience and to feel free to raise questions of the author about his or her assumptions about the world and people's relationship to one another; (2) to use one's imagination to retell the story in ways that it was never meant to be told in order to get at hidden truths and meanings embedded in stories; and (3) to take responsibility as a reader/interpreter/storyteller for the impact the stories we tell has on the lives of other women, men and children who hear them and try to live up to them.

From Reading to Liberation

Finally, an important part of womanist biblical criticism involves empowering readers to judge biblical texts, to not hesitate to read against the grain of a text if needed, and to be ready to take a stand against those texts whose worldview runs counter to one's own vision of God's liberation activity in the world. For example, the woman reader who insists that the story of the butchered concubine in Judges is divinely inspired or that Ezekiel, Jeremiah, or Hosea's use of sexually violent imagery to connote divine judgment is holy must be made aware of her role and responsibility each time she literally, that is, unthinkingly/uncritically, passes these stories on to the next generation.[4] One of the most effective ways to introduce women students and interested male students to a hermeneutics of liberation is by turning their attention to stories of rape and violence in the Bible and asking them what kind of world would our world be if stories like these were normative, if we duplicated, reproduced or transmitted them to the next generation without warning and comment. No wonder stories, whether religious or profane, ancient or contemporary, European or postcolonist, are potentially powerful tools for spreading liberation. After all, it is through the narrative, symbolic universe of stories that readers, ordinary readers, non-specialists—who rarely give their own lives a fraction of the same amount of attention—get to contemplate and talk indirectly about matters of culture, history, gender and identity, language, power relations, material conditions, all the things those of us in the bourgeoisie world of Academy tackle in more rarified, highly theorized, but no less subjective, ways (Conway 1998: 17).

Finally, working as a womanist scholar committed to a hermeneutics of liberation entails opening my mind and those of others to radically new and different ways that different people read, tell stories and testify to their understanding of God. Rereading for liberation is not done in a vacuum, nor is it a solitary enterprise. Liberation is the work of people reaching out to one another across the gulf of their real flesh-and-blood painful gender, racial, national, religious, and geo-political differences like we tried to do in Ascona. It means hearing people out, respecting the way they read and interpret stories, making room for them at the table, and sharing power with them. For what is liberation without power? And what is power? Power is the ability to take one's place in whatever discourse is essential

---

4. For my own discussion of sexual violent imagery and language in prophetic literature, see Weems 1995.

to change and having the right to have one's story matter regardless of how it is told, no matter how rambling the story, no matter how unconventional the telling, no matter how irritating the inflections, and sometimes no matter how unthinkable the tale. Rereading for liberation is risking failure and taking the plunge to divest yourself of some of your own power and privileges for the chance to enter another's world so as to understand and to make yourself understood to others.

BIBLIOGRAPHY

Brown Douglas, Kelly
    1993   'Womanist Theology: What Is Its Relationship to Black Theology', in James Cone and Gayraud Wilmore (eds.), *Black Theology: A Documentary History 1980–1992* (Maryknoll, NY: Orbis Books): 290-99.

Conway, Jill Kerr
    1998   *When Memory Speaks: Reflection on Autobiography* (New York: Knopf).

Dube, Musa W.
    2000   *Postcolonial Feminist Interpretation of the Bible* (St Louis: Chalice Press).

Haywood, Chanta M.
    2000   'Prophesying Daughters: Nineteenth-Century Black Religious Women, the Bible, and Black Literary History', in Vincent L. Wimbush (ed.), *African Americans and the Bible: Sacred Texts and Social Textures* (London/New York: Continuum Publishing): 355-66.

Jacqui, Alexander M., and Chandra Mohanty (eds.)
    1996   *Feminist Genealogies, Colonial Legacies; Democratic Futures* (New York: Routledge Press).

O'Connor, Kathleen
    1998   'Crossing Borders: Biblical Studies in a Trans-Cultural World', in Fernando Segovia and Mary Ann Tolbert (eds.), *Teaching the Bible: The Discourse and Politics of Biblical Pedagogy* (Maryknoll, NY: Orbis Books): 322-37.

Weems, Renita J.
    1991   'Reading Her Way Through the Struggle: African American Women and the Bible', in Cain Hope Felder (ed.), *Stony the Road We Trod: African American Biblical Interpretation* (Minneapolis: Fortress Press): 57-80.

    1995   *Battered Love: Love, Sex, and Violence in the Hebrew Prophets* (Minneapolis: Fortress Press).

Helping Each Other to Think
(A Series of Propositions in Retrospect by Viola Raheb, Palestine)

The theme of the conference offered a variety of challenges and opportunities. For some women the emphasis was on feminist issues, for others it was on biblical interpretation and hermeneutics or the issue of liberation, and for some it was the question of all aspects as a whole. Each woman's viewpoint was influenced by her context, by her personal experience and commitment.

The influence of context on each woman's agenda and methodology became particularly clear as I reviewed the different lectures and contributions. Feminist theology is not merely about information but more importantly about transformation. We need to develop a more holistic methodology of interpretation, one that is critical, experiential, dialogical, contextual and liberating.

At some point I had to think how women from the Southern Hemisphere are not only the object of patriarchal domination in theology but sometimes as well of a patronizing Anglo-American European feminist theology.

For some women, doing theology is a question of an academic career or profession. Yet for other women it is more an issue of survival, of life and death.

Some participants, especially those from the Southern Hemisphere, stressed the fact that 'first things come first'. But who determines what things are first? Have women come to agreement about what is first? If not, where do we meet? And how?

For me as a Christian Palestinian, Christianity is indigenous to my country and has a different context here than in South America or Africa. But at the same time, Western theology is an imported discipline that has brought a foreign interpretation to the Bible, one that often alienates Christian Palestinians from their own religion. This is a unique challenge for us.

Feminist theologies have developed more sensitive approaches with regard to questions related to 'anti-Judaism' in recent years. Yet, there are still many other 'anti' traditions in our theologies that need to be exposed and dealt with if feminist theology is to become liberating for women around the globe. I believe that is necessary to develop what I would call a 'hermeneutics of the marginalized', one that focuses on reading the Bible from the periphery.

It is evident in the various contributions that the Bible is often an ambivalent instrument, one that can be both liberating and enslaving. Accordingly, hermeneutics has to take this ambiguity into consideration. The question is, should theology focus on eliminating this ambiguity or on developing innovative and challenging methodologies of dealing with it?

Despite the fact that each participant came from a different context and had her individual story and experience, I left the conference with the feeling that we shared what I would call a 'meta-language'. This is a women's language of suffering, pain, joy and hope that connects our different stories and experiences and forms a bond of solidarity among us.

SOME REFLECTIONS ON FEMINIST BIBLICAL HERMENEUTICS
FOR LIBERATION

Adele Reinhartz and Marie-Theres Wacker

This essay is based on our observations of and responses to the sessions in which we participated throughout the symposion. It reviews some of the questions that have been discussed and provides a commentary from our own particular and situated points of view on how what we have done might fit into the broader context of feminist biblical hermeneutics.

Biographical Backgrounds

Marie-Theres Wacker (MTW): I would like to begin by setting the context and by saying a few words about myself. I am from Germany and I work within an academic context. As a German Catholic woman scholar I have had to struggle with being a member of a minority within a minority. When I was going to school and later on at the university, I was considered to have come from a background that was more backward socially than that of German Protestants. This was even more so for myself as a Catholic girl from the countryside. This experience illustrates the varieties of upbringing and identities among those of us who come from a Western European context. The fact that I am a Catholic is relevant to the ways in which I approach my academic work. I mention two points. First, the importance given to the Bible is somewhat different within Catholic theology than in the churches of the Reformation. While the Protestant churches focus on the principle of *sola scriptura*, Roman Catholics include also the tradition that has developed from the Bible as lived and taught within the Catholic Church. Because Roman Catholics may be more aware of reading the Bible in a given context, their hermeneutical conscience may tend to be more elaborated. Second, to be a Catholic woman theologian working in a context determined in one way or the other by the church is to have to contend with an ecclesiastical system characterized by rigid control. Silvia

Schroer is an example. She, a Catholic, was prevented by ecclesiastical authorities from teaching at a Catholic university. Discussions on feminist hermeneutics for liberation thus have special connotations for Catholics.

Adele Reinhartz (AR): Perhaps the most pertinent part of my social location is that I am a Jewish woman specializing in New Testament. For this reason I am almost always an outsider at academic gatherings, where I am frequently the only Jew and often one of only a handful of women. I do not lament this situation. In fact, I see it as a position of privilege because it allows me to observe and participate without necessarily becoming embroiled in the discussion in a very personal way. In the classroom too I have not found it a hindrance to be Jewish—quite the opposite. The classroom provides me with the opportunity to stand as a Jew in front of Christian students, to be able to talk about Jewish texts, the Sabbath and the dietary laws from an insider perspective. As a Jew I provide a different lens through which my students can view the Jewishness of Jesus and the early Christian movement and understand more sympathetically such Jewish groups as the Pharisees.

General Reflections

Setting the Table

AR: Perhaps the best way to describe our task here is to recall some of the metaphors that have emerged in our discussions together. One such metaphor was that of 'binding a sack together' or 'tying a bundle' so that we might put it on our shoulders and carry it home with us. According to this metaphor, our task on the last day of the conference is to help you fill or perhaps arrange the bundle and help you tie it up. This is a very descriptive metaphor but perhaps it does not quite capture our intention, for we do not believe that we can wrap or bundle the entire week together in a package that will include all things and that will be satisfying and meaningful to all participants.

A more fitting metaphor, in our view, is the banquet or feast. We would like to see ourselves as preparing a festive table and inviting you to sit down and join us for a meal. But you are invited not simply to taste the food that we are preparing but also to contribute your own spices, drinks and tasty dishes to the communal meal. We sincerely hope that we will not presumptuously serve someone's food before she is able to finish her cooking and is ready to share her food with us.

Of course, we have been sharing a meal together all week long. Because we two were charged with the task of presenting our views to you at the end of the week, we came not only as participants in the ongoing discussion, but also as observers. As the week went on we also began to think about what we would say and how we would be able to present our views to you. This does not mean, however, that we have an objective perspective. Even in the rich and enjoyable discussions between the two of us, in which we tried to work out what to say this morning and how to say it, we realized that there were some things that we agreed on, that we shared, that we had observed, and many other points which only one of us noticed or thought important. Thus, what you will receive this morning are only our impressions. Please do not think that we present them as 'closed bundles'. These are not intended as the results of our week-long conference but rather as reflections that can serve to initiate some discussion.

We begin with some remarks concerning the dynamics of our week together, as they appeared to us. We will then discuss briefly some of the topics that were presented. To invoke yet another metaphor, these topics are some of the threads that wove their way into our conversations throughout the week. We will then mention some threads that were begun but not continued, and others that might have been included but were not.

MTW: So, let us begin with some observations about the dynamics of the week. We appreciated very much the overall structure of this conference with its variety of presentations. Having only one major lecture per day allowed us to give each speaker the attention she deserved. The small groups provided the opportunity for intensive discussion and also a way for us to get to know each other better. The plenary discussions were a forum within which everybody could share her point of view with all the others. The panels and working groups gave us insight into work or research in progress or recently completed. Pasolini's film opened up new perspectives, while the morning meditations, the dances, the excursion into beautiful valleys of the region all enriched our time together in many different ways. Last, but certainly not least, were the marvelous celebrations, especially our dinner party yesterday evening. Through this variety of experiences we were not only intoxicated with words and our exhilarating work together, but we were able to communicate with one another on many levels.

Metaphors

AR: One striking element of the discussion was the use of metaphors. The first metaphor to be introduced into the discussion was the description of the Bible as a storehouse to which everyone can come to find things she needs for the sustenance of life and to meet other people who are similarly looking for what they need. A second metaphor was the 'poncho' as a weave of history, memory and inspiration for action. This textile metaphor seemed to suit many of us. Others took it up, wove it further and added other ponchos as well. Some reflected upon the figures woven into the ponchos, such as the dismembered goddess or the women and men engaged in struggles for liberation. Some spoke about loose threads that could be pulled out or unraveled, just as sexist, racist and androcentric views of the world need to be unraveled in order to make room for more inclusive perspectives.

Yet another metaphor was introduced in the African story told by Musa W. Dube yesterday evening concerning the princess who was pushed into the fire. Pushing someone into a fire is a powerful—and dangerous—metaphor for eliminating the people whom we believe to be responsible for our problems.

A fourth metaphor is the one that we are using again today, namely, that of a table set for a feast or banquet. This metaphor is rooted in biblical Wisdom Literature, where Lady Wisdom invites those who aspire to wisdom to her house. We prefer to think not of a single and authoritative figure like Lady Wisdom, but of a community of wise women, in many different places, preparing their meals and inviting others to join in.

This introduces yet another metaphor, that of geography. The structure of the week took us on a journey, beginning here in Switzerland with Silvia Schroer, moving with Elisabeth Schüssler Fiorenza to America, although with strong European connections and roots, and then to Brazil with Nancy Cardoso Pereira, a brief side trip to Italy through the lens of Pier Paulo Pasolini, the American South with Renita Weems, to Botswana with Musa W. Dube, and finally to Canada and Germany this morning. This metaphorical journey has a somewhat troubling undercurrent. Perhaps, unknowingly, we have been partaking of a 'white lady sandwich', beginning with Silvia Schroer and Elisabeth Schüssler Fiorenza and ending with Marie-Theres Wacker and myself, Adele Reinhartz. This metaphor is potentially troubling because it may be read as suggesting that all of the colorful and enriching discussions from the middle of the week were bracketed by or contained between the white and Eurocentric bread of the first and last days. Such a reading re-inscribes the intellectual and cultural religious imperialism that many of us are struggling so hard to change. Another, more positive reading is to suggest that what is important about a sandwich is not so much the bread upon which it is served but rather the filling. After all, when we order a sandwich in the restaurant we do not order a white bread sandwich but, let us say, a meat or cheese sandwich. This too, however, is ultimately troubling because it might imply that we are privileging one element of the week over others, contrary to what we believe were the intentions of the organizers. We shall ignore these more ominous interpretations and simply share our delight in the journey itself, through many countries and many cultures.

Another element that wove its way through the week—along with the ponchos—was the tendency to use polarizing or dichotomizing language: the other/the self, white/non-white, colonizer/colonized, First World/Third World or Two-Thirds World, intellectual/activist, academic/grass-roots, center/margins. Perhaps it is natural to think or to express ourselves in such terms. I have noticed in my own children that as they develop language and thought their initial tendency is to think in polarizing language as a way of trying to understand reality. At the same time, there was evidence throughout the week also of a measure of discomfort with the polarizing language. This discomfort was expressed in efforts to acknowledge the complexity of the issues that we were confronting. In this way we began to undermine, to subvert and also to expand the dichotomies. For example, by adding the notion of collaborator to the dichotomy of colonizer and colonized we were able to articulate the recognition that in different contexts we ourselves may take on these different positions. In some cases we have choices. For example, when reading a text we might decide quite deliberately to read from one perspective or another. In other cases our positions are imposed upon us by gender, politics, religion, sexual orientation or other elements of our identities within particular social locations and contexts. Nevertheless, we often recognize that these dichotomies need to be questioned and subverted.

The consequence of questioning accepted dichotomies often requires us to confront the paradox that the Bible can be both an instrument of oppression and an instrument of liberation. Of course, there are many women for whom the Bible does not hold either of these positions because they define themselves and their worldviews in other ways. Nevertheless, for those in whose lives the Bible plays a central role, this book can be simultaneously a source of pain and a source of joy.

Main Lectures

MTW: Having identified some of the core metaphors and other elements of our shared discussion, we move to a brief survey of the main lectures. This survey is not meant to summarize the lectures or to speak in place of their authors with respect to their central points. It is simply to share with you our own impressions of what we have learned and thereby to raise again some of the hermeneutical proposals that have emerged during the week.

Silvia Schroer's opening lecture introduced some general questions, such as: 'What does liberation mean?' and 'What kind of feminist interpretation of the Bible is liberating?' Silvia Schroer made a strong case for including images as well as texts as sources for the work of feminist hermeneutics of liberation. She argued that we should make use both of artistic renderings of biblical passages, which are just as much interpretations as are commentaries and other textual renditions, as well as images from the ancient Near East and the other ancient cultures among which biblical literature flourished. These latter enable us better to set the Bible within its historical setting. Silvia Schroer also suggested that we must not content ourselves with the work of deconstruction, but we must also engage in reconstruction. Reconstruction is essential to our commitments to the community or communities in which or for which we do our work.

Elisabeth Schüssler Fiorenza then outlined a set of useful tools for doing feminist theology in general, and feminist hermeneutics of the Bible in particular. She used the term 'kyriarchy' as a way of referring to the structures of multiple oppression in which gender is only one, albeit important, element. Other elements include race, class, age, sexual orientation and economic status. These as well as other elements of personal identity can be turned into oppression. She also gave us a simple but radical definition of feminism as the notion that women are people. This definition reminds us that women are still often denied the opportunity to live as fully human persons. To struggle for women means to struggle for a more human world. Third, Elisabeth Schüssler Fiorenza provided us with a sketch of what she calls a hermeneutical dance, that is, the hermeneutical struggle for a critical feminist interpretation of the Bible. She proposed seven steps for this dance. These steps are in effect seven battles through which we fight to deconstruct the power or the authority of the biblical text insofar as this prevents liberation. They also serve as tools for constructing meanings for the biblical text as a foundation for our struggle for liberation. It was clear that Elisabeth Schüssler Fiorenza wanted us not just to sit, think and discuss but also to act.

Nancy Cardoso Pereira's lecture focused on story-telling. She told a powerful story of massacre and resistance, woven into a poncho, and then expanded into several more ponchos. She showed us that Bible stories were often used in an oppressive way to condemn Latin American popular religion, a religion of poor and landless people. Her hermeneutics entails interweaving biblical stories with stories from Latin America's popular religious tradition. She illustrated this hermeneutic by presenting the Malinche in interaction with the biblical Judith. Her work illustrates the importance and power of images.

AR: The film by Pier Paolo Pasolini, *The Gospel According to St Matthew* (*Il Vangelo Secondo Matteo*, Pier Paulo Pasolini, Italy/France 1964), was presented by Suzanne Buchan, expert in film studies, not just as a diversion but also as yet another example of interpretation that we could take into account in our week of thinking about feminist biblical herme-neutics for liberation. The fact that many of us reacted against it did not diminish its usefulness. As an audiovisual medium, film presents us with a rich text, including words, visual images, music and, as Suzanne Buchan emphasized, also the technical aspects such as camerawork. All of these elements influence our interpretation of film. Film is itself an interpreta-tion, but it also presents a special interpretative challenge. Whereas in the many contexts in which we work we often emphasize the multiplicity of interpretation, a film-maker usually has to choose one particular line of interpretation or else risk losing his or her audience. Many of us were conscious both of what Pasolini emphasized in the film and what he omitted. In particular, we focused on the way in which women were presented or not presented. This film not only presents an interpretation of the Gospel of Matthew but also calls for our attempts to interpret the film itself. Among other issues, we also addressed questions of context. That is, we considered whether or not Pasolini's own context influenced the film and whether some understanding of his own social location helps us to understand his film.

The lectures by Renita Weems and Musa W. Dube, though coming from very different concrete experiences, converged on the experience of oppression. Renita Weems focused on the role of the reader of the Bible. She made a significant point: it is people who have power to oppress, not texts. Although we are used to speaking about oppressive texts, we should keep in mind that texts become oppressive in the ways that they are used by people. She also encouraged us to look critically at the issue of deconstruction and reconstruction and asked us to consider what happens to people who deconstruct the text and then find themselves bereaved of the text as a resource. Thus we who teach the Bible, in whatever context, must be sensitive to the impact of our interpretations on those to whom or with whom we are reading the text. What effect will our efforts to show the androcentrism, patriarchy and the oppressive potential of the Bible have on someone who might have profound need of this very text in order to continue her or his journey?

Musa W. Dube, like Nancy Cardoso Pereira, introduced song and story into her talk in a way that was very engaging. Musa W. Dube is a superb storyteller. In her story yesterday evening she introduced us to the contrast between the disobedient daughter who is non-compliant in her food preparation and is punished for it, and the obedient daughter who prepares such a wonderful meal for her future husband. Her presentation asked us to confront issues of colonization and post-colonization, and to consider the roles that we can take in reading as a colonizer, a collaborator or the colonized. She suggested that while the issues surrounding colonization and post-colonization are related to patriarchy and gender, they should not be subsumed under these categories. This point connects powerfully with Elisabeth Schüssler Fiorenza's emphasis on kyriarchy, and the intersecting elements of oppression. These reflections suggest that while we may focus on gender issues in our work as feminists, we must also consider other oppressive relationships which intersect with oppression based on gender.

Basic Problems within a Feminist Hermeneutics of Liberation

Three Main Points

MTW: We have offered our impressions of the main lectures as an 'hors d'oeuvres' before the main course of the meal. We continue now with what the French call 'le plat de résistance'. These are some basic foods that we hope you will all be able to digest. This course entails three points that have emerged from the week's discussion as being basic to the work of feminist biblical hermeneutics of liberation. The first point concerns the Bible as a foundational text for feminist biblical hermeneutics. While it is not necessarily a holy text for all who are concerned with feminist biblical hermeneutics, it is by definition central to the task. Furthermore, the Bible is a cultural classic that has impact worldwide even for groups and individuals for whom it is not a sacred text. For this reason the struggle with the biblical text is crucial for feminist liberation. The second point concerns the Janus-face of the Bible as an instrument of both oppression and liberation. The third point concerns the integral relationship between gender oppression and other forms of oppression.

AR: To these basic elements we will now add a variety of others to form a buffet of ideas. We share these in the hope that others will find them nourishing and tasty, but we know that it is the nature of a buffet that not every dish will appeal to every guest. Some dishes will be left over, others will be consumed completely.

The Bible as a Foundational Text
MTW: I want to present you a first set of thoughts. My comments will expand upon the first of the three basic points we have just mentioned, namely, the Bible as a foundational text. Although, as we have already noted, the Bible is not a sacred text for all, we must also acknowledge that for many, many people, women and men, it is in fact a holy text. But the Bible is considered holy not just in terms of its content but also in terms of its status as an object. In some cultures, as we have been told, the Bible is buried in a new house; in other cases, its pages are eaten. Whereas we often tend to focus primarily on the words of the Bible and their potential for both oppression and liberation, we must remember that it is also important to consider the oppressive and liberative potential of the Bible as an object in and of itself.

Related to the question of the Bible as sacred object and holy text is the issue of authority. To assent to the Bible as a holy or sacred text is to give authority to it. As Elisabeth Schüssler Fiorenza has indicated, there are ways to deconstruct and reconstruct that authority. The Bible should not be considered as an archetype, that is, as the unchangeable word of God, authoritative for all cultures and all generations, but as a prototype which inspires people to retell it in new contexts and in support of new actions of liberation. But these two words, prototype and archetype, are in themselves riddles. We must explain what we mean when we use them.

Third, it is not only Christianity that accords foundational status to an ancient book. This is a trait shared also by Judaism and Islam, as well as, to some extent, Asian religions such as Hinduism. The dilemma of how to deal with their ancient sacred texts is faced by all of these communities today. The problem of the Bible as a book can therefore be a starting point of inter-religious dialogue. Such dialogue would point out where these religious traditions converge as well as diverge. It would also help to see differences within each religious tradition, as, for example, between Catholicism and Protestantism, in general as well as with specific application to the role of the Bible in the oppression and liberation of women. In the German context such discussion has already been taking place between Christian and Jewish women, and is just beginning to include Muslim women as well. One issue that emerges in such dialogue is the different roads that intellectual history has taken. For example, the Islamic cultures did not pass through what we could call 'modernity' and its commitment to rationalism; hence they have by and large not had to consider the impact of what we call 'higher biblical criticism' on traditional faith in the Quran as divinely revealed. Such differences can affect the nature of the communication that takes place between Muslim, Jewish and Christian women on issues of liberation.

Fourth, one important issue that we did not address at length is the question of canon. Many feminist biblical scholars advocate challenging the boundaries of the canon. The book of Judith, to which Nancy Cardoso Pereira and Musa W. Dube referred, is not considered a biblical book by Protestants and Jews. Another way of challenging canonical boundaries is to include meaningful stories from outside the biblical tradition, for example, from indigenous traditions. Even if we choose not to refer to them as canonical, such stories can be used as intertexts that illuminate biblical stories, themes and structures, especially structures of colonialism. Some stories provide an interesting vantage point from which to critique biblical texts. These comments suggest that the issue of the Bible as normative, as canonical, as the Word of God, is in fact a wide and open field for feminist discussion.

Contexts

AR: Another set of dishes spread out on our buffet table reflect our different contexts or social locations. One of the richest aspects of this week has been the opportunity to talk with women from different countries, religious traditions and points of view. We have appreciated in particular the opportunity to hear from women from Eastern Europe, whom many of us in the First World often have no opportunity to meet. Their comments brought us face to face with the experience of the Cold War and the dismantling of the Soviet Union. As women interested in feminist liberation, we need to think both about those who considered Communism to be a liberating system and those who suffered under its oppression. As a

Canadian, I found myself also thinking of the experiences of native peoples of North America and the active discussion in North American media and society about the effect of the mission schools on young children who forcibly were taken away from their parents and their culture, who were forbidden to speak their native language and who were often subjected to sexual abuse.

Another aspect of our social locations concerns the contexts in which we work and to which we will return after this week is over. Our work situations will also influence what we take away from this week and what we hope to achieve by being here. Some of us are activists who spend our time travelling to villages, speaking with women and working for economic and social wellbeing. Some of us are teachers in different contexts, which can both provide opportunities as well as limit the kinds of things that we do. For some of us our activism is integrated with our paid employment; for others, such as teachers at secular universities, it is often separate from our paid work.

Theory and Praxis
MTW: An element related to that of activism is the inter-relationship between theory and praxis. Often these are expressed as a dichotomy that is linked to the contrast between the academy and grass-roots activism, and between Northern or Western thinking as imperial and the South as non-imperial. Our discussions this week have emphasized the need for praxis to inform our theories, and for our theories to remain open to new practical impulses. Our model for this is Elisabeth Schüssler Fiorenza, who is continually inspired by new practical experiences which she reflects upon and integrates with her feminist hermeneutical theories. Perhaps we might consider theory to be an intellectual framework that we can return to again and again in the course of our praxis. Perhaps, indeed, theory can be seen as a cupboard in which we store everything necessary to lay out the table and to prepare meals: cups, dishes, silverware, serving utensils. Storing things in the cupboard keeps them organized and available for use at any time. Within this metaphor, some crucial questions arise. Do we need one single cupboard for all of us? Or is it better to imagine many, many kitchens with different cupboards, each equipped with the things that are best suited to that individual kitchen? If we opt for a multiplicity of cupboards, how can interaction, mutual learning and understanding occur? These issues emerge powerfully in our era as we struggle with globalization in all aspects of our lives and within our communities.

Missing Issues

God-Talk

AR: In reflecting upon the week as a whole, Marie-Theres Wacker and I noted with some surprise that there was very little discussion of the Deity or deities, God, the Goddess, or gods and goddesses. For some of us this may have been a relief, but it is worth noting that the element of the divine is not irrelevant to feminist biblical hermeneutics. This observation leads me into the final category of items that we bring to the buffet table. These are foods that were not brought by anybody or perhaps not brought in sufficient quantity to be satisfying. We wish to reiterate here that our comments on this issue, as well as throughout our presentation as a whole, are entirely subjective and are not intended to be either representative of or normative for the group as a whole.

Historical Criticism

AR: One element that we felt could have been given more attention relates to the liberative potential of academic training in biblical studies and theology. Those of us with graduate degrees in biblical studies were often trained primarily in historical criticism. For many of us the historical-critical approach to the Bible, that is, the situation of the Bible into its Near Eastern and Roman contexts, was a powerfully liberating and exciting experience. Although we to realize that historical criticism is not enough and must be supplemented with other perspectives such as feminist hermeneutics, we do not want to ignore or forget the impact that such studies have had on many feminist biblical critics. Also important to mention is the exhilaration, the excitement of working with biblical texts. Acknowledging this experience does not negate everything that we have discussed thus far, such as the need to engage not only in theory but also in praxis.

MTW: I see yet another, more spiritual aspect to the historical-critical venture. Historical work allows one to encounter, however dimly, the women of the past, our fore-sisters, to whom we belong in some fundamental way. We might even see an eschatological element in this encounter. I can hope for them, I can trust in the God of all living, that in our historical work we can in some way join together at one table, the dead with the living.

Jewish-Christian Relations

MTW: One additional point that is linked to the historical origin of the Bible concerns the relationship between Judaism and Christianity. Judaism and Christianity have been intertwined from the very beginnings of the Jesus movement. The Christian Old Testament or the Hebrew Bible is entirely a collection of Jewish writings; the Jesus movement was a Jewish movement in its time; the so-called Christian Testament or New Testament writings were written at a time where one cannot yet speak of a distinct Christianity beside or outside of Judaism. Our Christian origins are linked with Judaism. We face this connection every time we open our Bible. Yet the historical relationship between Judaism and Christianity can be problematic. Christianity has had the tendency to deny itself over and against Judaism, to see Judaism and Jews as the Other. This tendency has influenced both theory and praxis. In theory, that is, in Christian theology, the Jews were considered to be the wife to whom her husband, God, has given the divorce bill due to her stubbornness and infidelity, including her unwillingness to recognize Jesus as the Messiah. This understanding of the Jewish role in Christian theology at times legitimated the persecution or even the murder of Jews. As a German woman I am aware of the terrible history of anti-Semitism that reached its most murderous expression in the Shoah. But anti-Judaism and anti-Semitism are not a problem for Germany alone. Jews have been discriminated in many other countries. Furthermore, anti-Jewish feelings are expressed in the Christian Testament itself. If we do not wish to discard the Christian Testament altogether, we must nevertheless acknowledge and come to terms with these anti-Jewish aspects of Christian Scripture. These issues arise even when reading the Hebrew Bible, which, when read from a Christian perspective, may also be used to denigrate the Jews. We Christians need an ethics of reading in order to prevent ourselves from thinking or acting out anti-Judaism.

Oppressive Readings

AR: These reflections return us to one of the themes that many of us here this week have commented on repeatedly, namely, the need to be sensitive to the ways in which our readings might oppress others. This principle goes far beyond the Jewish–Christian tension and inter-religious dialogue as such to touch many other issues pertaining to our personal identities and community affiliations. We must constantly remember and honor the fact that our own ways of looking at the world are not the only ways.

AR: Thus the buffet that we have set before you today is by no means complete. Our goal has been to provide you with some food for thought. To this end, we have presented some dishes and ingredients which you may or may not choose to use to make your own meal. Even if you choose to use them, you will no doubt have to add some from your own kitchen, from the kitchens of those who are present this week or perhaps from the kitchens of others who are absent. We have all taken much nourishment from the meals that we have provided for one another this week and hope that there will be other opportunities to share food, wine and our thoughts together again.

CHANGING SEASONS: ABOUT THE BIBLE AND OTHER SACRED TEXTS IN LATIN AMERICA

Nancy Cardoso Pereira

There are five seasons in Latin America:
winter, spring, summer, fall and massacre.

—Manoel Scorza

The Story of Dona Añada

Dona Añada wrote in ponchos. She was an old, blind woman who after years of domestic service in silence had returned to her village. She couldn't work any more, but she still could weave. And so she wove ponchos for the people of her village, ponchos woven in the style as they had been for hundreds of years.

But the people in her village soon noticed that Dona Añada wove life itself into her ponchos. A man recognized his ancestors in one of her ponchos. And soon all of the villagers learned to read the history of their village in the colors and figures of her cloth. Although blind, Dona Añada could see with an inner eye.

Battles, exploits and important persons from the past appeared in her ponchos. Events from the past that had been forgotten became visible, events that had been asking to be remembered: the beginning of her people's resistance, the blood that they had shed in massacres. And the goddess Inkari, broken in thousands of pieces, almost impossible to put together again.

But Dona Añada's ponchos did not remain fixed in the past. The threads moved quickly and changed scenes, new colors and new lines appeared, all joining together into the eternal fabric. Soon the villagers began to recognize themselves and their village in the ponchos. Dona Añada wove the present into her fabric. And toward the bottom the goddess Inkari appeared, frantically trying to put her parts together again.

In reading their own reality in the ponchos, the village community also was confronted by questions that their ancestors had asked: What if? Why not? Who knows what would happen if...? By learning to read Dona Añada's ponchos, the villagers learned to understand their own reality, a reality of oppression. They recognized their enemies, outer and inner. They saw the goddess Inkari rise to life again and heard her promise: 'When my people free this land from the oppression of foreign powers I will rise to join them in battle and will live among them once again'.

Many tried to read the future in Dona Añada's ponchos, but this was impossible. The future lay in the decisive moment of learning to read the texts that emanated from the old blind woman's hands. It was the past that opened the door to a present filled with secrets and promises.

The authorities confiscated Dona Añada's ponchos after they had heard of their secret texts and the talk of uprising. They brought in specialists to decipher the ponchos, but they could only find ordinary, everyday clothing.

The power to read lay in the eyes of the village community that felt the colors, the threads and the movements of the designs. The word was alive among the people. And their encounter with the ponchos was a revelation! The indigenous community was the fabric of the ponchos that were written on bodies of the poor.

The rebellion began. In the beginning was the poncho, and the poncho became flesh and lived among us. The goddess Inkari gathered her pieces together on the living and sacred earth.

This is a free reading of a section from a real and yet fantastic 1986 novel by Manoel Scorza, *A Tumba do Relâmpago* (*The Lightning Tomb*). Scorza was one of Latin America's great writers. His books deal with the unending battle of the Latin American people against oppression. At the end of Scorza's story the villagers are massacred and the ponchos and the body of the people torn to pieces.

The Fabric of Latin American Texts

There are many stories throughout Latin America that mix myths and fantastic realities with the eternal suffering of this continent's peoples. The beauty and the anger of these stories, novels and poems live in intensive dialogue with the history of the struggle for liberation of this continent. The battle against political, economic and cultural oppression has woven beauty and pain into these peoples' texts as well as on the bodies of the poor.

Whether by the landless in Brazil, the FARC in Columbia or the Zapatistas in Mexico, whether in Chile, Cuba or Guatemala, over the past decades hundreds and thousands of ponchos have been created by these populace movements and struggles throughout Latin America.

The struggles of women, in particular, have contributed to the fabric of these ponchos. And, similar to the Bible, another one of the many ponchos, these texts cry out to be read, to be embraced and to be believed. The challenge is to learn to read the Bible as well as the other sacred texts that have been written by the struggles of countless women. Feminists are clothed in ponchos, and the challenge for feminist theologians is not to allow these texts to be usurped by exegetical or scholarly methodology.

Existence, history or daily life, these can be read. They are primary, sacred texts that ask to be interpreted, remembered, revealed. But the fabric of these texts has taken on a dark shadow in Latin America.

Our history is not a peaceful and quiet history. Latin America's history is marked by invasion, capitulation and subjugation. 'Massacre' is a key word in our history. Being massacred has become a way of life. And the instruments of massacre are many—guns and books, flags and religion, the Bible and wealth, all telling us over and over again: 'This is natural! This is life!'

Our ancestors, mothers, fathers and children, cry out from the past, joined by their violated land: widowed forests, orphaned waters, grieving animals. In an enormous chorus they whisper: 'This is not natural! This is not life! This is a massacre!'

The Bible's Scars in Latin America

The massacre is also a religious massacre. Christianity arrived in Latin America as a gun, as a sign of power. It has functioned and still functions as a religion of oppression.

For women and for all native Afro-Brazilians the Bible was and is an instrument of massacre. It was the justification of the robbery of our land and the enslavement of our people. The Bible was an instrument of massacre because it was and still has been used to treat native religions as demonical, linking them with idolatry and superstition. The Bible was used to condemn native sacred dances, rituals and meals. And the Bible was used to forbid the full participation of women in Church and society, binding them in the bonds of temptation, weakness of the flesh and sin.

Moreover, the manner in which the Bible has been transmitted throughout history in Latin America has preserved it as an exclusive, elitist text for the illiterate poor. It has been used to sustain European concepts and visions ignorant of the realities and needs of the native Latin American peoples.

We cannot read or study the Bible in Latin America without opening these old wounds. The first step we must take—a hermeneutical and political one—is to locate ourselves in this pain, to open our memories and to take the risk of denouncing our own Christian tradition.

During the visit of the Pope John Paul II in Peru some 500 years after the invasion of our continent, a group of leaders of native communities wrote a letter and sent it to the Pope with a Bible saying: 'We, native peoples from the Andes and the Americas, have decided to use the visit of the Pope to give back your Bible because in five hundred years it hasn't given us love, peace or justice' (Richard 1992: 19).

The symbolic act of giving back the Bible is also a rejection of the religious model that it has imposed and its character of domination, not just colonial domination but also the oppression of women, children and nature. The bad news is that the Good News could not be tasted by our people without a spice of domination.

The journey of the theology of liberation from/with the Bible was a tremendous effort to free Christianity of its ideological commitments to the politics of domination. The use of sociological tools opened new perspectives and allowed integration into popular movements.

Thousands of communities have been touched by popular readings of the Bible or reading the Bible through the perspective of the poor. Thousands of activists from trade unions, land reform movements, socialist party leaders and feminists have been affected. Seminaries, schools, magazines, meetings, celebrations and struggles have been influenced by popular readings of the Bible…but this is just the first mile.

To understand the role of the Bible in Latin American culture it is necessary to walk the second mile and to talk about popular religion or, to be more exact, the religions of the poor.

The Religions of the Poor

The God of the poor is present in ordinary things, in the working hands of the people, in the struggle that becomes life's beauty, in work and food, the very now and the challenges of tomorrow, in a hug and in dancing and in the tenderness that dawn hopes. It's a God of taste. It's a God of love. The experts know nothing about God (they know without tasting) but the poor can feel at home in the arms of this God.

—based on a poem by Hugo Asmann

Let us consider some points about popular religion:
1. It is an alternative form of religious expression, not orthodox and not conformist.
2. It is not institutional, it is not controlled by priests or government agents.

3. Since it is not authoritative, popular religions is inclusive and plural, eclectic and syncretic, both in beliefs and in practices.

4. It is characterized more by celebration than by intellectual elaboration.

5. It is not dependent on literature but employs numerous cultural and theatrical resources; religious tradition is alive in food, dance, sacred objects, and so on.

6. It has a very loose relation with official religion and the Bible, freely selecting and employing symbols, images and metaphors.

The syncretic character of popular religion calls for an anthropological perspective that cannot be encapsulated by historical-critical or socio-literary hermeneutics. The cultural content of popular religion is incoherent and undisciplined; each thing is a lot of things at the same time. It is opposed to linear positions, denying any attempt to order what insists on remaining disordered. This opposition to order is a way of knowing, it is a way of resistance and beauty.

Popular religion has a very creative relationship with Christian tradition and the Bible. Narratives, images, miracles and rituals are important to this relationship. For example, the Bible opened at Psalm 91 in front of a house or a tent entrance is a powerful sign that protects the whole family. Someone can be blessed by placing the Bible on their head or their hand. Narratives from the Gospels are used very freely in songs and dramas with non-biblical stories. People dress in or eat fragments of biblical texts.

Traditional historical-critical methodology and its extremely refined rationalism have failed to incorporate life-embracing, holistic concepts. In order to contact the hybrid plurality of self in the biblical text it is necessary to immerse oneself in the complete spectrum of existence, including its sweat, sensuality, danger and creativity. Without this awareness, hermeneutics will remain an elitist and exclusive enterprise.

Let me share a statement from the group Atabaque, the Black Pastoral Agents:

> The Bible is one source among many. Sometimes it is not even the main one. For the poor and the black, the stories of the saints and of miracles stand side by side, for example, with the sung and danced stories of the *terreiro* of Candomblé. The Bible of the *terreiro* is a story that is danced and sung. It is not written, it cannot be read…but it is also a story of salvation and liberation. It builds black identity, family ties, dignity, health, organization, education and the promotion of life.

Black Pastoral Agents can proclaim an image of God that is and is not in the Bible.

The Bible is a source of light for dialogue and solidarity, but it cannot exist as the Book, the Word or the Truth. It will be accepted in dialogue, not in exclusivity. The challenge now is to learn to criticize interpretations based on just one paradigm, to learn to work with a plurality of paradigms without creating a hierarchy among them, whether of gender, of social and ethnic relations or of generations. The authority of the sacred has shifted from the book in itself to a dialogue with a plurality of living traditions.

Feminist Reading

The feminist reading of the Bible shares the same perspectives as native and Afro-Brazilian reflection and praxis. We share the same wounds and suffering. We have studied the Bible and used it, but always with doubts of its ostensible objectivity and its scholarly character. By 'we' I mean a whole first and second generation of biblical scholars that have worked under the motivation of the theology of liberation. While the first genera-tion—an exclusively male generation—studied in North America and in Europe, the second generation—including the first female scholars—has arisen from a popular reading of the Bible shaped by historical-critical methods but with very strong sociological accents.

But there was also a growing uneasiness about the treatment of women's concerns. It began as an unspoken need, a very old hunger that was used to not being feed. It was unaccustomed enough to talk about the poor, about the struggle for survival, about political changes that had to be made. We were part of the whole, but we were there masked as men. We had been reduced to non-women.

In the beginning it was enough to look for women in the Bible. We were happy just hearing our own voice speaking the names of women and recognizing ourselves as part of their history. But reading and interpreting is not a controlled operation. We realized upon returning home that we could have said other words, that we could have made other links, but we had not done so. We had remained silent in order not to disturb the process and not endanger our presence there. But we did start dreaming…

And that was the key to the second movement, the key to understanding the narrowness of traditional biblical hermeneutics and the invitation to speak at last our own words. Our marginal situation within Churches and theological institutions, as well as in society, gives us the strength and the motivation to create a new biblical hermeneutics in dialogue with other processes of empowerment of women and the transformation of academic methodology, society and Christian Churches.

Following a period of great interest in the historical books and the prophets in Latin American biblical reflection there was a shift to an interesting use of stories and poetry at the beginning of the 1990s. The use of biblical stories and poetry opened a dialogue with a spirituality concerned with everyday life and its links to culture and resistance. Ruth, Esther, Judith and the Song of Songs, at first glance this looks like an encouraging focal point for women's reflection. At the beginning it was enough just to find these characters in the Bible in order to confirm ourselves, Latin American women, as theologians or biblical scholars.

Although the methodology we have been developing uses traditional techniques (translation, textual criticism, semantic field study, literary criticism, internal textual structure, etc.), the recognition that the biblical text was shaped by a male consciousness and then disguised as a neutral tradition has challenged feminist hermeneutics to read through and beyond the text. Many times it means reading the text against itself, looking for underlying rhetorical possibilities, visualizing dissident experiences.

Sociological analysis of the text tries to overcome historical, economical or literary exclusivity while giving priority to anthropological tools and cultural dynamics. The hermeneutic exercise must be minimalist, artifactual, rhythmic, based on processes and gestures without intending a closed system or synthesis. Such procedures have as an aim 'that the rigor of the analysis never steals a people's lives from a text', according to anthropologist Carlos Brandão (1983: 74). Ivone Gebara (1998) likewise says that comprehending a text is not projecting yourself in an absolute form in the text, but exposing yourself to it. The text is, in this way, a mediation for a revelation of ourselves.

Reading Judith in Latin America

Using the popular reading method of seeing–judging–acting, the biblical narrative works as a mirror or a lens in order to reflect or to examine our own reality. The description of the political situation in the first chapter of the book of Judith serves as a starting point. The description of the tyranny of the empire contains many elements similar to our own situation. The figure of Judith thus appears as the expression of the situation of collective political suppression and as a model of resistance. Heroines are not unusual in the Bible, but the difference between heroes and heroines in biblical narratives is the fact that for men victory will always mean a step to a more powerful position, while for heroines it leads either to an anonymous honor or maternity.

In Judith's case the results of her actions will earn her recognition and praise but without changing her social position. In fact, her character is presented as a woman without social or political intentions. She is a virtuous widow and will remain so until the end of her days. The fact of her transformation into an erotic, seductive woman is for traditional hermeneutics not significant; her strong spirituality and her desire to defend the exclusivity of YHWH and the Jewish nation protect her.

But it is essential to recognize that the book of Judith does not want to give a historical description of a social reality; it is a carefully constructed fiction with strong didactic intent. The character of Judith is chained by these didactic aims. What is interesting about Judith is not what she is but what she can be. She is a female chameleon, but is she so through self-determination or by coercion? As she takes off her widow's clothes she makes a conscious political statement and thus transforms her body into a stage where a conflict between powers takes place. The dramatic prayer before her transformation stresses a woman in conflict with herself. She is part of a culture sustained by moral values that believes that an honorable woman is not allowed to be sensual or erotic.

The question of the abuse of Judith's body is central to the Latin American perspective. In a continent where rape, prostitution, sexual abuse, sex tourism and pornography are a significant part of our history and export goods, any attempt to functionalize the female body—even a symbolic attempt—must give rise to suspicion. The last bastion of conservative Latin American socio-political domination is sexual morality. Any expropriation of the female body—including subjective and objective sexual and erotic alienation—favors and reinforces the expropriation of human free will and the capacity to rebel (Maduro 1978).

The book of Judith represents, in fact, the expropriation of a woman's power to choose what she wants to be. Its didactic interests nourish the consolidation of monotheism, the exclusivity of a single, male god, the subjugation of women as well as the plurality of native culture. The idealization of the female character, the denial of her right to choose, is a reinforcement of traditional male models of spirituality, relationships and power.

Reading Other Texts

Stories from the indigenous and Afro-Brazilian tradition also have heroines. The difference to the biblical story of Judith lies in their complete absence of moral judgments that would bind them in accepted collected values such as honor or virtue. The myths of Brazil's indigenous peoples are characterized by pronounced erotic freedom void of censure or functionalization. They deal with social relationships with a clear accent on sexuality in a climate of contradiction, deception and creativity without recourse to higher national or collective interests.

I could mention many stories and novels here. Unique to all is an absence of taboos; there are no canons for these stories and their heroines. They are characterized by incest, greed, love, violence, compassion, oppression and war; the whole spectrum of life is brought to word in these stories (Mindlin 1997). (Two of these characters, Malinche and Iemanjá, are described in the Appendix.)

Moreover, the same story can even be subject to differing, sometimes completely contradictory accounts that provoke varying and liberating interpretations. For women who read, hear or perform these stories the lack of didactic, restrictive tones creates space for free interpretation. Ambiguity and plurality affirm female retrospection and consciousness.

Conclusion

The Bible should be read like the texts that live in the fabric spun by the hands of Dona Añada. The Bible should be read in the difficult but indispensable encounter with the myths written on the violated bodies of the Latin American people. It is necessary to learn to read the fabric of these texts in interaction with the history, fantasy, memory and utopias that nourish the fight of the poor, of poor women.

Work with the Bible should begin with fidelity to feminist struggles and their motivation. We must not allow male ethical preconceptions and conditioning to perpetuate in these texts or in our collective memory. The Bible must break free of the chains of programmatic discourse, didactic interpretation and rectified exegesis.

Contrasting Judith with La Malinche or Iemanjá means creating a dialogue between the biblical text and other positive female symbols in order to reaffirm women's rights over their bodies and their right to self-determination in fundamental political and cultural matters.

APPENDIX

La Malinche

The native woman 'Malitzin' or 'La Malinche' was given as a gift to Spanish conqueror Cortés by the Mayan military chief of Tabasco. She was loyal to her master, learned the Spanish language and assimilated the Spanish culture. She was thus able to carry out such activities as translating and interpreting languages, thus ultimately supporting the consolidation of the colonization of Mexico. Up until this day the term 'malinchista' is employed in a pejorative sense in order to describe an identification with other cultures that represents a betrayal of the Mexican national identity:

> 'La Malinche'. Slave, interpreter, secretary, mistress, mother of the first 'Mexican'. Her very name still stirs up controversy. Many Mexicans continue to revile the woman called Doña Marina by the Spaniards and La Malinche by the Aztecs, labeling her a traitor and harlot for her role as the alter-ego of Cortés as he conquered Mexico. They ignore that she saved thousands of Indian lives by enabling Cortés to negotiate rather than slaughter. (Lenchek 1997: 1)

La Malinche played an important role in the conquista. She could speak the Mayan and Aztec (Nahuatl) languages. The Spanish priest Jerónimo von Aguilar employed the Mayan language in order to translate what Malinche said, and she used the Aztec language when speaking to the emissaries sent by Montezuma, the great Tlatoani (the Aztec term for emperor).

Iemanjá

Iemanjá represents everything related to salt water and the oceans. She is regarded as the principle behind everything in relation to the earth, Oduduwa. Iemanjá is the ocean that provides nourishment, that links the corners of the earth, that gives the earth energy. But she is also the world's largest cemetery. And she represents the depths of the subconscious, the motion of rhythm and everything that takes place cyclically in the world, everything that repeats for infinity. Iemanjá is controlled force, equilibrium.

In one story Iemanjá unites with Oxalá, creation, and together they have four sons, Ogum, Exu, Oxóssi and Xangô. As her sons gradually leave her Iemanjá begins to feel increasingly lonely and decides to stream around the world until she reaches Okerê, where she is honored for her beauty, intelligence and elegance. King Alafin of Okerê falls passionately in love with her and wants her to become his wife. Iemanjá flees, but the king calls his army together and has her pursued. She is trapped by Oke (the mountains) and falls, thereby gashing her giant breasts, and this was the birth of rivers. Iemanjá thus became the mother of the ocean gods Oxum, Obá and Iansã.

Another story says that Iemanjá was so beautiful that her son Xangô could not resist and followed her with the incestuous desire to possess her. While fleeing she falls and gashes her breasts, thereby giving birth to all waters on the earth as well as to the Ibejis, the children of Xangô and Iemanjá. And still a different version recounts the pursuit in a contrary manner: it is Iemanjá who chases her son Aganju (firm earth), he is the one pursued.

Since Iemanjá represents the subconscious she is often considered the goddess of reason and good sense, as the one who gives balance and stability so that we can deal with our emotions and subconscious desires.

Other variations of the Iemanjá story recount that Olodumare created the world and returned back to the home of gods, then giving each god a realm to rule. Iemanjá was placed in charge of Oxalá's household and the education of his children. Iemanjá began her work but soon complained about her lowly position; all the other gods received offerings and homage while she had to live like a slave. Her complaints about her fate were unending, eventually driving Oxalá mad. When Oxalá was in hospital Iemanjá realized what she had done to him and cured him in a short time by giving him herbal baths, fresh water, kola nuts, white doves and sweet fruits.

Oxalá, once again healthy and eternally grateful, implored Olodumare to give Iemanjá the power over all heads. After that Iemanjá also received offerings and homage, especially before rites that dealt with increasing or strengthening reason and intellect.

BIBLIOGRAPHY

Brandão, Carlos
    1983   *Os deuses do povo* (São Paulo: Brasiliense).
Gebara, Ivone
    1998   'What Scriptures are Sacred Authority? Ambiguities of the Bible in the
                Lives of Latin American Women', in Kwok Pui-Lan and Elisabeth Schüssler
                Fiorenza (eds.), *Women's Sacred Scriptures* (London: SCM Press; Maryknoll,
                NY: Orbis Books) (= *Concilium* 34.3): 7-19.
Lenchek, Shep
    1997   '"La Malinche": Harlot or Heroine?', *Guadaljara-Lakeside* 14 (citation
                from: http://www.mexconnect.com).
Maduro, Otto
    1978   'Extracción de plus valia, represión de la sexualidad y catolicismo en Latino-
                américa', *Expresamente* 4: 33-39.
Mindlin, Betty, *et al.*
    1997   *Moqueca de Maridos—mitos eróticos* (São Paulo: Editora Rosa dos Tempos).
Richard, Pablo
    1992   'Hermeneutica Biblica India', *Revista de Interpretación Biblica Latino-
                americana* 11: 16-25.
Scorza, Manoel
    1986   *A Tumba do Relâmpago* (Rio de Janeiro: Nova Fronteira).

Joshua 2: Spies Sent to Jericho

[1] Then Joshua son of Nun sent two men secretly from Shittim as spies, saying, 'Go, view the land, especially Jericho'. So they went, and entered the house of a prostitute whose name was Rahab, and spent the night there. [2] The king of Jericho was told, 'Some Israelites have come here tonight to search out the land'. [3] Then the king of Jericho sent orders to Rahab, 'Bring out the men who have come to you, who entered your house, for they have come only to search out the whole land'. [4] But the woman took the two men and hid them. Then she said, 'True, the men came to me, but I did not know where they came from. [5] And when it was time to close the gate at dark, the men went out. Where the men went I do not know. Pursue them quickly, for you can over-take them.' [6] She had, however, brought them up to the roof and hidden them with the stalks of flax that she had laid out on the roof. [7] So the men pursued them on the way to the Jordan as far as the fords. As soon as the pursuers had gone out, the gate was shut.

[8] Before they went to sleep, she came up to them on the roof [9] and said to the men: 'I know that the LORD has given you the land, and that dread of you has fallen on us, and that all the inhabitants of the land melt in fear before you. [10] For we have heard how the LORD dried up the water of the Red Sea before you when you came out of Egypt, and what you did to the two kings of the Amorites that were beyond the Jordan, to Sihon and Og, whom you utterly destroyed. [11] As soon as we heard it, our hearts melted, and there was no courage left in any of us because of you. The LORD your God is indeed god in heaven above and on earth below. [12] Now then, since I have dealt kindly with you, swear to me by the LORD that you in turn will deal kindly with my family. Give me a sign of good faith [13] that you will spare my father and mother, my brothers and sisters, and all who belong to them, and deliver our lives from death.' [14] The men said to her, 'Our life for yours! If you do not tell this business of ours, then we will deal kindly and faithfully with you when the LORD gives us the land.'

[15] Then she let them down by a rope through the window, for her house was on the outer side of the city wall and she resided within the wall itself. [16] She said to them, 'Go toward the hill country, so that the pursuers may not come upon you. Hide yourselves there three days, until the pursuers have returned; then afterward you may go your way.' [17] The men said to her, 'We will be released from this oath that you have made us swear to you [18] if we invade the land and you do not tie this crimson cord in the window through which you let us down, and you do not gather into your house your father and mother, your brothers, and all your family. [19] If any of you go out of the doors of your house into the street, they shall be responsible for their own death, and we shall be innocent; but if a hand is laid upon any who are with you in the house, we shall bear the responsibility for their death. [20] But if you tell this business of yours, then we shall be released from this oath that you made us swear to you.' [21] She said, 'According to your words, so be it'. She sent them away and they departed. Then she tied the crimson cord in the window.

[22] They departed and went into the hill country and stayed there three days, until the pursuers returned. The pursuers had searched all along the way and found nothing. [23] Then the two men came down again from the hill country. They crossed over, came to Joshua son of Nun, and told him all that had happened to them. [24] They said to Joshua, 'Truly the LORD has given all the land into our hands; moreover all the inhabitants of the land melt in fear before us'.

(NRSV translation)

JUMPING THE FIRE WITH JUDITH:
POSTCOLONIAL FEMINIST HERMENEUTICS OF LIBERATION*

Musa W. Dube

Killing a Beautiful Princess

Ngubani o ngamala lapha? Nqo
Yemi ngamla. Nqo
Ufike utshele umama lo baba, Nqo
Uthi Utentelezandlane ka sekho, Ngo
Ngoba bamqebela mhlathini we bundla, ka kusa iwa.

Once upon a time. *Kolobetsa.*[1]

There was a beautiful girl called Utentelezandlane. *Kolobetsa.*

She was a princess, the daughter of the queen and king of the village. *Kolobetsa.*

Everybody spoke about her beauty, her kindness and her luck. Everybody loved her. *Kolobetsa.*

Soon the other girls in the village also began to talk about the princess. 'It is as if we are not beautiful and kind too.' 'Oh, how can you even expect anyone to notice us? As long as Utentelezandlane is alive, no one will ever notice us. Utentelezandlane, Utentelezandlane, that's all they see and talk about.' 'When are we ever going to be noticed, when is someone ever going to speak about our beauty and kindness, just like the princess?' 'We've got

* I wish to thank Dr Johanna Stiebert and Dr Gosbert Byamungu, who heard and read this paper. I particularly appreciate their attempt to clean up my postcolonial 'English' so I can take the 'voyage' into Western centers and readers disguised in the 'Queen's' language. *Leka muso Bagaetsho!*

1. The word '*kolobetsa*', which may appear in different versions, depending on the ethnic group, simply means 'carry on, go on, keep telling us' or 'yes, we are listening' to the story. It is the role of the listeners who become 'participant listeners or active listeners'. Indeed, in some cultures this interjection can become elaborate and listeners become co-storytellers.

to do something to be noticed.' 'There, you are. You have finally hit the horn of a cow on its tip!'

That very afternoon they went to see the princess. 'We are going to gather firewood in the forest. Don't you want to come with us, princess?' 'I would love to.' 'Come on. Let's go!' And off they went to the forest. The girls kept on walking further and further into the forest. When the princess asked why they had to go so far, they said, 'We want the best firewood'. Right in the heart of the forest they started gathering firewood. Soon every girl had a nice bundle of firewood, well tied and ready to be put on their heads and to head back to the village. Just as they were about to leave someone said, 'How about playing a little game?' 'Game? What kind of game?', asked another. 'Since we have so much firewood, we can build a fire.' 'And then?' 'We could see who can jump the fire?' 'Jump the fire! What a great idea!', they chorused. And soon a big fire was blazing. And the girls took their turns and jumped the fire until it was the princess' turn. 'Let's see if our beautiful princess can jump the fire', they said. And all eyes were on the princess. She jumped and they all said, 'Yeah, let's do it again!' And so they did. But when the princess' turn came around, someone pushed her into the blazing fire. They dug a hole, they buried her, they built another fire on the grave to eliminate all traces. They picked up their bundles of firewood, they put them on their heads, they hurried back to the village.

The sun was about to set when they arrived. 'Where is Utentelezandlane?', asked the queen. 'Oh, is she not back? She didn't go far with us. She returned complaining of a headache. She should have been here a long time ago.' When the sun went down and Utentelezandlane was still nowhere to be seen, the king called his servants and asked them to take their horses, dogs and lamps and go searching. And so they called out everywhere and searched through the grass, under the trees and on top of the boulders, but all remained silent. At midnight they went home and slept. In the morning the king sent the whole regiment to search for his beloved daughter, Utentelezandlane. But all to no avail. The queen and the king began to believe that their daughter had been eaten by an animal or captured by a stranger. They mourned and gave up.

One day a farmer went out to search for some nice long logs for his kraal. He walked deep into the forest and began to cut logs. As he was cutting he heard a voice singing and saying,

Ngubani o ngamala lapha? Nqo
Yemi ngamla. Nqo
Ufike utshele umama lo baba, Nqo
Uthi Utentelezandlane ka sekho, Ngo
Ngoba bamqebela mhlathini we bundla, ka kusa iwa.

It was the princess singing from her grave, telling her story. The girls were arrested for their crimes of jealousy and murder. But was the crime of patriarchy ever punished?

My grandmother used to thrill us with this little story every evening as we sat around the fire. No matter how often we had heard the story, we still asked for the tale of Utentelezandlane. I guess we wanted to be the beautiful princess, loved by everyone, rich, kind; we certainly did not wish to kill or to be killed—which is why I am standing before you today singing a song of resurrection and telling my own story.[2]

But how come the village girls killed a beautiful and beloved princess? The answer is provided in the story: they wanted their beauty and kindness to be seen and appreciated too. In a typical patriarchal[3] society where women are largely denied access to resources such as land, money and other sources of income, beauty and kindness are essential for one's status. They can help a woman in selecting a man, and consequently in getting a richer husband with more resources. Beauty and kindness, therefore, can be a woman's biggest assets for surviving and succeeding in a patriarchal society.

Circling Around a Patriarchal Orbit

As feminist[4] readers seeking the liberation of women from patriarchy and other forms of domination, we may even side with the village girls. We may say the girls of the village sought their own space in the deep forest, in the periphery of the patriarchal institutions; they plotted to seize power from the throne of patriarchy by killing the beautiful and beloved princess, for she was the embodiment of patriarchal values. By so doing, we could say, the girls of the village are rejecting patriarchal values that exalted Utentelezandlane, using her to buttress its values against all other women. Yet some feminist readers will, rightfully, regard the village girls as

---

2.   The bulk of this paper is an attempt to summarize my ideas, expressed in many different papers, which I shall repeatedly refer to.

3.   There are too many different systems of patriarchy to define it as a universally uniform practice. As used here, patriarchy defines social, economic and political institutions that are structurally arranged from a male point of view, giving power primarily to males and relegating the majority of women, certain groups of people such as homosexuals, blacks, youth and lower classes to social margins. The system is usually supported by an ideology engrained in religion, culture, law, etc.

4.   Although the word 'feminist' is used here, most Two-Thirds World women prefer to use other terms, such as 'womanist' (African Americans), 'Mujerista' (Hispanics) and many others prefer to speak of 'women's interpretation or theology'. This reservation is due to the fact that white feminists were also involved in the racist and colonizing discourse of Two-Thirds World people.

embodying rather than resisting patriarchy. They may well say, 'the princess resurrects!' She sings from her grave, refusing to die for the crimes of patriarchy.[5] Either way, there is a feeling that the reader has returned to the starting point, where patriarchy welcomes her/him!

In our trained feminist ways of reading texts, we often highlight the gender constructions of a story, how they serve as ideological tools that normalize the subordination of women and other groups. Often we also make efforts to seize the story and reinterpret it to further the empowerment of women and the creation of a just world, since highlighting a problem without advancing an alternative will hardly change the situation. This, indeed, seems to be a larger part of our strategy given that biblical feminists are readers and interpreters of texts (and theories) that are mostly written by men about women. Feminist readers in the fields of biblical literature and its institutions, the Academy and biblically related faith institutions try to inscribe or wrench the empowerment of women and the creation of a just world from these patriarchal stories. The circle of reading and re-reading, exposing and highlighting, formulating and reformulating multiple readings, applying and formulating this and that theory in feminist biblical hermeneutics can be heady.[6] This is particularly pronounced in biblical studies (unlike literature, where unknown, neglected or disguised women authors can be recovered and new women authors can rise to classic status), where the canon is 'closed' and where extra-biblical texts are still largely, if not exclusively, male-authored texts that uphold patriarchal values. In biblical studies, feminist hermeneutics of liberation can recover some neglected and marginalized 'women texts' such as the *Acts of Thecla*, the book of Judith and, possibly, some interpretations of women.[7] They can extend the canon by reading it in unconventional manners that do not preserve its patriarchal status and its values of violence.[8] But the circle of feminist hermeneutics of liberation sometimes feels like

5. See Dube Shomanah 1999: 11-17, where I read this story from the perspective of the singing princess who resists death.

6. See Dube Shomanah 1998, where I hold that the creative stance of feminists has been hijacked by multiple readings, which, while undoubtedly liberative, nevertheless also keep feminist readers focused on patriarchal texts and theories.

7. See Schüssler Fiorenza (ed.) 1994. This publication in particular with its method of 'transgressing the canonical boundaries' represents this move.

8. In general, feminist methods debunked the biblical canonical authority by showing that the biblical texts harbored violence against women and other groups to equate it with the authoritative Word of God. Further, feminist readers insisted that authority is in the hands of communities that are struggling for liberation rather than in the biblical text.

driving a different car on the same road, embarking on a feminist rocket on a patriarchal orbit. It more often than not brings one back to ponder on Audre Lorde's statement that 'the master's tools can never dismantle his house!' (Lorde 1984: 110-13).[9]

Returning to the story of Utentelezandlane, in this paper I narrate this Southern African tale not only in memory of my grandmother, not only out of a desperate need to read from the canon of black Southern African cultures, but also to make the statement that for me to read biblical texts alone is not only to be caught circling around a patriarchal orbit, it is also to circle around the imperialist web.[10] The story is used here to call attention to the global village, to its bank of stories (patriarchal as they are) and to the fact that some of us can hardly be re-reading the biblical stories alone without feeling the bitter taste of subscribing to imperialist oppression (especially since biblical texts were employed as instruments of our imperialist domination by suppressing our own stories). The story is used here, therefore, to call attention to the need to develop a multicultural and interdisciplinary approach in feminist biblical studies. I am, therefore, employing this story to put across 'my'[11] postcolonial[12] feminist interpretation(s) as a quest for liberation from both patriarchal and imperialist forces, as the assertion that biblical texts were too involved with modern imperialism to be read on their own without easily asserting their coloniz-

9.   In general, feminist scholarship has disregarded this warning; much time is spent elaborating and applying theories of male scholars and reading male texts rather than generating new ones from feminist perspectives of a just world.

10.   As used here, the word 'imperialism' shall define the imposition of economic, political and cultural institutions of some foreign nations on other less aggressive nations as well as the reconfiguration of the latter's institutions to serve the interests of the invading nation rather than to benefit its own citizens. Colonialism is a manifestation of imperialism when it includes geographical possession, but sometimes this dividing line is blurred, especially when a foreign nation is very much in control of the economic and cultural situation of another country, for example, through high debts.

11.   Although the letter of invitation to the symposium at Monte Verità stated that speakers should expound their feminist hermeneutics, I am hesitant to add 'my' since I regard what I write as raising and reflecting the many voices of Two-Thirds World women as well as men of various backgrounds and many postcolonial writers. At the same time, I accept that this paper does not and cannot represent them in their vast diversities, hence 'my' also applies, indicating my particular context and limited vision.

12.   The word 'postcolonial' defines the historical and global impact of imperialism/ colonialism and how it has shaped and informed international relations in the past and present. As used in literature, it seeks to highlight the role of texts in the power struggles of imperialism between the dominated and the dominators.

ing 'right' of suppressing other cultures (Kwok 1994: 8-19). Undoubtedly, imperialism is a relationship of domination and subordination, which involves the imposition of foreign political, economic and cultural institutions of more aggressive nations on less aggressive ones. The methods of subordination stretch from conquest and exile to ethical claims of saving the natives from their own shortcomings/sins/paganism or claims such as 'taking up the white man's burden'. The story is, therefore, read here to highlight that postcolonial feminist hermeneutic(s) of liberation is a search for a relationship of liberating interdependence between genders, races, nations, countries, cultures, economies and political establishments—at national and international levels.

Tricking or Treating Patriarchy?

This story of the beautiful and beloved princess leads me to ask whether the girls[13]/feminists of the global village play the game of jumping the fire? Do we talk about each other, about who is getting noticed and who is not in the patriarchal and imperialist global village? Do we push each other into the flame? The age of globalization[14] is more rife with competition, domination and indifference than with ethics of cooperation, solidarity and compassion (Lind 1995: 40-42). There will, no doubt, be many answers to these questions. Many of us may be planning and executing the death of patriarchy by killing a beautiful princess who embodies these values. But some of us may want to kill the princess because we want to have a place in the patriarchal structures. It might be that we sing a defiant song of resurrection against the patriarchal powers that have buried us. We may be telling our own stories on the periphery, yet at the center of the forest. But I can only hope that we are not telling our resurrection story to another man, who shall go back to the village and ensure that the patriarchal laws are fully enforced upon all other oppressed women. While the story gives us many different answers to this question, one thing is clear from the

13. As used here, the term 'girls' does not refer to the male use, which often denotes the perspective that women are children; rather, it is drawn from the story and used to evoke friendship among women with common interests and struggles.

14. As used here, 'globalization' refers to what has been defined as 'the process whereby producers and investors increasingly behave as if the world economy consisted of a single market and production area with regional or national subsections, rather than of a set of national economies linked by trade and investments flow' (Anonymous 1996), or what some have dubbed 'the absorption of all countries and systems into one' (van Drimmelen 1998: 8).

story: girls can trick and kill other girls in the bid to survive within patriarchal systems, which are designed to disadvantage them. But by killing each other are we tricking or treating patriarchy?

In the book of Judith we meet Judith, the pious, beautiful and beloved Jewish widow. She does not become a victim, she is the killer. We find that Judith can deceive and behead an unsuspecting army commander, who had come brandishing the agenda of imperialism in her city. Judith can lead the whole city in a song of triumph against the imperialist forces of invasion and urge most of us here to join the chorus. But in all her roaring success we are left with the question: If Judith kills imperialism, does she arrest the crimes of patriarchy as well? If, for example, I adopt Judith as decolonizing heroine, which suits her well, can I adopt her as a depatriarchalizing model? The answer to the latter is negative. Judith does not challenge patriarchy. She works within patriarchy; she leaves it intact. For me, Judith reminds me of the strategy of 'first things first' (Holst Petersen 1995), which was advocated by African males during the struggle for independence. That is, women were urged to fight against imperialism but not to fight against patriarchy. To adopt Judith as a feminist heroine is, therefore, to be involved in the game of jumping the fire—it is a dangerous game and it does not free women from the traps of patriarchal oppression. It is the game of jumping the fire since both stories were created about women but not for women. The stories feature women without featuring their interests; indeed, the stories feature the prescription of patriarchal values. Both stories force us to reconsider the old feminist question of 'can the master's tool dismantle his house' or just dent it, repaint it, renovate it, but not transform it? But above all, I want to believe that when we ask these questions we also wish to cultivate a transformative and revolutionary path—a path that leads away from all forms of oppression towards a more just world.

Should Feminists Trick or Treat Imperialism?

No doubt, the great patriarchy–imperialism divide, or should I say, the great imperialism–patriarchy divide has kept feminist liberation practices of First and Two-Thirds World hermeneutics at loggerheads.[15] While for many so-called First World feminist intellectuals, readers and activists imperialism could sometimes be forgotten, for Two-Thirds World practi-

---

15. For an elaborate discussion of this tension see Ashcroft, Tiffin and Tiffin 1995: 249-83.

tioners it was more like being caught in the crossfire of two battles—a woman cannot take one and ignore the other without compromising her search for liberation.

But one may ask why feminists or Two-Thirds World women should be concerned with the general struggles for liberation if it does not guarantee gender empowerment. Why should Judith, for example, fight against imperialism if patriarchy remains intact? The issue here is that imperialism/ colonialism heightens the gender oppression of women in colonized areas. While imperialism affects both men and women, it is not an exaggeration to say that it, more often than not, exposes women to more violence and poverty. This is because under normal circumstances most women have less direct access to power and resources in their nations. But in colonized contexts, where even men are denied political, economic and cultural power, women are inevitably worse off. Women become exposed to more violence and subordination because in colonized settings, where men are disempowered, men tend to assert the little power they have left on women, by controlling their dress, their movements and insisting on the most strict adherence to patriarchal traditions.[16] Culturally, in imperialized places where national cultures are invaded by a foreign one, the tendency is to insist on nativism, which, more often than not leads to increased subordination of women.[17] In addition, the colonizers bring their own forms of patriarchy to superimpose on the existing national ones—claiming that these exemplify the behavior of civilized women.[18] Women in imperialized areas are, therefore, subjected to an intensified subordination in all three spheres of their lives: cultural, political and economic.[19] The struggle

16. See Tohidi 1991, who highlights how Islamic fundamentalism (while ignited by various socio-economic factors) is a movement which cannot be totally separated from resisting Western cultural and economic imperialism. Its rise, however, has had an adverse impact on the lives of women in such countries. See Fanon 1994; Cabral 1994; Harlow 1987.

17. Sometimes during the struggles for liberation women can be exempted from their gender roles, for example, to participate in guerilla warfare, but national cultural resistance often entails nativism. See the literature mentioned in the preceding note.

18. See Spivak 1994, who discusses how the British colonizers abolished the *sati* but at the same time introduced their own Victorian gender construction on Indian women.

19. See Amadiume 1987. Focusing on one Nigerian group, Amadiume's sociological study highlights how the colonial phenomenon affected the lives of Nigerian women and how the native gender system was transformed into a much more exclusive system that relegated relatively public women into the private sphere with little or no access to property and leadership rights. This was achieved through the introduction of male orientated schools (training church clergy and colonial clerks), religion and colonial jobs.

against imperialism is, therefore, far from being peripheral to the feminist struggle for the empowerment of women.

Postcolonial feminist hermeneutics of liberation are, therefore, practices that seek liberation from both patriarchy and imperialism by realizing that gender empowerment cannot be realized while these two structural forms of oppression exist. Thus, postcolonial feminist interpretations of liberation seek to understand how the two work, how they affect women and to cultivate relationships that do not subscribe to either of them. Postcolonial feminists have learnt from history that while women's liberation is closely tied to the struggle of and for all, nevertheless, 'the women's question should not be relegated to the days after the revolution' anymore (Tohidi 1991: 260). Rather, postcolonial feminism seeks to ensure that women's empowerment/liberation is included at all levels and forms of the struggle for liberation in the national and international arena.

The play between patriarchal and imperialist oppression thus marks one of the concerns of my postcolonial feminist hermeneutics, and those of many other Two-Thirds World women. That is, Two-Thirds World women who have found themselves oppressed because of colonial and patriarchal structures are seeking ways to understand how the two operate, how they differ, how they are similar, how these two forms of oppression interact with class, race and gender and how they can be counteracted. Postcolonial feminists seek to engage ways of reading that will promote liberating interdependence of nations, races, gender, classes as well as of cultural, economic and political systems (elements that beat too close to their lives and hearts to be ignored) by taking both of these forms of oppression seriously and by seeking to articulate liberation that flows into all aspects of women's and men's lives.

It is on these grounds that I believe we have something to harvest by focusing on Judith, for white Western feminism has by and large not integrated an imperialist critique in their discourse. I therefore believe that by focusing on Judith—the woman who rises to resist the threat of the empire that is holding her people under siege—we can begin to expound a feminist hermeneutics of liberation that does not subscribe to imperialism and its related oppressions. Judith goes all the way in resisting the empire and seeing to it that it does not progress any further. Bless her heart. For me, she underlines that imperialism is oppressive and must be combated with all seriousness.

Since imperialism worsens the situation of women, it should indeed be confronted by all feminists who are committed to justice. I hope, then, that our gathering here in the middle of this forest (Monte Verità) focusing on

Judith will mark our commitment towards understanding imperialism and how it affects women's access to resources, leadership and their rights as human beings; I hope too that it will lead our feminist hermeneutics of liberation to adopt an even more committed stance towards eradicating imperialism along with patriarchal oppression.

Patriarchy and Imperialism: Are They Always Twins?

The question of the relationship of patriarchy and imperialism/colonialism is worth some pondering. While we can say that different forms and degrees of patriarchal systems are found in almost every society, one cannot say that almost every patriarchal society is also imperialist. I definitely come from a patriarchal society, but it is neither imperialist nor does it have such a history. This is not to claim that my society is not riddled with its own set of social evils—but it is not imperialist. Therefore, in my post-colonial feminist perspective I do not equate patriarchy with imperialism. I acknowledge that there is an overlap insofar as imperialist actions are often executed by men from patriarchal societies and in that respect they represent both forms of domination; the two, however, are not identical. For example, while patriarchal systems primarily involve male-centered social institutions that primarily marginalize women, men of lower classes, homosexual orientation and youth, imperialism involves women and men of lower and higher classes, of heterosexual and homosexual orientations, from foreign, aggressive nations imposing their economic, cultural and political systems on different nations. In imperialism, both women and men of certain nations participate together in oppressing women and men in distant countries. In fact, the lowest classes and the despised from a colonizing nation rise in stature in the colonized land by virtue of their race or status as colonizing agents. They are elevated through claims of superiority, whether based on race, religion, origin, science or civilization. On the other hand, men and women of all classes are affected in the colonized land. Imperialism also includes ruling other wealthy men and women, those who do not necessarily depend on their subjugators although the system is constructed as such. Among the colonized, it is the lowest classes, the despised genders and other groups located at the margins of society who suffer the most.

That patriarchal resistance does not translate into colonial resistance is attested by the fact that feminist work, focusing on counteracting patriarchy, does not necessarily counteract imperialism. Imperialism is, in fact, often oblivious to the manifestations of feminism in the texts they read, save when feminist readers make deliberate efforts to become decolonizing readers.[20] Similarly, decolonizing readers of the Two-Thirds World share a lot with feminist practitioners insofar as they both seek freedom from oppressive institutions. Yet, unless they make deliberate efforts to advocate gender empowerment, their discourse is often blind to patriarchal oppression. In short, biblical feminist readers do not necessarily counteract imperialism[21] while liberation activists and theologians from the Two-Thirds World do not necessarily champion feminist concerns,[22] although many overlapping spaces of interaction definitely exist. This condition, therefore, necessitates the need to propound postcolonial feminist hermeneutics of liberation.

Postcolonial Feminist Hermeneutics of Liberation

Postcolonial feminist hermeneutics of liberation, as practiced in its various forms, therefore seek to take imperialist oppression just as seriously as it takes patriarchy. It assumes that just as we can say that different societies have operated under different and varying degrees of patriarchy from ancient to contemporary times, that the same can be said of imperialism. It emphasizes that these two forms of oppression intensify the oppression of women in colonized regions. It holds that resisting one form of these oppressions does not always translate into the other. Postcolonial feminist hermeneutics of liberation thus seek to understand and to identify the methods and ideologies of patriarchal and imperialist discourse both in texts and in real life. Postcolonial feminist hermeneutics of liberation seek to understand how these forms of oppression manifest and justify them-

---

20. See Dube 2000: 168-84, where I offer an analysis of Western biblical feminist readers and their position towards imperialism.

21. One good example here is that Western feminists have made a hard critique of historical-critical methods and their claims of objectivity, showing how such claims have actually suppressed women and served the interests of male readers. However, we have hardly heard any criticism from these same Western feminist readers about the imperialist/colonizing edge, origin and ideology of this method. This has been highlighted by Two-Thirds World readers. See Segovia and Tolbert (eds.) 1998; Kwok 1998.

22. See Amoah and Oduyoye 1990. In this article the authors discuss African male theologians' construction of Christology. While traditional African ancestorhood or spiritual mediators include both men and women, male theologians have constructed an exclusively male Christology. In this article, Amoah and Oduyoye attempt to build an inclusive African Christology.

selves.[23] They seek to read for decolonization and depatriarchalization, for both oppressions compromise women's rights to complete dignity and liberty as human beings. Thus postcolonial feminist hermeneutics of liberation seek to analyze how colonialism affects gender oppression of women by focusing on:

1. How colonialism is implemented and justified, including the use of women's bodies to articulate positions of subordination.
2. How it uses texts and how it is manifested in texts.
3. How the imposition of cultural, economic and political forms of the colonizer affects colonized women, given that women are often at the bottom of these institutions.
4. How to counteract patriarchy on a national level and imperialism and patriarchy on an international level.

Given that imperialism/colonialism defines international relationships that affect colonized women in their particular areas and involves Western women in their countries, Two-Thirds World postcolonial feminist readers urge First World feminist readers to take into cognizance the fact that we are, more often than not, working within imperial frameworks of past and present times. Feminists, especially biblical ones, read texts that were largely written in colonial contexts, which either resist, collaborate or openly endorse imperialist domination. Therefore, unless feminist biblical readers make deliberate efforts also to become decolonizing readers (Dube 1996), their feminist discourse of liberation will be found subscribing to the cultural, economic and political oppression of Two-Thirds World women and men.

Expounding on postcolonial hermeneutics of liberation, Kwok (1998b: 110) holds that it:

> 1. Challenges the totalitarian forms of Western interpretation, exposing its co-option by imperialist interest and destabilizing its frame of meaning; 2. It is a counter-hegemonic discourse, paying attention to the hidden and neglected voices in the Bible; 3. It places the Bible or any particular religious text within the multi-scriptural contexts of diverse settings; 4. It encourages and welcomes contributions from the marginalized groups that have been neglected; the Dalits, the indigenous people, the migrants, people in the Diaspora and in the borderlands, and especially women in these communities; and 5. It learns from the debates with other hermeneutical frameworks...

23. For an ideology that justifies the domination of one nation by another, see Bailey 1995.

Some Proposals

In the light of the above discussion, I propose a few strategies and tactics that should assist concerned readers to read for decolonization, depatriarchalization, and for liberating interdependence.

Decolonizing Questions in Feminist and Other Liberation Works

To avoid a feminist reading that subscribes to colonizing ideologies in the text, the following questions can be put to a text:

1. Does this text have a clear stance against the political imperialism of its time?
2. Does this text encourage travel to distant and inhabited lands, and if so, how does it justify itself?
3. How does this text construct difference? Is there dialogue and mutual interdependence, or condemnation and replacement of all that is foreign?
4. Does this text employ gender representations to construct relationships of subordination and domination?[24]
5. Which side am I reading from: the colonizer, the colonized or the collaborator?

These questions should be accompanied by gender-feminist questions of analysis.

An Open Space in a Multi-Cultural Setting[25]

I have also called for an open space (open space here does not suggest lack of political engagement) for global women to do their feminist hermeneutics in a multi-cultural setting, where other cultures/religions are recognized and read alongside (not above or below) the Bible. Given that the Christian Bible was a central text in suppressing other religions in modern imperialism, biblical feminists cannot afford to ignore the voices of Two-Thirds World women who are calling for the affirmation of their colonized traditions.[26] If biblical feminist movements call women of the Two-Thirds World to the forest in order to push them into the fire, that is not liberation, it is just girls killing other girls, and not even to protect their own interests but those of patriarchy and imperialism.

---

24. These questions are tabulated and applied in Dube 2000: 56-58, 128-30.
25. See Dube 1997: 23.
26. See Dube 2000: 31-33.

Cultivating Feminist Cultural Studies as Hermeneutics of the Bible[27]
I have also proposed that feminist biblical studies need to further cultivate
a cultural studies approach. In view of the fact that the Bible has been an
instrument of suppression in colonial agendas, it has gained the status of
being the colonizers' 'First World' instrument of power. It can be studied
on its own at the risk of re-inscribing its colonizing status, which holds
that Christianity is the only viable religion. And, given that other cultures/
religions have interacted with the biblical traditions, under friendly or
unfriendly conditions, they deserve to be studied together. Finally, given
that the world consists of many diverse religious texts (written and oral),
studying the Bible as if it is the only religious text can be viewed either as
our vehement support of imperialism, our collaboration therewith or its
hegemonic power. Feminist biblical studies can cultivate a cultural studies
approach by making efforts to study the Bible with the suppressed and
neglected ancient and contemporary, high and popular cultures of the
world. There is no need to claim that these 'other' cultures/religions constitute perfect entities or alternatives. There is also no need to claim that
the non-biblical cultures are savage, exotic, static cultures of pagans.
Rather, the focus should be on how they shape human thinking and experience of the world; how they interact or can interact with each other; how
they function in texts, in history and in institutions; how they have participated in the oppression of women; and how they can participate in the
liberation of women and other human beings. My use of the singing
princess to read both Judith and Rahab signifies this practice.

Reading through 'Rahab's Reading Prism'
I have also proposed a reading strategy which I have termed the 'Rahab
Reading Prism' (Dube 2000: 12-124) as a form of reading that takes cognizance of both patriarchal and imperialist forms of oppression and how
they often utilize women's bodies. It is a prism in the sense that it seeks to
lay bare, as much as possible, the colors of a text for its ideological tones
and impact. Here Rahab is more like Two-Thirds World women who have
suffered colonialism, who have crossed over to the colonial centers having
betrayed their own cultures, economies and political institutions. But as
used here, the Rahab reading is not only a self-conscious colonized
subject, but one who has resurrected from the colonial grave and insists on

27. See Dube 1998b: 240-43. On the subject of cultural studies, see Smith 1999;
Easthope 1991; Inglis 1993; Exum and Moore 1998.

her liberation from both imperialism and patriarchy—she is a singing princess.

Recognizing Type Scenes of Land Possession

Given the long role of literature in the various colonial/imperialist histories, I have held that texts of entrance or colonial contact/target tend to bear flexible but recognizable literary features, which I have elsewhere termed 'type scenes of land possession' (Dube 2000: 117-20). This highlights how colonizing literature has reproduced certain literary forms to articulate the desire or agenda to colonize or not colonize a foreign land and that this form often features metaphoric women characters.

Reading for Liberating Interdependence[28]

From ancient to contemporary times, it is clear that nations, races, genders, cultures, people of different sexual orientation, and economic and political institutions of various nations/peoples around the globe have always been in contact with and dependent upon each other. Globalization indicates that this will hardly abate. The question, therefore, for feminist practitioners, is to ask what made/makes the relationship of the past/present so oppressive and how they can promote relationships of 'true' interdependence between these diversities in God's world. Postcolonial feminist interpretation(s) of liberation thus call(s) for feminist practices that seek for relationships of liberating interdependence between nations, regions, cultures, genders, races, classes, different sexual orientation, and political and economic systems. This/these interpretation(s) seek(s) holistic liberation that affirms the diversity of women in their different settings to operate within cultural, economic and political systems that affirm all people as fully entitled to their human rights.

BIBLIOGRAPHY

Amadiume, Ifi
    1987   *Male Daughters, Female Husbands: Gender in an African Society* (New York: Zed Books).
Amoah, Elisabeth, and Mercy Oduyoye
    1990   'The Christ for African Women', in Mercy Amba Oduyoye and Virginia Fabela (eds.), *With Passion and Compassion: Third World Women Doing Theology: Reflection from the Women's Commission of the Ecumenical Association of Third World Theologians* (Maryknoll, NY: Orbis Books): 35-46.

28. See Dube 2000: 185-201.

Anonymous
1996   *Globalization and Liberalization* (New York: United Nations Conference on Trade and Development).
Ashcroft, Bill, Gareth Tiffin and Hellen Tiffin (eds.)
1995   *The Postcolonial Reader* (New York: Routledge).
Bailey, Randall
1995   'They're Nothing but Incestuous Bastards: The Polemical Use of Sex and Sexuality in Hebrew Canon Narratives', in Fernando Segovia and Mary Ann Tolbert (eds.), *Reading From This Place*. I. *Biblical Interpretation in the United States* (Minneapolis: Fortress Press): 121-39.
Cabral, Amilcar
1994   'National Liberation Culture', in Williams and Chrisman (eds.) 1994: 53-65.
Drimmelen, Rob van
1998   *Faith in a Global Economy: A Primer for Christians* (Geneva: World Council of Churches).
Dube, Musa W.
1996   'Reading for Decolonisation: John 4.1-42', in Laura E. Donaldson (ed.), *Postcolonialism and Scriptural Reading* (Atlanta: Scholars Press): 37-60 (= *Semeia* 75).
1997   'Towards a Post-colonial Feminist Interpretation', in Phyllis A. Bird, Katharine Doob Sakenfeld and Sharon H. Ringe (eds.), *Reading the Bible as Women: Perspectives from Africa, Asia, and Latin America* (Atlanta: Scholars Press): 11-26 (= *Semeia* 78).
1998   '*Go, Therefore and Make Disciples of All the Nations* (Matt 28.19a)', in Segovia and Tolbert (eds.) 1998: 224-46.
2000   *Postcolonial Feminist Interpretation of the Bible* (St Louis: Chalice Press).
Dube Shomana, Musa W.
1998   'Scripture, Feminism and Post-colonial Contexts', in Kwok Pui-Lan and Elisabeth Schüssler Fiorenza (eds.), *Women's Sacred Scriptures* (London: SCM Press; Maryknoll, NY: Orbis Books): 278-87 (= *Concilium* 34.3)
1999   'Fifty Years of Bleeding: A Storytelling Feminist Reading of Mark 5.24-43', *The Ecumenical Review* 51: 11-17.
Easthope, Antony
1991   *Literary into Cultural Studies* (New York: Routledge).
Exum, Cheryl, and Stephen D. Moore (eds.)
1998   *Biblical Studies/Cultural Studies: The Third Sheffield Colloquium* (JSOTSup, 266; Gender, Culture, Theory, 7; Sheffield: Sheffield Academic Press).
Fanon, Fants
1994   'On National Culture', in Williams and Chrisman (eds.) 1994: 36-52.
Harlow, Barbara
1987   *Resistance Literature* (New York: Methuen).
Holst Petersen, Kirsten
1995   'First Things First: Problems of a Feminist Approach in African Literature', in Ashcroft, Tiffin and Tiffin (eds.) 1995: 251-54.
Inglis, Fred
1993   *Cultural Studies* (Cambridge: Basil Blackwell).
Kwok, Pui-Lan
1995   *Discovering the Bible in the Non-Biblical World* (Maryknoll, NY: Orbis Press).

1998a	'Jesus/Native: Biblical Studies From a Postcolonial Perspective', in Segovia and Tolbert (eds.) 1998: 69-85.
1998b	'Reflections on Women's Sacred Scriptures', in Kwok Pui-Lan and Elisabeth Schüssler Fiorenza (eds.), *Women's Sacred Scriptures* (London: SCM Press; Maryknoll, NY: Orbis Books) (= *Concilium* 34.3): 105-12.

Lind, Christopher
1995	*Something is Wrong Somewhere: Globalization, Community and Moral Economy of the Farm Crisis* (Halifax: Fernwood Publishing).

Lorde, Audre
1984	*Sister Outsider: Essays and Speeches* (California: The Crossing Press).

Schüssler Fiorenza, Elisabeth (ed.)
1993	*Searching the Scriptures.* I. *A Feminist Introduction* (New York: Crossroad).
1994	*Searching the Scriptures.* II. *A Feminist Commentary* (New York: Crossroad).

Segovia, Fernando
1995	'And They Began to Speak in Other Tongues', in Segovia and Tolbert (eds.) 1998: 1-32.

Segovia, Fernando, and Mary Ann Tolbert (eds.)
1998	*Teaching the Bible: The Discourses and Politics of Biblical Pedagogy* (Maryknoll, NY: Orbis Books).

Smith, Abraham
1999	'Cultural Studies', in John Hayes (ed.), *Dictionary of Biblical Interpretation* (2 vols.; Nashville: Abingdon Press), I: 236-38.

Spivak, Gaytri
1994	'Can the Subaltern Women Speak?', in Williams and Chrisman (eds.) 1994: 66-111.

Tohidi, Nayereh
1991	'Gender and Islamic Fundamentalism: Feminist Politics in Iran', in Chandra Mohanty *et al.* (eds.), *Third World Women and the Politics of Feminism* (Bloomington: Indiana Press): 251-60.

Williams, Patrick, and Laura Chrisman (eds.)
1994	*Colonial Discourse and Postcolonial Theory: A Reader* (New York: Columbia University Press).

Feminist Biblical Interpretation
and the Hermeneutics of Liberation:
An African Woman's Perspective

Philomena Njeri Mwaura

Introduction

The symposium on feminist biblical interpretation and the hermeneutics of liberation provided an opportunity to become acquainted with various frameworks and methodologies in these areas of endeavor from diverse parts of the world. It was quite challenging and fascinating to experience and learn the types of hermeneutics and exegesis that prevail in different contexts and in which ways they are liberating and for which type of women. It was quite obvious, however, that although there are major identifiable categories in current feminist biblical interpretation, there is no single method of a feminist biblical hermeneutics of liberation. As Barton rightly observes regarding mainstream biblical scholarship: 'the quest for a correct method is, not just in practice but inherently, incapable of succeeding' (Barton 1995: 5).

What seemed to emerge nevertheless may be summed up by Schüssler Fiorenza's assertion that

> a feminist critical interpretation for liberation insists on the hermeneutical
> priority of feminist struggles in the process of interpretation...liberation
> theologies of all 'colors' take the experience and voices of the oppressed
> and marginalized, of those wo/men traditionally excluded from articulating
> theology and shaping communal life, as the starting point of hermeneutical
> reflection. (Schüssler Fiorenza 1998: 78)

Hence, the task of interpretation is not just to understand biblical texts and traditions but also to change the powers of oppression documented throughout history and their effects on the lives of Jews, women of all colors and creeds, homosexuals and peoples of other faith.

Depending on the context and issues at stake, feminist biblical hermeneutics of liberation should focus on the experience and voices of the marginalized and have as its goal the transformation and realization of a vision of a new world with empowering inter-human relations.

In my reflection on the conference theme from the social-cultural background of Africa, I will focus on the question of methodology and the issue of the authority of the Bible as it relates to the lives and experiences of women in Church and society.

The Question of Method and Authority

Generations of African biblical scholars have been trained in the Western tradition; some have unquestioningly accepted the assumptions, biases and distortions of this scholarship, which has been tinged with Western social models and concerns. In essence, this scholarship was dominated by methodological questions relating to historical criticism, termed 'the scientific method'. More recently, however, the tradition has been challenged by the emergence of new approaches and methodological questions 'arising out of structural narrative, reader response, feminist, liberationist and post-structuralist or deconstructionist criticism' (Mojola 2001: 90). Since the emergence of feminism, gender-sensitive men and women biblical scholars have sought in a variety of ways to include the women's approach and perspective in biblical scholarship. The current quest for a critical feminist interpretation for liberation evolves around the paradigm shift caused by critical social theory, the theologies of liberation and post-colonial studies.

Critical feminist biblical interpretation in Africa employs a variety of methodologies that already exist in feminist biblical scholarship and are mainly grounded in liberation theology and post-colonial studies. Few women in Africa have been trained in biblical studies, hence, the methodology used in feminist biblical scholarship can only be deduced from a popular reading of the Bible and theological studies. African women theologians thus must double as biblical scholars except for the few that have been so trained. African women theologians have not yet coined a term for their interpretative efforts. They generally vacillate between the terms 'African women's theology' and 'African feminist theology', and they have given it their own particular content, for Africa is a vast continent with a variety of cultures, peoples, religions and problems. Teresa Okure rightly points out that 'African women do not as a cultural rule start with methodology. Their primary consciousness in doing theology is not method but life and life concerns, their own and those of their own people' (Okure 1993: 76).

Nevertheless, one can still talk of a distinctive method used by African women scholars of theology. It has been described as 'doing theology from women's perspective' (Okure 1993: 76; Phiri 1997: 54). This approach is inclusive. It encompasses men and women, scholars and non-scholars, rich and poor, and utilizes ordinary, popular methods of reading the Scriptures as well as the 'scientific' and the critical. The articulation of women's perspective in African women's 'feminist biblical studies' has been done particularly within the Circle of Concerned African Women Theologians and the women's commission of the Ecumenical Association of Third World Theologians (EATWOT). Though EATWOT invites men to indulge in feminist biblical scholarship and theology, the number of men engaging in it is negligible despite their call for an inclusive Ecclesia. Mercy Oduyoye laments this situation when she charges that: 'African men theologians are beginning to own up the reality that African women have unveiled (injustice). Few will however admit to their privileged position derived from their being men, and few seem to be reading what African women theologians write' (Oduyoye 1995: 20).

She further observes that most of Africa's progressive theologians, 'inculturationist, liberationist, translationist and reconstructionist are nothing but "smokescreens" from under which Western Christian patriarchy and African Christian patriarchy engage in a combined offensive against African women' (cited in Maluleke 2000b: 7). Male-stream African theology has marginalized women or women's issues despite its emphasis on contextualization of the Christian theology into the African culture. It is erroneous, it has been realized, to assume that African women's experiences—that is, their interaction with God, oneself, community and the way they interpret and appropriate the biblical message—are the same as those of men. The Circle was thus formed to bridge this anomaly. Furthermore, as Musimbi Kanyoro rightly argues, African culture is not liberating for all as African male-stream theology assumes. It is, in fact, a 'double-edged sword' and the arena of women's oppression. To her, culture is to African women's liberation theology what race relations are to African American womanist theologians (Kanyoro 1997b: 368). In both private and public spheres, the roles and images of African women are socially and culturally defined. African culture is full of cultural practices that dehumanize women, ranging from taboos regarding food and relationships, widowhood rites, child betrothals and early marriages, domestic and cultural violence, female genital mutilation and lack of access to and control of family and sometimes national resources. Culture has thus silenced women in Africa and made them unable to experience the liberating promises of God.

Although there are aspects of African culture that may be liberating to women, others diminish them and they are embraced by both men and most women without considering their harmful nature. Furthermore, scriptural texts and misogynist Christian traditions have reinforced some negative aspects of our cultures and legitimized them.

African women theologians and feminist biblical scholars are calling for a 'cultural hermeneutics' as an important first step to biblical hermeneutics in Africa. According to Musimbi Kanyoro,

> the culture of the reader in Africa has more influence on the way the biblical text is understood and used in communities than the historical facts about the text. Not knowing the nuances of the culture of modern readers of the Bible has more far reaching repercussions on biblical hermeneutics than normally acknowledged. (Kanyoro 1997b: 364)

African women theologians like Mercy Oduyoye (1986; 1995; also Oduyoye and Kanyoto [ed.] 1992), Elizabeth Amoah (1987), Teresia Hinga (1992), Anne Nasimiyu-Wasike (1995) and others[1] have demonstrated the importance not only of reading the Bible from a women's perspective, but also of the specific African Cultural experiences grounded in African life and religious practices. They examine cultural practices already mentioned, rites of passage, priesthood and Church ministry as they relate to women and society in general as well as by bringing African culture and the Bible into conversation. There is also the recognition that the culture in which the Bible was written has a close affinity to African culture. Hence it is approached both critically and creatively.

African feminist theologians and biblical scholars also recognize other factors that impinge on their reading of Scripture such as race, ethnicity, gender, class, patriarchy and the global experience of imperialism past and present and their implications on politics, economics, language, the environment and other issues. The postcolonial feminist biblical perspective that Musa W. Dube effectively applies in her critique of biblical texts not only addresses gender oppression and affirms the agency of women, but it also deals with wider concerns such as how to read the Bible given its role 'in the subjugation and exploitation of one's nation and context' (Dube 1996: 122). This is reading for decolonization. She, too, calls for cultivation of a feminist, cultural studies hermeneutics of the Bible. This is a recognition that the Bible as a colonizer's tool for power has interacted with other religious traditions and cultures under 'friendly or non-friendly

---

1.   Cf. the bibliography at the end of this contribution.

conditions'. Such studies, without being judgmental, can show how culture shapes human thinking and experience of the world (Dube 2000: 13). This approach in biblical hermeneutics, which has been labeled as 'social-scientific', has been in operation since biblical scholars began to recognize the role that the social sciences can play in the reconstruction and understanding of biblical phenomena (Gottwald 1992: 79).

With the above in mind one may therefore ask: How do African feminist theologians read the Bible and what does a liberating hermeneutics mean to them? African women theologians approach the Bible from two angles. They recognize that although the Bible is the Word of God, it has explicit patriarchal bias and is colored by subtle androcentricity in the worldview of its authors. Having been written in a patriarchal culture, male theologians who interpret it tend to make women invisible and present them negatively. At the same time, the Bible provides to most African women Church-goers a reason for being. It is affirming, offering them liberation from social and cultural stigmatization and oppression through a relationship with Jesus, whose liberating message they find in the Bible. In the words of Phiri, 'the same Bible read from a woman's perspective is used to urge for the liberation of both women and men in the church' (Phiri 1997: 55).

In order to appropriate the liberating message, several methods have been employed. One method has been to separate biblical culture, which is historically conditioned and therefore limited in application to a particular period in history, from the gospel, which is universally true, though always in relation to particular cultures. The argument used here is that it is the gospel that leads to salvation. There is also the recognition that the Bible contains what Phyllis Trible calls *Texts of Terror* (Trible 1984). Are these also to be taken as the inspired Word of God and therefore authoritative and for all time? How are women and men to relate to them? Do they have universally acknowledged principles? What purpose do they serve in a context where women are abused overtly and covertly? Kanyoro argues that for women to find justice and peace through the texts of the Bible, they have first to try and recover the women participants as well as their possible participation in the text. Second, women need to read the Scriptures side by side with the study of cultures and learn to recognize the boundaries between the two. African women theologians, like other feminist biblical scholars, particularly in the Two-Thirds World, use their context as the springboard for reading the Bible. They call attention to how the Bible has been used to subjugate them and go beyond the text to reconstruct and re-imagine it, to seek its relevance and transforming power for the current generation (see Tamez 1994). As Renita Weems asserts, 'People...have power, not texts'.[2]

Besides the scholarly approach to biblical interpretation by African women theologians, there is the popular reading of scriptural texts that goes on in Bible study groups, African Instituted Churches (AICs),[3] Neo-Pentecostal Churches and within fellowship groups in the Churches. In most of these contexts the Bible is taken literally as the Word of God. In the AICs, for example, it is accorded a mystical value. Its interpretation is also mystified and the approach becomes what Mosala calls 'hermeneutics of mystification' (Mosala 1996: 55). It is used as an instrument of deciphering anomalies in one's life and relationship with God and the rest of the community. It is also a tool for healing, for it is the physical contact between it and the sick person that is believed to hasten healing. The Bible is not only appropriated in terms of what it says, but in terms of what it stands for: a canonical authority. It has authority, but there are other sources of equal authority—the Holy Spirit, in particular, who calls the prophet-healers, both men and women, and breaks barriers of race, class, gender ethnicity or creed. We agree with Maluleke when he observes that African Christians 'view the Bible as part of a larger package of resources and legacies which include stories, preaching, language mannerisms, catechism manuals and a range of rituals and rites' (Maluleke 2000a: 95). These other resources emanate from their culture and are also important to their spirituality.

Musa W. Dube, in a study of Botswana AIC women's reading of Mt. 15.21-25, discovered that a variety of methodologies were used, particularly during a sermon on the passage. There was communal interpretation where others, in addition to the minister, could engage with the text from their context. There was also participatory interpretation through use of songs, dramatized narrative and repetition. She identifies (1996: 125-26) a complex and desirable hermeneutics which has four tenets:

1. The Semoya framework—a mode of reading that resists discrimination and articulates healing.
2. A creative integration of the different cultures faiths and experiences in the 'reading' of 'texts'.

---

2.   Cf. Renita J. Weems' 'Re-Reading for Liberation: African American Women and the Bible' in this volume (quote from p. 26).

3.   African Instituted Churches emerged out of the interaction between Western Christianity and culture and African culture and religion. They were started under African initiative in a quest for African spirituality. They are highly indigenized.

3. A 'feminist' model of reading by women 'tutored by the spirit'.
4. The use and understanding of healing 'as an articulation of political resistance and survival'.

This mode of reading is evident in AICs as elsewhere. These African Christians have mainly an oral disposition, acquiring textual information through socialization in Churches by way of songs, sermons, drama and narrative. Hence they appropriate only scant knowledge of the texts. However, there is evidence that the personal experience of the readers or hearers is the starting point of their engaging with scriptural material. These ordinary readers 'read' themselves into the text. They see their experiences of poverty, deprivation, illness and suffering captured and reflected in the text. They see themselves as those who went to Jesus for healing and teaching. Therefore, discussing a text in this context means discussing the lives of the people without making a distinction between method and content. As Kanyoro says, 'reality and biblical text merge and become one, each casting light on the other and competing for attention' (Kanyoro 1997b: 364). Okure underscores this fact when she states that 'experience is the primary context for doing theology and reading the Bible' and that before the text was written 'there was the life' (Okure 2000: 202-203). Hence life is the central hermeneutical key of understanding the scriptures for African women and men. This type of 'reading' is liberating for it gives meaning to people's lives today. It is also a way of reformulating the principal of biblical authority.

Conclusion

It is evident from the foregoing that for African women theologians and feminist biblical scholars a liberating feminist biblical interpretation is one that is grounded in life. African women see the Bible as a community book whose message is addressed to both men and women in their context of struggle against dehumanizing conditions such as poverty, disease, ignorance and the impact of globalization at macro and micro levels. They are also aware of the patriarchal context of the biblical text and message and have developed a methodology that enables them to distinguish between oppressive cultures and the gospel of life. This approach is to be found written both from the academic perspective and the people's readings in the Churches and lives. The methodology of feminist biblical interpretation and the hermeneutics of liberation adopt the traditional procedures as well as liberating ones that go beyond the text, and as Cardoso asserts, 'reading the text against itself, looking for underlying rhetorical possibilities, visualizing dissident experiences'.[4]

BIBLIOGRAPHY

Amoah, Elizabeth
    1987   'The Women Who Decided to Break the Rules', in John Pobee and Bärbel von Wartenburg-Potter (eds.), *New Eyes for Reading: Biblical and Theological Reflections by Women from the Third World* (Oak Park, IL: Mayer Store Books): 3-4.

Barton, John
    1995   *Reading the Old Testament: Method of Biblical Study* (Philadelphia: Westminster Press).

Dube, Musa W.
    1996   'Readings of Semoya: Botswana Women's Interpretation of Matt. 15: 21-28', *Semeia* 73: 111-29.
    1997   'Toward a Post-Colonial Feminist Interpretation of the Bible', *Semeia* 78: 11-23.
    2000   *Postcolonial Feminist Interpretation of the Bible* (St Loius: Chalice Press).

Gottwald, Norman K.
    1992   'Sociology of Ancient Israel', in David Noel Freedman (ed.), *The Anchor Bible Dictionary* (6 vols.; New York: Doubleday, 1992), VI: 79-89.

Hinga, Teresia
    1992   'Jesus Christ and the Liberation of Women in Africa', in Oduyoye and Kanyoro (eds.) 1992: 183-94.

Kanyoro, Musimbi R.A.
    1997a   'The Challenges of Feminist Theologies', in Musimbi Kanyoro (ed.), *In Search of a Round Table: Gender Theology and the Church Leadership* (Geneva: World Council of Churches Publications): 176-82.
    1997b   'Biblical Hermeneutics: Ancient Palestine and the Contemporary World', *Biblical Hermeneutics Review and Expositor* 94: 363-72.

Majola, Aloo Osotsi
    2001   'The Social Sciences and the Study of the Old Testament in Africa: Some Methodological Considerations', in Knut Holter *et al.* (eds.), *Interpreting The Old Testament in Africa* (Nairobi: Nairobi Acton Publishers): 89-99.

Maluleke, Tinyiko Sam
    2000a   'The Bible Among African Christians: A Missiological Perspective', in Okure (ed.) 2000: 87-112.
    2000b   'Reflecting Christ Crucified Among Africa's Cross-Bearers', unpublished paper presented at the IAMS Conference, 26 January 2000, Hammanskraal, South Africa.

Mosala, Itumeleg J.
    1996   'Race, Class and Gender as Hermeneutical Factors in the African Independent Churches' Appropriation of the Bible', *Semeia* 73: 43-57.

4.   Nancy Cardoso Pereira, in her contribution to this volume—'Changing Seasons: About the Bible and Other Sacred Texts in Latin America' (quote from p. 54).

Nasimiyu-Wasike, Anne
 1995 'Christology and an African Woman's Experience', in Robert J. Schreiter
    (ed.), *Faces of Jesus in Africa* (Maryknoll, NY: Orbis Books).
Oduyoye, Mercy A.
 1986 *Hearing and Knowing: Theological Reflections on Christianity* (Maryknoll,
    NY: Orbis Books).
 1995 *Daughters of Anowa: African Women and Patriarchy* (Maryknoll, NY: Orbis
    Books).
Oduyoye, Mercy A., and Musimbi Kanyoro (eds.)
 1992 *The Will to Arise: Women, Tradition and the Church in Africa* (Maryknoll,
    NY: Orbis Books).
Okure, Teresa
 1993 'Feminist Interpretation in Africa', in Elizabeth Schüssler Fiorenza (ed.),
    Searching the Scriptures: A Feminist Introduction (New York: Crossroad):
    75-85.
 2000 'First was the Life, Not the Book', in Okure (ed.) 2000: 194-214.
Okure, Teresa (ed.)
 2000 *To Cast Fire Upon the Earth* (Pietermaritzburg: Cluster Publications).
Phiri, Isabel Apawo
 1997 'Doing Theology as an African Woman', in John Paratt (ed.), *A Reader in
    African Christian Theology* (London: SPCK): 45-56.
Reinhartz, Adele
 1997 'Feminist Criticism and Biblical Studies on the Verge of the Twentieth Cen-
    tury', in Athalya Brenner and Carole Fontaine (eds.), *A Feminist Companion
    to Reading the Bible: Approaches, Methods and Strategies* (The Feminist
    Companion to the Bible, 11; Sheffield: Sheffield Academic Press): 30-38.
Russell, Letty M. (ed.)
 1985 *Feminist Interpretation of the Bible* (Philadelphia: Westminster Press).
Schüssler Fiorenza, Elisabeth
 1985 *Bread not Stone* (Boston: Beacon Press).
 1992 *But She Said: Feminist Practices of Biblical Interpretation* (Boston: Beacon
    Press).
 1998 *Sharing Her Word: Feminist Biblical Interpretation in Context* (Boston:
    Beacon Press).
Sugirtharajah, R.S.
 1998 'A Post-Colonial Exploration of Collusion and Construction in Biblical
    Interpretation', in R.S. Sugirtharajah (ed.), *The Postcolonial Bible* (The Bible
    and Postcolonialism, 1; Sheffield: Sheffield Academic Press).
Tamez, Elsa
 1994 'Women's Re-Reading of the Bible', in Mercy Amba Oduyoye and Virginia
    Fabela (eds.), *With Passion and Compassion: Third World Women Doing
    Theology: Reflection from the Women's Commission of the Ecumenical Asso-
    ciation of Third World Theologians* (Maryknoll, NY: Orbis Books): 173-80.
Trible, Phyllis
 1984 *Texts of Terror: Literary-Feminist Readings of Biblical Narratives* (Philadel-
    phia: Fortress Press).
West, Gerald
 1991 *Biblical Hermeneutics of Liberation: Modes of Reading the Bible in the
    South African Context* (Pietermaritzburg: Cluster Publications).

The Book of Ruth and a Group of Prostitutes in Costa Rica
(A Story Told by Irene Foulkes, Costa Rica)

Bible stories can help women talk about their lives in dialogue with other women—especially women outside the establishment, even outside the borders of respectability. Women who are looked down on, even despised by other women. I have been studying the Bible during the past few months with a group of prostitutes. They are not called sex-workers in Costa Rica, but 'women of the happy life', 'la vida alegre'. It is a small group of some eight women who would like to leave prostitution and who were brought together by an energetic Christian woman who doesn't represent a particular Church or institution. There were a few more at the beginning, but some of them returned to the streets. They live on their own, and that, of course, provides all sorts of pitfalls for them, and yet it seems to be the best way for them to become independent of their former profession.

How can Bible stories help these women talk about their lives? Let me give you an example from a study of the book of Ruth that we had a few weeks ago. Here is what they found: it's a story of two women who become friends and collaborators. The women talked about the fact that in prostitution no one is a friend to anyone else. Nobody would take another's interests into account. It's everyone for herself. There is a certain amount of trust between the two women in the story of Ruth and Naomi; and the women in this group are learning to trust each other, and to help each other.

There is also an intergenerational element in the story, and in this small group of eight women there is a mother and a daughter. All the women have children, and in the case of the mother and her daughter, both have young babies. The mother is about 32, the daughter is 15 or 16, and she has been brought up in an area where prostitution is practiced openly. Can the mother look out for her daughter's change into a new life? Can the daughter support her mother in this joint enterprise? They saw that Ruth and Naomi worked out strategies together to build a new life. The older woman and her daughter-in-law wanted something for themselves when they arrived in Judea, especially Naomi, bitter in her emptiness.

We live in a culture that is 'machista' [sexist, male chauvinist]. How do women make a machista society work for them? How do they find space for their own needs? Naomi and Ruth made that space for themselves. The women in our group found that the book of Ruth is not a story about a good man, Boaz, who rescues a helpless, hopeless young woman, for his own benefit perhaps. They found that the two women are the ones who develop a strategy to get the man to provide what they want and need. One woman said: 'How different this Bible study is with all women! Last year we read this story with a priest and it wasn't that way at all. The hero of the story was Boaz.'

These women talk about their lives, and they see their lives in the story of Ruth. Finding a husband is important to these women; they have had many, many men, but they want one man, one who will be a real companion. They had a lot of trouble with the scene of Ruth and Boaz at the threshing floor at night. In academic study we view it as a story of seduction and that doesn't bother us, but these women all said: 'No, that's not it!'

They identify with Ruth; they want a relationship with a man that isn't determined by sexual need. And they want children. Children are important for establishing an identity and a goal in life outside prostitution. When we reached the end of the story the women reveled in the domestic scene; it gave them hope that their own strategies would also be vindicated.

WOMEN IN CONTEMPORARY PALESTINIAN SOCIETY:
A CONTEXTUAL READING OF THE BOOK OF RUTH*

Viola Raheb

'May God recompense!' A Palestinian family hears these words at the birth of a baby girl; it is a greeting that reflects society's attitude towards women. It is thus not surprising that families are often sad at the birth of a daughter. It is a feeling well expressed in the Arab proverb: 'The burden of a daughter is felt until the tomb'. From the moment they are born, women's lives in Palestine are not easy (Azzouni Mahshi 1995). The Palestinian society is a patriarchal society with a hierarchical structure that defines roles and norms for men and women. As in other traditional societies, men in the Palestinian society dominate the public sphere while women dominate largely the private one. A superficial look at the situation of women in Palestine today gives the impression that much has changed. Upon closer examination, however, it is clear that women's lives in Palestine are still bound to the traditional structure of the society. This paper aims at explaining the situation of women in Palestine today through the window of the story of Ruth, the Moabite woman, who made her way to Palestine thousands of years ago.

Women in a Peasant Society

The Palestinian society is traditionally a peasant society. Our forefathers and foremothers were peasants. This fact has had great influence on the formation of the society. One sign of this is found in the extended family structure of most Palestinian families, often with several generations living in the same family home. This structure is of great importance when it

*   This article is an extended English version of an article previously published in German ('Frauen in der palästinensischen Gesellschaft heute', *Bibel und Kirche* 3 [1999]: 131-33). The English version was written specifically for the present publication.

comes to the issue of inheritance, an issue at the heart of the story of Ruth as well.

Upon arrival in Palestine Ruth had to search for a source of living. The only possibility was to work in the fields at harvest time. Historically, Palestinian women have worked in these same fields, and as in Ruth's story, this work was mainly on family-owned fields. Accordingly, Palestinian women worked on their family's land as long as they were single. Upon marriage their work shifted to the land of their in-laws. Since they were working within the 'family business', women's work was without pay. One could say women worked for food and lodging.[1] Today, however, the situation has changed. The Palestinian society is no longer a peasant society and agriculture is no longer the main source of income.

Accordingly, the areas of work for women have become more diverse. Within the last few years Palestinian women have made their way into different fields of employment (e.g. tourism, medicine, law, etc.). Yet, this development does not necessarily mean that the right of women to work has become more accepted by today's society due to a change in the patriarchal structures. Rather, this development has to be seen in light of the difficult economic context in Palestine and the challenges arising from it. In a context in which one source of income is no longer sufficient for the basic needs of a family, women working is a matter of survival rather than a recognition of their right to do so or a right of equality. At the same time it is important to note that although some Palestinian women have made their way into previously male-dominated professions, the majority of Palestinian women who work outside the private sector today are still working in the traditionally accepted female professions such as nursing, teaching or secretarial work. Sixty-five per cent of the business administration students at Bethlehem University are women. However, statistics are often misleading. A look at the careers these female business administration students have after their graduation makes it clear that they differ immensely from their male colleagues in terms of position.[2]

---

1. Hammami 1998: 'Despite the fact that one finds high numbers of women employed in West Bank agriculture, the majority of them are working as an unpaid family laborer. In other words, most women (unlike men) are not engaged in agriculture for pay—as wageworkers, or as tenant farmers. As such, agricultural labor is not an income generation option for most women but a labor responsibility they inherit through husbands and fathers.'

2. The percentage of women in the labor force in Palestine is 11.4 per cent.

Widows

Ruth's story viewed from a contemporary European or North American context is far from the present-day reality, especially with regard to what takes place following the death of her husband (which is the main story). Most women in Western societies are no longer defined through marriage. In Palestine, however, women are still defined by their marital status. Accordingly, the highest social goal for a woman in the Palestinian society is to get married. Female children thus are trained and prepared to fulfill their roles as wives and mothers from a very early age. A woman's highest fulfillment comes from marriage. In the eyes of the society, a woman reaches 'full womanhood' the moment she gets married, the moment she becomes a mother and, most importantly, the moment she becomes a mother of sons. But even this fact has to be seen in the light of the existing context, where children and mainly male children are considered a sort of 'social security system' in a land in which such a system does not exist. It is interesting to note that marriage is considered the highest level in the social development of the life of women, while, in contrast, it represents only one level in the life of men.

The structure of the Palestinian family determines the role of a Palestinian woman. Until marriage, a woman lives in the family into which she was born. With marriage, women go from the custody of one male (father) to another (husband). In the case of a woman who remains single, she continues to live with her family, regardless of her age, level of education or profession.

Therefore, being defined through the lives of the men in her life, a married woman's life seems to come to a standstill at the death of her husband. Widows often have to remain with their in-laws, particularly if they want to retain custody of their children or keep their right in regard to inheritance. It is therefore of no big surprise to us to read that Ruth decides to stay with her mother-in-law Naomi instead of going back to her family, a choice of survival rather than one of ideology.

In the story of Ruth, Naomi appears to be a very open-minded, understanding and sympathetic figure. Naomi even goes as far as to help her daughter-in-law find a new husband. At a certain moment, Naomi gives Ruth very clear and detailed instructions in regard to what we might call today 'ways to find a husband'. She even explains to her how to seduce Boaz. Have you ever thought about how strange it must seem for a mother-in-law to give such advice? Yet, isn't it the issue of survival that leads

Naomi to do this? Isn't it the case that after the death of all male relatives, both women have no one except themselves to count on? Isn't it the case that in Naomi's securing the future of Ruth she was ultimately securing her own?

Another interesting aspect in the story is that of the remarriage of a widow. A look at the current reality in Palestine shows certain schizophrenia. When a man becomes a widower, his family and the society are involved in trying to find him a suitable new wife as soon as possible. In many cases, men remarry within less than a few months of the death of their wives (and of course everyone will see to it that his new wife is much younger—after all, she should serve him in his old age!). On the other hand, when a woman becomes a widow, she is expected to remain faithful to her late husband—no matter how old she is.[3] It is highly interesting to listen to discussions on the subject. Men seem to be perceived as too helpless to live on their own, without women to care for them. (An image that does not correspond to the 'macho' image of a man in a patriarchal society.)

Inter-Religious Marriages

Reading the story of Ruth from today's inter-religious perspective is also very interesting. 'And your God will be my God' (Ruth 1.16), says Ruth, making it clear to Naomi that she wants to stay with her. Yet, the question is whether it is so easy to adopt a new religious identity in a context in which religious affiliation is a major social factor. Therefore, the question is whether Ruth's decision was one of religious openness or of social survival. In the situation where women make the decision to marry across religious boundaries, the issue of social belonging becomes a major factor in determining women's identity. Therefore, in order to understand Ruth's words we first have to ask ourselves whether she really had another choice or whether her decision was the only choice for a Moabite woman who decided to marry a Jew.

For quite some time now Palestinian society has been undergoing an interesting development. Increasing numbers of Christian Palestinian women are marrying Muslim men. The reasons for this phenomenon are manifold. To state but a few:

---

3.   In the Palestinian society it is more likely for a Muslim widow to remarry than for a Christian. This is linked to the issue of religious and social acceptance.

1.   In light of the political situation, the Palestinian society is a much-politicized society. Accordingly, young people often define themselves by their political affiliation rather than by their religious one.
2.   Since the opening of Palestinian universities, the chance of interaction between young Palestinian men and women from different religious and social backgrounds has increased, thus creating new friendships, some of which end up in relationships leading to marriage.
3.   Many young Christian Palestinian men go abroad to study. Upon returning they either bring along a wife from the country in which they lived and studied or marry a young Palestinian woman in her mid-twenties. Thus, the number of Christian Palestinian single women in their late twenties is on the increase.

Yet, the issue of inter-religious marriage is highly complicated. First, in the context of the absence of civil marriage in Palestine, which also applies for Israel, marriages are handled by religious institutions. This means that every marriage is contracted religiously, which implies that one of the partners will have to convert to the faith of the other partner. In a patriarchal society most often the woman has to convert to the tradition of the husband. The issue of converting may be considered a strictly private decision, but in an extended family society like the Palestinian one it has enormous consequences both for the individual and for the family as a whole. Practically speaking, such a decision means the casting out of a woman from her family, which in a context like the Palestinian one is a matter of social death. Possibly, this was a consequence that was also evident for Ruth when making her decision. Therefore, the words of Ruth, 'Your God will be my God', are accompanied by 'and your people my people'. Yes, the moment Ruth decided to convert from her religion to that of her husband, she realized also that her social belonging would have to change too.

Second, in a traditional society such as the Palestinian one, marriage is a decision made by two families rather than by two individuals. A marriage contracted without the families' blessings is a societal taboo. In most cases, women are the ones behind marriage arrangements. The same is true in the story of Ruth, where her mother-in-law Naomi is the active one seeking a husband for Ruth, consequently deciding whom the appropriate man is.

Third, in some cases of inter-religious marriages between Christian Palestinian women and Muslim men, women formally convert to Islam, though this is not a necessity in Islam. Yet, women do this mainly to safeguard their rights (e.g. inheritance, custody of the children, etc.). The crucial moment arises when children are born and the two parents are confronted with the difficult question as to which religious principles they ought to follow in raising them.

Fourth, tragedy unfolds when intermarriages end. Traditionally women return to their own families in the case of a divorce. However, to whom can a Christian woman turn when her own family has expelled her? An example of this can be illustrated by the story of one such woman:

> A few months before the conference a Christian Palestinian woman, in her late thirties and well educated, married a Muslim man. She eloped with him to become his wife and converted to Islam. The news spread within a few hours and her family's reaction was predictable: the daughter was cast out by her family. The family even went as far as to hold a mock funeral for her, declaring her dead. The woman had to hide in fear for her life. She had no contact with her family and lost her job in the aftermath of the marriage. Yet, the story turned into a larger tragedy sometime later when her husband divorced her and sent her away. Where was she to go now? The only place that opened its door for this woman was a monastery. The irony here is that the woman who had converted to Islam ended up seeking refuge in a Christian monastery.

Many centuries have passed since Ruth the Moabite woman set foot in Palestine. However, many socio-economic factors of women's lives seem to be true even today. Ruth's story was recorded in history; her voice has not been silenced. Palestinian women today are struggling to find a way into the history of their people and a way not to be silenced completely.

BIBLIOGRAPHY

Azzouni Mahshi, Suheir
    1995   *My Daughter Deserves a Better Future* (Palestine: Women's Affairs Technical Committee).
Hammami, Rema
    1998   'Integrating Women into Wage Work in Palestine: Obstacles, Strategies and Benefits', an unpublished paper presented at the International Conference on Employment in Palestine, May 1998, Ramallah, Palestine.

A Secular, Jewish, Feminist Look at the Bible

Tal Ilan

Social Location

The 'Holy Book' has been used by various groups, sects and peoples throughout history as a source of inspiration, hope, spirituality, provocation and even despair. Women from all parts of the world speaking about the Bible from their social location, each upholding her vision of this document and presenting her prooftexts of reality embedded therein, provide an impetus for others to identify, define, uphold and defend their personal Bible with its unique prooftexts.

A Jewish atheist is not a contradiction in terms. It is a widespread phenomenon, prevalent particularly in Israel, a land thriving on dichotomies and contradictions. The 'either/or' nature (either Jewish or Arab, either European or Oriental, either religious or secular) of political and ideological loyalties are defined in my country at an early age; it is not possible to maintain a position of skepticism between two poles for long. I grew up in a socialist kibbutz. Among the many contradictions that the Jewish State has given birth to is one of the only working secular socialist societies in history—the kibbutz. Admittedly, the kibbutz is a voluntary socialist (and completely democratic) organization within a thoroughly capitalist society. It has its problems and limitations, but having grown up in it, it should come as no surprise that I view the socialist ideology favorably. The socialism of the Jewish kibbutz developed in the revolutionary atmosphere of Eastern Europe before these countries became socialist against their will. The ideology of the Jewish kibbutz was a strong reaction against the traditional Jewish way of life and all that it stood for—Torah study for men, childbearing, poverty, hard work and ignorance for women. The kibbutzim were founded by people who had escaped Europe before the Nazi threat of extermination became imminent. But the founders of the kibbutzim were not just socialists who agreed with Karl Marx that religion was the opium of the masses, they were also Zionists. They belonged to a larger national liberation movement that upheld the biblical vision of the Promised Land as the only politically realistic solution to anti-Semitism.

Incidentally, the kibbutzim have always supported and upheld equality among the sexes in theory, offering equal education and opportunities regardless of gender, maintaining an open-minded approach to sexual permissiveness on the part of both sexes. In practice, however, the kibbutzim suffer from real problems with regard to the division of labor between the sexes, the secondary role women actually play in the kibbutzim, and the use of subtly manipulative messages to instill certain values in young kibbutzim women (Sered 1994: 182-84).

The Bible as a Cultural Document

For these reasons the Bible has never been a source of indoctrination, frustration, subjugation or liberation for me. Yet it was not absent from our curriculum. The revival of the Hebrew language as part of the Zionist movement's national program had incorporated the Hebrew Bible into the new Zionist tradition. Biblical expressions became part and parcel of our linguistic repository of images. This was our history, our heritage in the land in which we now lived. The plants mentioned in the Bible were real for us. The mandrakes that Reuben had brought his mother Leah were plentiful in the fields. The tamarisk tree that Abraham had planted was a common sight in our region. The places mentioned in the Bible were real places we could visit. Beer Sheva, where Abraham had dug wells, was a 20-minute drive from home. Kibbutz Lahav, where I grew up, was located at the foot of a biblical archaeological site occasionally under excavation. The national commission for names thought it might be Ziklag, the place where the Philistines were stationed when David fled to their camp to escape from the wrath of King Saul. The secular national traditions celebrated in the kibbutz were Jewish and thus biblical. The Exodus, celebrated by Jews the world over on Passover, was of no less significance to us. The members of the socialist kibbutz envisioned themselves as the slaves who had escaped their oppressors (in the Diaspora), wandered in the wilderness (under the British mandate in Palestine) and finally arrived in the Promised Land—the State of Israel. The collective memory of Israel's enslavement promoted socialist ideals such as the obligation to eradicate slavery. When Purim—the festival which commemorates the revocation of the decree to annihilate all the Jews—was celebrated in the kibbutz, the connection with the holocaust and the miraculous escape of a few to the Promised Land was not lost. One need not believe in God, eat Kosher, fast on Yom Kippur or observe the Sabbath (none of which we did in the kibbutz) in order to experience these things.

Thus the Bible was and has remained for me a historical and literary document of great aesthetic value and moral fiber. Yet it was never more than a cultural document equal in basis with other cultural documents that we studied (such as the works of Shakespeare). Education was of major importance in the situation I grew up in. Books were everywhere. Reading was encouraged. A sympathetic view of the world, its peoples and its diversity was promoted. At the same time, criticism of the Bible and the institutions deriving from it (criticism of all cultural documents, for that matter) was never viewed as a blasphemous activity in the kibbutz. The socialist Jews had long rejected the authoritative character of the Bible or its divinity. The idea of Israel as the chosen people was soon rejected in our education to make way for an ideology of human equality. In the same vein we rejected the colonialist vision of the book of Joshua, the xenophobic approach of the books of Ezra and Nehemiah and the notion of original sin and the 'natural' division between the sexes suggested in the first chapters of Genesis.

This intellectual standpoint is rooted not only in socialist ideas but also in the eighteenth century humanist enlightenment movement. On the one hand, it replaced God with humankind as the center of the universe, and on the other hand, it developed a rationalist critical approach to the world, and the Holy Scriptures. I have always viewed the success of these Western intellectual movements as a great achievement for the human race. The use of the term 'objective' to describe the results of research generated by these movements did not seem problematic to me. I cannot imagine any other way of reading the Bible except by critical examination. I remember well deciding for myself while reading the book of Samuel in fifth grade that King David, even though a model for the Jewish ideal of kingship, was in fact a bad example to follow. Many years later I was able to translate my opinion into solid scholarship by comparing David's literary and historical character with that of Herod, a supremely evil king for Jews as well as for Christians (Ilan 1998).

Role Reversals

Feminism as a discipline has overturned some of my optimistic suppositions about the world and the value of scientific inquiry. A better understanding of the mechanism of patriarchy and the oppression of women in all economic, political and sexual power structures has, of course, also made me critical of the naive feminism with which I grew up. The kibbutz had displayed a facade of equality between the sexes but at the same time upheld and maintained the social stereotypes of women as stupid, incapable and unimportant. Meeting women from other countries, cultures and perspectives at Monte Verità reminded me of the very different impacts the Bible has on other peoples. The encounter with Christian women from Eastern Europe for whom faith in the texts of the Bible had given hope during the time when their religion was oppressed by a socialist system brought home something that I had known for a long time—namely, that socialism as an ideal may have envisioned a beautiful utopia, but in reality it produced some of the most oppressive systems of power in the world. Upholding atheism as an ideal contradicted the idea of religious tolerance as part of my upbringing. Atheism can be as religiously intolerant as any religion.

Our education taught us to view ourselves as the subjects of the biblical text. It is a text about an oppressed Jewish minority, enslaved (in Egypt), threatened (in Persia) and abused (by the Philistines). As Viola Raheb showed in her reading of Ruth at Monte Verità (cf. Viola Raheb's article, 'Women in Contemporary Palestinian Society: A Contextual Reading of the Book of Ruth', in this publication), it is possible for Palestinian Christians, people who live in the same land and experience similar biblical family structures and institutions, to read the same text with a reversal of roles. It is possible to interpret us as the oppressive biblical enemy against whom another 'Israel' struggles. A thoroughly secular Israeli television sitcom written by the renowned Israeli satirist Ephraim Sidon conveys this message well. It is called 'Half of Manaseh' (Josh. 13.7) and takes place in a little village (Besir Aviezer, Judg. 8.2) in the territory of the tribe of Manaseh—Samaria or the northern part of the West Bank today (Josh. 17.7-12). It is the time of Judges. The Philistines occupy the land (e.g. Judg. 15.11). Two Philistine soldiers stationed at the village represent the occupying power. They look, talk and behave a lot like modern Israeli soldiers. One of them is short and smart. The other is a big bully, very stupid and violent. He speaks only Philistine. One of the Israelite villagers is a member of Samson's guerilla organization—'Samson's Foxes'. This name is not only reminiscent of the biblical account of Samson's retaliation against the Philistines (Judg. 15.4-5) but was also the name of a real military unit in the Israeli army during the 1948 war (of independence).

The other villagers include a widow and her daughter (who is betrothed to the guerilla fighter), a priest and a sojourner from the tribe of Ephraim who, according to the book of Judges, cannot pronounce the sound 'sh' (Judg. 12.6). The situations developed in this series are comic, loaded with biblical quotations and allusions, but at the same time refer to the problems and predicaments of modern Israel. It also drives home the message that the situation of the Israelites under Philistine occupation then was a lot like the situation of the Palestinians under Israeli occupation now. The use of the Bible in this manner demonstrates well the impact of the 'Holy Book' on the Jewish secular society in Israel.

I would like to conclude this short summary of my personal struggle with a feminist biblical interpretation rooted in a secular Jewish background with my own reading of a biblical story—that of Michal, the daughter of King Saul. In this reading I will show how a woman's experience can be read in the Bible without theology, much like one reads a great classic or modern novel—Jane Austin, Toni Morrison, Amy Tan. The story is very modern in its conception of love. It would make a great movie. It is easy for a woman growing up in a Western society to identify with Michal. Her experience is both universal and specific. The former makes her predicament understandable; the latter makes her exotic and interesting.

The Story of Michal

Michal is mentioned in four episodes of David's life: her love for him and their marriage (1 Sam. 18.20-29); her part in saving his life when he escapes Saul's wrath (1 Sam. 19.11-17); her forced marriage to another and David reclaiming her (2 Sam. 3.13-17); and finally her derision of David for making a fool of himself in front of the people and her banishment from court (2 Sam. 6.20-23). David is the apparent hero in all of these episodes (Exum 1993: 16-60), but by employing the feminist technique of placing the woman in the center we can discern a completely new story, one that has been there all the time waiting to be told. It is a story about women's emotions, entrapment and our predicament (Schüssler Fiorenza 1998: 88-104).

Michal meets David when he is young, handsome and has just earned fame and glory by defeating the Philistines. Michal's social location is important. She is a princess. David is from another social class altogether and is perhaps not a suitable match for her. The issue of class difference is raised by David himself (1 Sam. 18.23). Here we encounter the typical fairytale theme. Since David cannot pay the bride-price for Michal, he must risk his life in a terrible ordeal in order to win her—kill 100 Philistines and display their foreskins to the king (1 Sam. 18.25). Yet, as we have already seen in the story of Goliath (1 Sam. 17), David likes a challenge. Without much ado he goes out and slays the Philistines. We know nothing of David's emotions but are twice told that Michal loved him (1 Sam. 18.20, 29). This, of course, does not surprise us. We all know how romantic love works, how images of romantic heroes are created and how easy it is to become completely besotted with such an image. David, according to the Bible, was steadily acquiring just such an image. Women sang out his praise (1 Sam. 18.6-7). The marriage between Michal and David was an arranged marriage. The king's daughter could have been married off to anyone the king felt would benefit him. Yet she was married off to the man she loved. Michal must have thought herself very lucky indeed. She was the wife of David's youth. Most fairytales end here.

Yet the story of David as told in the two books of Samuel is not a fairytale. It is a story of the rise to power. It is a story of the preservation of power. It is a story of the price of power—a very modern story indeed. On the way to achieving power one loses innocence and righteousness. The books of Samuel tell these facts, too. The handsome, hopeful, musical young man Michal met and fell in love with was destined to become someone completely different. The struggle for power is clearly at the background of the next episode that features Michal. Discord has set in between her father the king and her husband, whose ambitions the king suspects. Her loyalties are put to the test. Who will she support? Her father and her family, or her beloved? Typical of romantic love stories, she opts for her lover. In a key scene she lowers him by a rope through her window while the king's guards are knocking at her door. She could be saying the words of the Song of Songs to him at this moment: 'Flee my love as a gazelle and be like a fawn on the perfumed mountains' (Song 8.14). In our imagination we see Juliet lowering Romeo from her balcony and sending him off to Mantua. We have left the realm of fairytale and entered the realm of tragedy. David and Michal's families are now mortal enemies. The lovers are entangled in an impossible marriage and the separation that follows real love can be fatal.

In Shakespeare's *Romeo and Juliet* tragic love ends in tragic death. But the story of David and Michal is not a tragedy and love is not its main concern. We enter into a long digression from Michal's point of view concentrating on David's exploits and victories as he goes from being an outlaw and an outcast to a legitimate contender to the Israelite throne. His conquests include women and additional marriages (1 Sam. 25). What was Michal's parallel and separate story? The Bible does not tell us. It is apparently not interested in her fate or her emotions. In passing it is mentioned that the king, her father, had given her hand in marriage to someone else—a certain Palti ben Laish (1 Sam. 25.44). The rest we have to fill in. We may imagine that Michal had taken a certain amount of risk upon herself when helping David escape. She alone must bear the consequences of her actions. The king is furious with her. He must punish her. Of course, he can kill her, but he chooses what he views as a fate worse than death— he marries her off to another. Her act of loyalty to her husband-lover, over and against her father, results in the couple's relationship being severed.

We can imagine her anguish. After her brief moment of strength and courage Michal is faced with an eternity of frustrated love and sexual abuse. Being a princess does not help now. She is trapped within the machinations of a patriarchal system. Her father, the almighty ruler in the household, has the last word. The idea of this other marriage must be seen in modern romantic terms as an impossible hardship for a woman truly in love. It would be viewed as rape, sexual violence and abuse in the worst sense of the word. Is this really what happened? The Bible surprises us here. What we are told about Michal's second marriage is nothing if not touching. The man to whom Michal was now given fell in love with her.

Many years later King Saul dies. David is about to become the next king of Israel. When he eventually sends for Michal she is taken away by force. Her husband is, of course, aware of the finality of the situation. He realizes that David's orders must be followed. The Bible says: 'She was taken away from her husband, from Paltiel ben Laish. Her husband went with her weeping after her all the way to Bahurim. Then Avner said to him: "Go, return", and he turned away' (2 Sam. 3.15-16). We have no idea what Michal feels and how she sees this event. We can only imagine it from what comes next. This is how I imagine it. Michal was forced into a marriage her father chose for her. She was miserable. She missed David and was very worried about his wellbeing. She knew that he was in no position to save her from her fate. But then time went by—years even. He was no longer weak. She heard stories, rumors. At the same time she realized with surprise that the man she was now married to was kind, tolerant and understanding. He genuinely loved her. Their relationship developed into a comfortable existence. David was a far-off myth, a teenage flame. She followed his exploits with less concern. She grew used to the idea that the episode with David in her life was over. She was sure he had forgotten her. She almost forgot him. She went on with her life. This is no longer a fairytale or a tragedy, it is a soap opera.

But David had not forgotten Michal. It was not romantic love but rather possessiveness that drove him. At this point in his life he had developed into a carefully oiled machine whose only objective was to acquire more power, more territory, more wealth. He fought ruthlessly to defend what was his. Michal also belonged in his list of possessions. Now that he had power he wanted her back. He took her back. For Michal, what David had to offer came too late. She was a king's daughter. She was not dazzled by his wealth. Distance from him also may have reawakened her family loyalties. She must have realized that David had become her family's mortal enemy. Moreover, her comfortable life was disrupted against her will; her reunion with David brought with it none of the old excitement. This time Michal saw right through him. She saw that all his charm was only there to sweep people off their feet and make them slaves to his ambitions. She certainly did not like the new David that she saw.

The final episode in their lives shows Michal's disillusionment with David (2 Sam. 6.20-23). She sees him dance in the streets with all his admirers and is disgusted. Unlike the author of Samuel, she is not impressed by his ability to mix with the simple folk. She sees his actions as manipulative, hiding what is really going on in his court from the public. I think the issue on which Michal criticizes David is just an excuse. The scene is constructed so as to demonstrate the end of their love. When love ends we are able to see the truth about the object of our love. Despite the fact that the lovers are restored to one another this story does not have a conventional happy end. The two are not lovers anymore. They are two estranged human beings. David never touches Michal again. From now on she will be lonely, sexually frustrated and punished by the worst curse of patriarchy—childlessness. More than anything else, this story, like a Thomas Hardy novel, is about the quality of human relations. It never ends where we would have expected it to end conventionally. It shows us what comes after the end of a marriage of love, what comes after the end of a tragedy, what comes after the lovers' reunion, because, as we know, life simply goes on.

This last scene between David and Michal is interesting from an atheist point of view because it is also the first time God comes into their relationship. In answer to her spite and criticism, David claims for himself the status of God's chosen one, over and against Michal's family (2 Sam.

6.21). After he had used every trick in the book to oust the previous ruling house, after he had shown far greater treachery, ruthlessness and lack of principle than his predecessors to establish his position of power, he then claims God as his agent of murder and bloodshed. This comes as no surprise to atheists. Humans like David, we claim, create God in their image and likeness. We, however, should not make the same mistake by assuming that David's hunger for power was indeed God's will.

The story of David and Michal can also stand as a metaphor for my own youthful beliefs and the disillusionment of middle age. King David stands for all the norms and values of Israel. Michal's love for him is the love we imbibe in our youth for our country, our culture, our values. Michal's love of David was justified. He was indeed endowed with the qualities she loved. He was a man of action, he was brave, he had integrity and he had a healthy ambition. However, Michal is justified also in her disillusionment. David changed. His interests changed. Of all the impressive attributes of his youth, only his ambition was left. He had become pleasure-seeking, self-indulgent, cruel and pompous. Absolute power had indeed corrupted him absolutely. So, too, am I also justified in my disillusionment—not much is left of the Israel I grew up in, except an unquenched ambition. Pleasure-seeking, corruption and cruelty are everywhere. I no longer live in the kibbutz either, not least because of some of its socialist applications. This, of course, has nothing to do with God or his chosen people (if such a thing exists at all).

BIBLIOGRAPHY

Exum, J. Cheryl
    1993   *Fragmented Women: Feminist (Sub)versions of Biblical Narrative* (JSOTSup, 163, Sheffield: Sheffield Academic Press).

Ilan, Tal
    1998   'King David, King Herod and Nicolaus of Damascus', *Jewish Studies Quarterly* 5: 195-240.

Schüssler Fiorenza, Elisabeth
    1988   *Sharing her Word: Feminist Biblical Interpretation in Context* (Boston: Beacon Press).

Sered, Susan
    1994   '"She Perceives her Work to be Rewarding": Jewish Women in Cross-Cultural Perspective', in Lynn Davidman and Shelly Tenenbaum (eds.), *Feminist Perspectives on Jewish Studies* (New Haven: Yale University Press): 169-90.

The following statements were selected by the editors from the transcripts of the panel discussions. Although we have edited them for redundancies and clarity, we have attempted to retain their original oral character. The selection and order of these statements do not correspond to the symposium program. Rather, they have been organized according to the various themes that arose in the main presentations and following discussions and which also are reflected in the various contributions to this publication. The editors have refrained from naming the individual speakers, in part in order to emphasize the fact that the ideas behind these statements are not bound to or limited by specific geographical, religious, cultural or social backgrounds (which was reflected over and over again throughout the symposium); they have a general significance for the discussion of (feminist) biblical hermeneutics as a whole.

Critical Feminist Biblical Scholarship and Gender

What do we mean by using terms such as *critical* feminist biblical scholarship and *critical* feminist biblical analysis? What is a feminist biblical scholar if she weren't doing that kind of critical work that you have in mind?

['What do I mean by *critical*? Since the words *critique* and *critical* are often unterstood in a negative, deconstructive, and cynical sense, I use these terms in their original sense of crisis. This expression is derived from the Greek word *krinein/krisis*, which means judging and judgement, evaluation and assessment. A critical approach is interested in waging, evaluating and judging texts and their contexts, in exploring crisis situations and seeking their adjudications. Its goals and functions are opposite to those of a positivist approach of "pure" science'.[1]]

How can we deal with these very theoretical and critical issues without killing the text or the readers? How can we put the text into a concrete social framework of power and then struggle against these structures while failing to create another way of closing interpretation in the text? Do we, for instance, assume that people, grass-roots people, can understand and can interpret for themselves? Do we conclude from this that what is sacred is already present and evident and does not need our critical perspective in order to be something?

If you look at women's movements in the Southern Hemisphere, the struggle they are focusing on is not that of women. That is not their primary focus.

What are these struggles focused on, if they are not focused on women? Women are half of the population!

Feminism or feminist criticism is not enough if it is just gender analysis. It also has to acknowledge economic oppression, etc. But is it not also the case that feminist criticism risks becoming so large and ambiguous that it somehow loses its 'bite', its power, its particular sting. Let me put this a bit more personally. One of the reasons why I sometimes find the term so offensive is that you eventually are confronted with the question—particularly by Anglo-feminists: Why do you want to use the word 'womanist' or 'mujarista' or anything else? We've already got that included in the word feminist. Class criticism is already included in feminist criticism; ethnic criticism or criticism against ethnic oppression is already included in the word feminist! So why do you want to do *that* in particular? We already have a concept that includes all of this. And thus this term becomes imperialistic, totalitarian. The word itself almost becomes oppressive and is certainly not useful to people in different contexts.

Isn't setting a common methodology kind of alienating to the people in the South?

---

1.   Elisabeth Schüssler Fiorenza, *Rhetoric and Ethic: The Politics of Biblical Studies* (Minneapolis: Fortress Press, 1999), p. 9.

Reading Critically—Reading Differently

There is a song in Brazil about a gypsy woman reading the hand of Paulo Freire, one of the country's most important educators. It is about another way of reading. There is a kind of oppression in asking people to utilize systematic analysis when they have been used to analyzing reality and systems of power by reading hands or storms or myths. Sometimes it feels as if we have to pay a tribute for this very Western way of systematic analysis. Isn't it also possible to utilize this tradition of creative ambiguity as a way of understanding and producing knowledge and beauty in a new hermeneutics?

It is necessary to critique religion and culture both positively and nega-tively. We have seen that our cultures are very enriching, but, depending on who is determining the framework, negative parts or issues oppressive to women can be used, reinforced by biblical passages also oppressive to women, and that is depicted as the norm.

Word—Text—Image

There are images that can help break the bounds of the canon and invite a new interpretation, and in that new interpretation then invite others to explore their own imagination in dialogue with the biblical text, but also going beyond the biblical text. One of the things that I find happening among some of the students that I work with is that they are exploring their own areas of creativity, be it art or music, as alternative ways of doing theology and biblical interpretation.

There is a lot of similarity between the cultural and social backgrounds of Brazil and Kenya, particularly in the creative way the Bible is used in popular religion. And when I talk of popular religion, I mean the kind of Christianity that is practiced in the indigenous African Churches. In some countries like South Africa, or in East and West Africa, these form over 50 per cent of the population and hence they can be called 'mainline Churches'. Here the Bible is used as an instrument of healing. Some psalms, for example Psalm 35 and Psalm 40, are used in healing rituals. The experi-ence and the lamentation of the psalmist are used to express the situation of the people. The Bible itself is often physically used in healing rituals, it is placed on parts of the body, it is used to exorcise demons. I heard about a situation in Mozambique where it is actually eaten; pages of the Bible are torn into pieces and people eat it, or it is burnt into ashes and mixed into water and people wash their bodies with that water because of the power they believe is in the Bible. It has a power that is very important to them regardless of whether it is read or not read, but it is true that when it is read it has had the power to inspire people into activism or even nationalism. Actually, in our context it was the Bible that enabled people to fight for liberation, despite the fact that it also contains oppressive texts.

What is most significant is that most of the healers in these African indigenous Churches are women. They don't use the texts the way we do because most people are not literate in these Churches. They creatively use the texts, having read them, using songs, sayings, proverbs, and so on. So whether in the context of worship or in the context of healings there is a lot of interaction with the texts they have derived from the written texts. This is the site for a spirituality of resistance and a spirituality of struggle for these women. In their songs you will find the affirmation of their Christian identity and their dignity as women. These are sources of inspiration and strength in order to persevere in their lives.

I occasionally ask myself, even as an African American, if we do not sometimes romanticize popular religion. Do we not sometimes go so far as to suggest that women or people considered different fared well under popular religion? That everything was just and equal and Christianity came in and corrupted it, this pristine world?

In Switzerland, popular religion is an odd mixture of Christian heritage, astrology, esoterica, etc. It works to reinforce the state of things, it doesn't challenge the world in general. Moreover, it claims elements from other cultures and mixes them together in a way that I perceive as neo-colonialistic. They claim bits of North American indigenous religion, bits of Asian religion, and make a mix to suit themselves. And I as a Christian theologian with my conviction that this world must change, I have to challenge this popular religion.

The Authority and Sacredness of the Text

There are people who grow up in an environment where there is no religious upbringing or education and yet the Bible is still there, usually as a work of literature.

The more concrete we are in our work, the less we work with 'the Bible' and the more we work with specific texts. This is also the case for the phrase 'the Word of God', which still exerts power over us. I think we can best liberate ourselves from this by examining what it signifies in these texts themselves. For example, it can simply signify a powerful or a particularly special word. It is a human word, for this or that prophet can claim to speak the Word of God. Or it is exactly the opposite of what they claim. It is important to free ourselves from this claim to authority. There is authority that is imposed, and there is authority that is earned. Texts can earn authority for us because of our experience of them or because they have proven themselves, but not because someone merely says that they are sacred or the Word of God and thus they have authority.

I agree that the sacredness of the Bible should not be understood literally, but where is the boundary where I can discern that it is a holy book that is different somehow from other books and texts? And to what extent do I have the freedom to make a completely different story out of the biblical story? Let me ask the question in this manner: What does it mean that the Bible is holy or that it is a religious book?

I don't begin anymore from the assumption that the Bible is a holy text that cannot be questioned. To me, just because it's holy doesn't mean it cannot be questioned, and that's not just to me the trained academic, it's also to me as a person who was raised in a community where questions were asked. And I don't think that with my history I could afford not to have asked that question. If we hadn't asked questions I would still be a slave.

It was interesting to hear Nancy Cardoso Pereira saying that in her culture in Brazil the Bible is an imported poncho. Now, first of all, we have to claim responsibility for that in the Middle East because we were the first to export the Bible as such. For us, the Bible and Christianity are indigenous to the land, yet, what is imported are the theologies. I have a connection to the Bible, but I'm alienated to the theologies that arose from the usage of the Bible in Western culture. Second, we are talking about people reading the Bible, and this is a connecting point to Palestine for me. Very often we theologians think that we are challenging the institution of the Church, but I say that this is a myth. In the Third World context it is people at the grass-roots level who are actually challenging our theologies.

Women need to weave a common ground, not only as women, but also as women who are concerned about people who live at the margins. That's the concern for which we are doing feminist theology.

The Bible has always been a good companion to the people who had to pass through the hard decades of communism in Romania. It gave hope and faith to them. Even in those times the Bible was considered a sacred book. It was placed in a prominent location and when a new member was born into the family his or her date of birth was entered into it. It was thus not only a book that was literally valued by everyone, but it also represented a living, continuing tradition. We know what dangers it represented in communist times: when it happened—very rarely—that we could travel abroad, we were asked at the border whether we were carrying any guns or Bibles or religious books with us. Or when friends from Western countries sent us Bibles because we couldn't buy them here, then they were confiscated at the border and recycled into toilet paper. It wasn't unusual to discover fragments from the Bible in toilet paper. You may not have been aware of this, but it can help you to understand the very special significance the Bible has for us. Even if we don't take it word for word, it gave hope and strength to many people in those difficult times. And now we are in a dire strait in our country and therefore need the Bible more than ever. I don't consider this to be a naive belief.

As a person from the Orient, one way for me to liberate myself from the domination of the Bible was to view it as an oriental market, a place where you can find everything that you could possibly need and more. You only need the patience to look, and to consider what you want to purchase and which price you want to pay.

Taking Action; Change and Struggle

Feminists have spent a lot of time, thought and energy on trying to change education, but they have not spent the same time, thought and energy on trying to change religion.

Only after you have rhetorical analysis can you really enter into action, that is, a transforming action that can illuminate ritual and cultural expression.

Textual interpretation is a kind of neutral tool for me. It can be applied to any text; it can be applied to a Hindu text or it can be applied to a biblical text. But the question remains what will we do after we have applied the tool in analysis? When does it become action?

I have never felt that interpreting the Holy Scripture would ever make me able to change anything in the world. My only interest in interpreting these texts has been purely academic. I don't have any problem comparing the biblical stories with any other sort of stories in the world—there isn't any difference between them. I always make comparisons between these stories and any other form of literature; I don't see a difference in the presentation of the human condition between this sort of literature or the other. The difference for me personally is that I like to read Jane Austen very much as a hobby and I read the texts of the Bible professionally.

How do the struggles of people at the grass-roots level shape feminist hermeneutical methods?

It's very important to meet other persons coming from situations where they also always have to fight on different levels. It is empowering.

Dialogue

I like the term 'feminist theology'. It does not specify *Christian* feminist theology, *Hindu* feminist theology or *Muslim* feminist theology. And from the Indian background, I really have tremendous admiration for Hindu women who are also theologizing in their own field.

There are different languages of dialogue. I would describe one as the intellectual dialogue and another as the dialogue of life. On the level of the intellectual dialogue, scholars of Hinduism, Christianity and Islam come together and enter into dialogue at inter-religious centers. They discuss matters such as our understanding of God or the meaning of life, important issues, very theoretical, very intellectual, very much related to a scriptural understanding of religion. The dialogue of life, on the other hand, is taking place where popular religions interact. This is where activists and ordinary people confront each other's lives.

We have come together with the vision that we are contributing to change. We have to be conscious that change always takes time. Let me use the image of a mosaic. Each one of us in her own way is contributing one of the beautifully colored stones. The whole mosaic might not get finished in our generation, we might not know what it will look like in the end, but we will be contributing to it so that perhaps the generation of women after us will be able to give birth to the world with it.

Globalization

Globalization has led to a questioning of categories such as First World, Third World, North, South, etc. We need to work on an analysis of globalization, which will most likely be the dominant system for the next 20, 30, perhaps even 50 years. What is the meaning of the fact that I soon might have more in common with someone in India or in Africa because we share the same status in terms of education, economics and social position than I have in common with the woman down the street who is on welfare?

Nevertheless, we still need one kind of language, one kind of terminology that will allow us to communicate with each other. And here we come back to the global situation, because one sign of oppression lies specifically in the Western ideology that defines the other in such terms that it is not possible to have anything in common, that the other is by definition inferior.

In some parts of feminist criticism there is an understanding that not all women are alike, that there are differences. There is a polite acknowledgment in feminist criticism that we all stand at different places in our contexts and in our interpretations. But at the same time this criticism doesn't define a methodological moment when you must consider who you are in your interpretation and then take responsibility for the fact that once you interpret as a European, African, Asian or American feminist your interpretation can have an enormous effect for other people across the world. It can have implications to Caribbean women, it can have implications for South American women, because once I empower, for example, African American women, that will have an effect upon how they deal with other women. As a methodological point, this becomes very important.

Center and Periphery

I would like to talk about a hermeneutics of reading the Bible from the periphery. One of our major problems is that we always have been reading the Bible from the perspective of the majority, from the center. But for the Bible to be a liberating force we must rediscover the perspective of the marginalized, those who are nameless and speechless in the Bible.

Haven't we all at one time said that we are outsiders, that we have been marginalized? And now I ask myself what or where the center is from which we have been marginalized. Hasn't the world changed so much that we don't have a center any more? And consequently marginalization does not necessarily follow, but perhaps something else?

Political Aspects of Colonialism and Colonization

We cannot keep talking about colonialism, because to some extent the colonizers have left. And if colonialism has been removed and patriarchy has remained, what has been added to patriarchy to explain the current situation? What have we done? Especially for or to women?

The truth is, imperialism is still very much alive, built on cultural, economic and political levels throughout the world. I think we should be careful to avoid thinking that it is not part of our contexts as well.

We have to talk about exclusion. The majority of the Brazilian population, for example, is illiterate. Yet this process of globalization focuses to great extent on the possibilities of studying and doing research. What good is it to create possibilities for some to study and do research, to write and to travel, if it means excluding others?

I appreciate that you do not equate patriarchy with imperialism, because I see imperialism as a wider umbrella. It encompasses more than what patriarchy represents in feminist studies or in feminist criticism. In interdisciplinary discourse it covers social and economic issues as well as political and cultural issues.

The social location of the reader is extremely important. From a postcolonial perspective, the reader has been informed not only by who she is in terms of gender but also by the social location of the situation in which she was colonized. There is also the dimension of one's cultural background. For instance, as a first-generation Christian I have to take into consideration the Confucian background I come from. So there are multiples identities or multiples issues that I have to consider when reflecting on my social location.

Post-Colonial Biblical Interpretation

The Hallelujah Movement in Indonesia condemns all of the tribal traditions and in this respect is even harsher than the mainstream Churches in Indonesia. But why do so many people want to be members of the Hallelujah Movement? Because life is very difficult in Indonesia now, and when they go to the mainstream Churches they cannot clap or laugh as they are used to do in their Indonesian culture. But the mainstream Churches inherited the European tradition, and this means you have to sit, listen and not clap your hands. But in the Hallelujah Movement you can cry, you can shout, you can say 'Hallelujah'. And they say that they don't get anything from the mainstream Churches, not even from the pulpit. But with regard to the issue of condemning tribal traditions, let me give you another example of a major difficulty that I encounter: How can you teach the story of Elijah when he kills the priests of Ba'al if it represents a condemnation of your own tribal religion? It is very difficult for my students and for many Indonesians to accept the truth that is present in their own tribal traditions because these have been condemned as evil and sinful for so long by the Churches.

How am I involved in promoting cultural domination? How can I, in my own very little way, resist the mainstream reading and interpretation of the Bible?

Each time we come to a text we raise the question as to which perspective we are reading from. Are we reading from the perspective of the colonizer, are we reading from the perspective of the colonized or are we reading from the perspective of the collaborator? And I think, I'm in all of these positions. Sometimes we are collaborators, sometimes we are colonizers and sometimes we are colonized. It depends where we are. In a situation such as the one here, where I'm supposedly a representative of the Two-Thirds World, I would rather say: 'No, that is not true. I'm a privileged person. I've been educated in the West, I've become a colonizer.' Thus, my position can shift.

One of the things that post-colonial criticism does is that it gives us a heightened sense of self-criticism. But feminist criticism and all other criticism fail to give us a tool. A step in our dialogue with the text is that we must ask ourselves: Where do I stand in this text? Am I a collaborator, am I a colonizer or am I part of the colonized?

It is important to realize that many apparently liberative feminist interpretations actually continue to promote imperialism. I therefore have focused on and studied as much as possible the category of imperialism and its various faces, from ancient times to the present. Imperialism has not taken on only one face; its strategies are constantly changing. If you examine the biblical texts, for example, you find the tradition of conquest killing, as in the book of Judith. How is the story of Judith used to endorse patriarchy? Even when Judith is lifted high for us, how is she also used against us? We all have to be self-critical of the positions that we are in because we are bound by structures and ideologies. We must constantly be on guard against taking positions of domination with regard to others.

I'm not sure if there is such a thing as a liberating text. Because as soon as we limit ourselves to looking for a liberating text we give up the dynamic character between the text and the context. If you are talking about the land, for example, then you have to be aware of whether you are talking about the land when the Israelites were in the land or when they were in the exile or during the time of post-exile, each situation is different. The Bible itself is very contextual in terms of the liberating nature of its texts.

Interdependence

I like to think that we are one world, despite our differences, whatever they are. When we interpret the most ancient texts like the Hebrew Bible, *the Odyssey*, etc., they show us that there had been an interaction of people of different races, gender, cultures and nations. That should be a sign for us that we need each other, that we are interconnected.

Because we all come from different contexts it may well be that a text that is liberating for me is not necessarily liberating for you or for another. This is probably the reason why we want to communicate and to dialogue and to listen, knowing that we are interdependent and interconnected. The moment I start talking about my own liberation I am also saying something that might involve the oppression of the other. I therefore have to listen. I have to be willing to learn that what I say can be oppressive to the other person. I have to be willing to build on a continual dialogue, for liberation is an ongoing process.

Can we theologize without the analysis of the socio-political dimension? What are we then theologizing about? Are we theologizing in a vacuum? Is there content to our theology? Do we fear analyzing experience and the situation of oppression? How can we produce a theology that does not relate to socio-political liberation? These two things are not separate, we cannot divide them into two camps.

Difference and Liberation

You talk about postcolonial hermeneutics as a liberating hermeneutics, that it is reading for liberating interdependence. But how do we work that interdependence out? I call for a celebration of differences, but that is also very discomforting and problematic for some people.

What is liberating to me, is perhaps not liberating to others, but do we have a vision that we all share, a vision of liberation?

We need to learn to celebrate our differences. We are different. Let's not pretend that we are all one.

Every woman here has left her own context in order to come here and hear others speak of their contexts. And if I speak about something that is liberating for me, it might not be liberating for any of you. There isn't a single text in the Bible that is liberating for all of us, because in all of these texts there are several perspectives. You have to bring them out, and in some respect they can be liberating for me but not for you, etc. Let's talk about the tools to bring this out of the text.

Interpretation and Secularization

My experience of liberation has come from words like 'enlightenment' and 'rationalism'; they have been liberating elements in my education and upbringing. I remain within the Western, rationalist perspective. I'm not trying to say that it's any better than other perspectives, but we have to be aware of the fact that we're so strongly socialized into our forms of thinking that it is almost impossible to do anything else.

Don't some people somehow internalize the feeling that being religious makes you morally better? That people who have lost their religion have also lost their moral values, that they can no longer distinguish between what is moral and immoral? I think this is an extremely problematic manner of looking at the world.

Since I have been part of the feminist movement I have learned that certain philosophies and doctrines have been disqualified as no longer feminist. This, however, presents me with the dilemma that we apparently have a very equivocal relationship with modern and post-modern thought, with the mediatory role of modern thought and moreover with Jewish, Christian and biblical traditions. And this also includes a more precise definition of theology and its significance, of God (or Goddess, if you will), of what liberation is.

Construction—Deconstruction—Reconstruction

The first generation of Christians in Korea consciously made the choice to convert to Christianity from Buddhism, Confucianism or Shamanism, and therefore we don't have this tradition of deconstruction. Christian women in Korea want to learn and realize something new and liberating from Christianity. And it is just because of this that we have difficulties as feminist theologians. They are very disappointed if we begin to deconstruct the Bible. What are we doing here? I thought we were doing theology here? I want to learn something new from this old, well-known story; what are we going to do with it? We feminist theologians and women in the feminist movement have to help the women in this first generation of Christians to liberate themselves from the patriarchal clergymen who have complete control over them. For they want to learn something new without losing their identities as Christians.

Let me use the image of a knitted sweater to explain what I understand by deconstruction: I'm looking for that little thread, I'm just looking for that one piece of thread in the argument that is loose. I think in everybody's argument, my own included, there is a thread that is loose. And I'm trying to pull that thread, I'm trying to unravel that garment. In this case I might end up naked, and that, too, is not what I want to do. Even as I see that thread, even if I am really intrigued to unravel all of it, I don't pull the whole thing. I've recognized that people belong to communities, and sometimes it's within communities that you have to go back and rebuild.

What does the Bible have to say to us positively? It is the daily experience of the community of believers. Stories, persons or words from the Bible can give us strength, hope and understanding to meet the joys and sorrows, challenges and crises of our daily lives, strength to continue on, to continue to live, to bear the burden, to not abandon the struggle. That is why we don't want to forsake the Bible; it is the good news for us and for future generations.

Semper reformanda means deconstruction and reconstruction for me. For *reformare* also means reconstruction and indicates how you should deal with deconstruction—that is, through the control and renewal of your theology. For this purpose we should listen to the people at the grass-roots level and place their problems in a theological perspective.

THE STOLEN BIBLE

Elżbieta Adamiak

I did not expect to receive an invitation to the symposium at Monte Verità, nor did I expect the symposium to turn into such an important personal experience. The diversity of the participants at the symposium and their many views did much to relativize the apparent polarity between Western and Eastern Europe that I had encountered at prior conferences. Suddenly, we—women from Central and Eastern Europe—could (or had to) try and explain our viewpoint not only vis-à-vis woman theologians from the West but also vis-à-vis women theologians from all corners of the world. In this context we represented those parts of Europe that had never been colonial powers but had in many cases been conquered themselves and had had to suffer the dominance of foreign powers.

'Our viewpoint?' Is there a common Central and Eastern European view of theological and hermeneutic issues? I have been thinking about that question for a long time and I do not know whether I can answer it. As a systematic theologian I am interested in hermeneutic and exegetic discussions. Admittedly, I regularly venture into the land of feminist Bible interpretation by writing on 'women in the Bible'. Therefore, my primary objective at Monte Verità was to learn from women exegetes. What I learned was in reference to my context, my self-understanding and my approach to the Bible, which is based on practical experience rather than explicit reflection.

On the other hand, looking at my situation within a Central and Eastern European context, I have to admit that I was and still am in a privileged position. First, I come from Poland, a country where Churches could act with relative freedom in the communist era. Second, I have witnessed great changes that have allowed me to do many things I could only dream of before: I have been able to study theology—in the West, even. I have written a thesis on a feminist theological topic. I am working as a theologian. I am teaching at the theology faculty of the university. All of this is ample reason to rejoice—even though the imbalance between the majority of clerics and the minority of lay theologians on the teaching staff is making my work difficult (cf. Adamiak 1995 and 1998). A further privilege is the continually improving economic situation in Poland.

All keynote presentations at the symposium dealt with the interpretation of the Bible. The common subject, however, led to an emphasis of the differences of the cultural and social contexts among the participants. Thus, my experiences at Monte Verità culminated in two basic questions: Is there a specifically Central and Eastern European context in theology? And what common ground is there between the theological systems and methods developed and employed by women from our and from other parts of the world?

Is There a Central and Eastern European Theology?

When talking about Central and Eastern European countries one generally refers to those Second World countries essentially linked by the common experience of post-war communism. Of course, there are also deeper historical, religious and confessional roots which reveal not only connections and similarities among these countries but differences, tensions and conflicts as well. Central and Eastern Europe is not a uniform region. 'The differences among the countries in Central and Eastern Europe in spirituality, culture and society are greater than among the countries and regions of Western Europe... From a socio-cultural perspective Central and Eastern Europe can certainly not be seen as homogeneous' (Tomka 2000: 311).[1]

Many people—at various levels of the Church—have been moved by the question as to the significance of recent historical developments for faith and theology. 1991 saw the first congress of Central and Eastern European theologians in Lublin (Poland), and for the past few years now woman theologians from our part of Europe have organized regional conferences within the framework of the European Society for Women in Theological Research (ESWTR)—1998 in Prague (Czech Republic), 2000 in Lublin (Poland), 2002 in Riga (Latvia) and the next one is scheduled for 2004 in Varna (Bulgaria). There seems to exist a great need to jointly reflect on our past, present and future from a theological perspective. The diversity of our contexts, however, makes it difficult to define a common ground.

---

1.   Together with P.M. Zulehner, Tomka managed the project 'New Departures' for the Pastorales Forum in Vienna, the results of which are published in the series 'God after Communism'—see Tomka and Zulehner 1999.

One example of a shared past is the experience of atheistic propaganda and the oppression of Christian Churches. The circumstances, however, were very different from country to country. An avowal of Christian faith could, for example, lead to many years in prison or even spell death for persons whose influence was particularly feared. In other contexts/countries/periods it might 'only' have put a lid on career opportunities. Two factors can serve as a gauge: access to the Bible, and access to theological training. Whereas in some countries the Bible was a forbidden book, in others it was 'merely' impossible to find. In some countries permission to study theology was only given to those who agreed with the communist authorities, whereas in other countries students of theology faced a lack of professional perspectives. The existence of the Churches was threatened not only in the Soviet Union but also in Czechoslovakia and Hungary. Those two countries saw the emergence of a Catholic underground Church. Yugoslavia and Poland, on the other hand, were among the countries who showed more tolerance.[2]

The difficult situation of the Churches and their isolation from the world Church led to a reaffirmation of its deeply rooted ties with tradition. The consequences can still be felt today in the revival of national thinking or the renaissance of a theology taught before World War Two, in a Catholic context, a pre-Council theology. In some countries the reforms associated with the Second Vatican Council have yet to be introduced. In other countries the degree to which the spirit of these reforms has permeated the life of the Church is unclear. The fall of the Berlin Wall and the opening to the world has also brought a confrontation with the contemporary world.

> The 'total' upheaval of societies leads to existential fears and produces (in part emotional-fundamentalist) solutions from a national past. In this respect a rift can be observed between the East and the West. Western Europe is pragmatic, professional and forward looking—also rational. Among Eastern Europeans, however, the weight of history, pathos, anger and a feeling of injustice is pervasive. (Máté-Tóth 2000: 279)

All attempts to design a Central and Eastern European theology stem from different variations of a theology of suffering: a theology of Gulag (Halik 1993 and 1997) or a theology of Kolyma (Chrostowski 1991; see Nosowski 1992). Kolyma is the name of a river adjacent to the Arctic

---

2. For more specific information see Tomka and Zulehner 1999; and the entire issue of *Concilium* 36 (2000) on 'Religion in Communism' (especially Máté Tóth's contribution [Máté Tóth 2000]).

circle where one of the most terrible Soviet forced labor camps had been built. It was a place comparable with Auschwitz. Gulag stands for an entire system of violence and repression that existed between the early 1920s and the mid-1950s. 'Class enemies' were arrested in waves depending on the situation: the farmers who fought against collectivization; the populations driven from Polish and Baltic areas in 1939; the potentially disloyal segments (e.g. the Volga Germans during World War Two); those suspected of sabotage; believers; people who had contact with relatives and friends abroad; independent thinkers who did not toe the party lines; and also criminals. Most prisoners, however, were innocent. As a consequence of the harsh climate, the very long working hours and the inhumane treatment, roughly a tenth of those imprisoned died every year. From 1920 to 1956 between 15 and 30 million people are estimated to have died in the Gulag. The exact figures will never be known. The Soviet labor camps were the worst, but there were in all more than 400 such camps throughout Central and Eastern Europe.[3]

A theology of Gulag or Kolyma strives for an understanding that grows as the special fruit from past, unhealed suffering. Why did God permit such persecution? Why were some Churches almost condemned to death? Why did they not die and are on the road to revival now? Why did some Christian men and women become martyrs, and why were others ready to compromise with the powers that were? What is the meaning of the experience of suffering? How can the experience of suffering help to create an identity and a future within the new context of an opening to Western Europe, which has traveled other paths? Such questions are always burning. The answers, however, grow from Church practice rather than from theological publications. At the same time, a theology of suffering raises the basic question about the life-creating power of hope and thus serves as the litmus test of other theological systems and methods, feminist ones included.

Rapid change brings not only freedom and hope but also new suffering such as poverty, unemployment, social differences hitherto unknown and surging violence. Instead of developing individual theological viewpoints, those developed elsewhere (mainly in the West) are being translated into our languages—in the Polish Catholic context, primarily the viewpoints of the great theologians from the time of the Council rather than currently

3.   See the web sites of the Open Society Archives with the exhibition on Gulag: www.osa.ceu.hu/gulag.

active theologians. 'The new cups are often filled with old wine... The dogmatics of salvation, biblical hermeneutics, critical social teachings, practical theology and modern religious pedagogy are still viewed with great skepticism', says a Hungarian theologian (Máté-Tóth 2000: 285).

What does this briefly sketched past mean for our approach to the Bible? It means first of all that the Bible was unknown to many people. It was a forbidden book, considered to be subversive and dangerous by the former powers. It was a tool to criticize the ruling ideology. To some it was a symbol of the spiritual force of the Church, a bastion, a haven in times of insecurity. It was a holy and socially relevant book. It represented the tradition and identity of many people. The communist dictatorship robbed the people not only of their tradition and identity but also of the Bible. When we Central and Eastern European women theologians went to Prague in 1998 to reflect on our new situation and the challenges that it represented, one of us used the metaphor of 'the stolen Bible' in our discussion; I have taken this metaphor for the title of this article. At that time we used it mainly to refer to our common experience of limited access to the Bible during the communist era. It can, however, be understood in a much broader context—also in a feminist one. 'Stolen' means that something has been taken away by force, something that was mine or part of me, something I now miss and long for. Emotionally the metaphor is filled with sadness and bitterness, but also with joy in the Bible and the desire to approach it again.

The worship of the Bible on a symbolic level seldom went hand in hand with general and traditional knowledge of theology and Bible interpretation. A critical reading of the biblical texts, in particular from the perspective of feminist theology or the theology of liberation, could have been exploited to serve the purposes of communist propaganda. This led to an apology of the Bible from the side of the Church. For that reason the historical and critical method was received with great caution. It was known among specialists and students were made familiar with it in outline only. Applying it in lectures is still seen by some as an attempt to undermine faith. 'There is a wish to see and encourage theology as a discipline with definite answers and not as a discipline with open questions' (Máté-Tóth 2000: 285). Nevertheless, the theological tradition which understands theology as the art of formulating questions also lives on (Adamiak and Majewski 1999: 35-43; Adamiak 2000). Today, feminist questions have become part of those significant questions.

Is There a Common Ground Worldwide for Feminist Theology?

A further aspect shared by Central and Eastern European countries is the change in the situation of women. We need to take another look at the often fictitious equality between men and women hailed by communist propaganda. The former rulers did not care so much about women but about the changing demands on the labor market, with the corresponding adaptations in ideology related to women. Studies show that when power was actually at stake in different protest or reform movements the number of women in positions of power dwindled quickly (Fuszara 2000: 21-30). This pattern can be broadly observed after the demise of the Berlin Wall in 1989. The transformation processes adversely affected the situation of women (e.g. the financial discrimination of typically 'feminine' professions; more widespread unemployment among women; the discrimination of women by the new insurance system—examples from Poland).

There is thus a great deal of work to be done by contemporary feminists from our part of Europe in order to overcome the ideological representation of the women's movement. One of the difficulties they will encounter is the asynchronicity of the developments in the West and here. Many developments that took place in stages have been considered and accepted contemporaneously yet separately by different groups. Feminism itself is sometimes understood differently, if not contradictorily—depending on the tradition or the periods of the women's movements quoted. And some women are attracted by the post-feminist approach. The growing feminist interest goes hand in hand with a revival of the interrupted tradition of the Church or ecumenical women's organizations which were banned during the communist era. The networks of critical Christian women, however, have remained few. Individual efforts prevail. Even we few Central and Eastern European women theologians who represented our part of the world at Monte Verità could not agree on the significance of feminist approaches to our theology. While my Hungarian sisters, who work primarily as pastors, were rather skeptical towards feminist theology, the feminist dimension of theology is of great importance to me. To be sure, that kind of argument is typical for our context. The reservations against feminist theology are not limited to its feminist aspects only. What is at stake is an encounter with another, critical kind of theological thinking.

Given our subject, the most important questions are: How can we read the Bible from a viewpoint critical of all ideology, even though the Bible itself proved to be the best tool in criticizing Marxist and atheist ideology?

How can we, women from Central and Eastern Europe, reclaim our own Bible once again without raising the suspicion in our Churches that we are ideologizing the Bible? Is it not our main duty to catch up on the years lost by introducing and familiarizing women with the Bible? Does this mission therefore take precedence over criticism?[4] Once we leave the safe haven of the gospel to interpret the biblical text according to extra-biblical criteria, do we not tread uncertain ground in that every criterion can be replaced by new ones? The hermeneutic diversity at Monte Verità clearly demonstrated that women's liberation is not an unequivocal criterion but is understood differently depending on the context. Are we thus helping women with a feminist criticism of the Bible or are we depriving them of the best support they have had? What is our responsibility as theologians? How can we find a third way, both recognizing the sacred aspect of the biblical text while also criticizing it? Is a literal and uncritical rendition of the Bible not a continuation of the process by which women, all women in a certain sense, had been robbed of the gospel?

At the end of our symposium at Monte Verità we were invited to sit down at a well-decked table (not only symbolically), with the fruits of our search for understanding collected over the week.[5] They were given to us participants to nourish us on our ways. Inspired by that metaphor we might ask to what degree we are nourished by feminist exegesis. Does it convey strength and hope to live? What diet does it recommend? Is enough time spent on the preparation of a hearty meal or has criticism eliminated foods that still are and could remain nourishing for many?

How can we in Central and Eastern Europe build on the perception of the (at least) twofold 'theft' of the Bible and avoid falling into the 'criticism' trap? Should we follow in the footsteps of our theologian sisters from the so-called First and Third Worlds or find our own issues and ways? Is the answer here, too, in taking a middle road? Why should we not be inspired by the work of other women? In order to answer these questions we need to acquaint ourselves with existing feminist-theological systems and methods in the so-called First and Third Worlds. There are two levels of feminist-theological thinking, one of which is so fundamental that it can be applied also in our region (e.g. problems like the absence of women in decision-making bodies of the Church, the biases of existing theology, the

---

4.   The incisive formulation of these issues arose in lively discussions with Heike Walz, a Western European participant at the symposium.

5.   The 'buffet metaphor' was raised by Adele Reinhartz and Marie-Theres Wacker (see their contribution to the present volume).

exclusivity of language). Those general problems, however, are connected with local traditions, so that feminist-theological thinking also will need to be reformulated on the second level. Our task for the future is to find out what that means in practical terms (Adamiak 1997).

I would like to conclude my essay with another metaphor from the opening meditation of the ESWTR conference 2000 in Lublin. A woman opens the Scriptures and bows. She closes the book, wraps it, lifts it, embraces it, dances with it, lays it in a crib and watches over it. The Bible, the Word, brings life in our midst. It is in our hands, however; it needs our care to remain alive. By interpreting the Bible we interpret ourselves, our lives. We look for our lives in the Bible. We want to protect life and its dignity and care for it. My wish would be for feminist theology to render this life-giving force more visible.

BIBLIOGRAPHY

Adamiak, Elżbieta
1995   'Feministische Theologie in Polen? Ein beinahe unmögliches Thema', in Angela Berlis *et al.* (eds.), *Women Churches: Networking and Reflection in the European Context* (Yearbook of the European Society of Women in Theological Research, 3; Leuven: Peeters): 106-12.
1997   'Zerrissen zwischen Osten und Westen', *Schlangenbrut* 15.56: 5-7.
1998   'Kirche und Feminismus in Polen', in N.J. Njorge and I. Askola (eds.), *There Were also Women Looking on From Afar* (Studies from the World Alliance of Reformed Churches, 41; Geneva: World Alliance of Reformed Churches): 57-64.
2000   'Vrouwen en theologie in tijden van overgang', *Fier* 3: 7-9.
Adamiak, Elżbieta, and Józef Majewski
1999   'Teologia między Odrą a Bugiem. Kilka pytań o stan teologii polskiej w czasie przełomu' ('Theology between the Oder and the Bug: Some Questions on the Status of Polish Theology in Changing Times)', *Więź* 42.10: 28-46.
Chrostowski, Waldemar
1991   'Filozofia po Kołymie' ('Philosophy after Kolyma'), *Spotkania* (4 December 1991).
Fuszara, Małgorzata
2000   'Udział kobiet we władzy' ('Women's Participation in Power'), in *Kobiety w Polsce w latach 90. Raport Centrum Praw Kobiet* (*Women in Poland in the 90s: The Report of the Center for the Rights of Women*) (Warsaw: Fundacja Centrum Praw Kobiet): 21-42.
Halik, Tomáš
1993   *'Du wirst das Angesicht der Erde erneuern': Kirche und Gesellschaft an der Schwelle zur Freiheit* (Leipzig: Benno-Verlag).

1997   *Wyzwoleni, jeszcze nie wolni. Czeski katolicyzm przed i po 1989 roku (Freed,*
            Not Free Yet: The Czech Catholicism Before and After 1989) (Poznan: W
            drodze).

Kirchen in Osteuropa
2001   'Themenheft', *Junge Kirche* 62/1.

Máté-Tóth, Adrás
2000   'Eine Theologie der Zweiten Welt? Beobachtungen und Herausforderungen',
            Concilium 36: 278-86.

Nosowski, Zbigniew
1992   'Theology after Gulag', *The Tablet* (30 May 1992).

Tomka, Miklós
2000   'Die Marginalisierung der Christen in Ost-Mitteleuropa', *Concilium* 36:
            311-22.

Tomka, Miklós, and Paul M. Zulehner
1999   *Religion in den Reformländern Ost(Mittel)Europas* (Vienna: Pastorales
            Forum–Förderung der Kirchen in Ost[Mittel] Europa).

FREEDOM, LIBERATION AND CONTEXT AS HERMENEUTICAL TASKS

Sophia Bietenhard

Feminist Hermeneutics and Contextual Diversity

The international symposium at Monte Verità provided me with a number of valuable insights. The most important was probably the confirmation that a single methodology for the interpretation of biblical texts does not exist. The feminist discussion of various traditions of understanding and interpretation made it clear to me that in certain contexts it is important to enter into dialogue with the text, with oneself and with the environment utilizing a methodological basis. If the process of interpretation is to be meaningful, then history must be interpreted, the present must be recognized and comprehended, and choices must be made with regard to the future, both within and for a specific context. Moreover, I also realized once again during the presentations and discussions how important the persons involved in the process of interpretation and their whole backgrounds are.[1]

The recognition of the diversity of interpretive methodology gave rise to even more questions. If biblical interpretation is influenced greatly by context, then is it possible for outsiders to these contexts to comprehend the respective interpretations? In view of this diversity, what are the common elements, without which a profitable exchange could hardly succeed? Social, cultural, intellectual, political and economic differences are apparently so profound that they divide not only North and South or East and West but also every society in itself.

What significance does this have for feminist exegesis and what are the consequences for a discussion about the (feminist) hermeneutics of liberation? This division into contextual micro-regions is at odds with the classical vision of the political feminist movement on which Christian

---

1. Kessler (1999: 66) succinctly noted in his commentary to the book of Micah that 'feminist manners of reading raise the compelling question of how "we" appear in a text'. Cf. Noller 1995: 82-90.

feminist theology has been based, that is, of women around the world working (united) to overcome all forms of oppression. What does this mean for every specific context? For example, can the claim of the Western European *Kompendium Feministische Bibelauslegung* (*Compendium of Feminist Biblical Interpretation*) that 'Christian anti-Semitism, Western colonialism and all forms of racism must be battled concurrently with the oppression of women' (Schottroff and Wacker [eds.] 1998: xiv) have equal meaning and validity for others? During the symposium it became very evident that many of the mainstays of traditional Christian belief are no longer tenable. The reality of a pluralistic world, the growing realization among liberal Christians that they make up only a part of the diverse inter-religious world concert, and the experience of the rapid, global transformation of values and norms were reflected in many statements made at the symposium. The hermeneutical and theological conclusions based on this do not simply stop at the question of God, the problem of the unity of the Canon or the authority of Scripture. And more dependable allies are not to be found in the force of tradition, on the basis of classic academic methods of interpretation or the institutional Churches. Unless, that is, they are used as the premise for the necessary transformation. Sarolta Püsök, the Hungarian reformed theologian from Romania, pointed out during the final podium discussion that in her reformed tradition the Church has a responsibility for constant renewal and therefore must face contemporary challenges such as biblical hermeneutics, the question of the Canon or the authority of Scripture.

I find this statement very appealing, particularly since I also grew up in a critical, reformed tradition. At the same time, I doubt the chances of its successful realization. As a Western European I have developed a natural skepticism with respect to institutionalized directives, even those in reference to processes of transformation or renewal. The Church offers room for discussion only to the degree that I, as an autonomous subject, am willing or able to take it up.[2] I do not want to say that this space is not needed, but that it exists as only one of many possible choices for me. I also do not doubt any less the capacity of the theological schools to meet the demands for renewal; I had to find for myself through praxis the connections between the tools for historical-critical exegesis that we learned, scholarly theology

---

2.   With regard to the function and significance of religious communities and institutions, of the national Churches and religiousness in Switzerland, a number of sociological and theological studies have recently appeared, e.g., Dubach and Campiche (eds.) 1993.

and everyday praxis. An invaluable assistance for me, and for others, was the feminist movement in the Church and feminist theology because of the regular exchange between theory and praxis that they gave rise to. The annual Women's World Day of Prayer is a good model of how to bridge the gap between theory and praxis, between contextual biblical hermeneutics and openness in face of other contexts, and between one's own self-understanding and the acceptance of others (Bechmann 1993 and 1998). But I would also maintain that a critical, analytical discussion of questions of belief is a necessity in my context, for therein lies the potential for tolerance, one of the fundamental values of the Enlightenment. It is thus my obligation to discuss alternatives for thought and interpretation with respect to this given background from a foreign contextuality. Other than by means of discourse, I can neither esteem nor defend nor contextualize the differences of foreign lifestyles and foreign thinking.

The Relationship between Liberation and Freedom

The perception of differences and tolerance are obviously mutually conditional. But how do we make the step from our own identity to an understanding of other opinions and beliefs? The perception of differences alone is not sufficient here. Aside from the fact that contexts hardly can be unequivocally defined, I do think that the perception of the other is present in the concept of liberation as well as in the nature of reading the Bible.

It is evidently useful to examine the concept of liberation in order to discuss this question. It plays a central role in recent hermeneutical biblical debates. But as far as I am aware, feminist biblical interpretation that bears the label 'liberative' rarely explains what this precisely means. With the exception of Elisabeth Schüssler Fiorenza's contribution, this was no different at Monte Verità, a symposium held under the title of the hermeneutics of liberation! In my opinion, however, the difficulty of understanding how an inter-contextual feminist interpretation of the Bible might be defined is related to the fact that the differing contexts are accompanied by differing concepts of freedom and liberation on the epistemological level.[3]

The following thoughts might serve to motivate the work of clarification that is necessary; they are to be understood as arising from my intellectual and analytical context. During the symposium the representatives from the

---

3.   Nagl-Docekal (2000: 29-37) points out the significance of this discussion for gender studies.

Southern hemisphere rightly pointed out that they consider the definitions of the framework in which freedom and liberation should be discussed as given by hermeneutic scholars from Europe and the United States to be a new form of colonialism. This objection is even more justified given the fact that liberation theology has been formulated primarily with respect to various contexts in the Southern hemisphere. The clarification of my own terms and definitions, however, allows me to look for links for an inter-contextual discussion of the conditions for freedom and liberation in biblical interpretation.[4]

I proceed from the assumption that the term 'liberation' has been derived philosophically from the term 'freedom' and that it represents a concrete manner of conduct. Freedom is the basis and goal of human existence (in Classical philosophy the term is utilized in reference to citizens) with regard to will as well as to conduct; it is thus a truly fundamental precondition for responsible human existence. Liberation, on the other hand, is a reference to breaking free (theological redemption) from social, political and economic forms of dependence (Dussel 1995; Fornet-Betancourt 1988; Segundo 1995). There are various theories of freedom, each of which shapes the understanding of its respective concept of liberation. I would like to demonstrate this using the example of Elisabeth Schüssler Fiorenza's feminist hermeneutics of liberation.

Schüssler Fiorenza understands the goal of feminist biblical interpretation as the liberation from the patriarchal or kyriarchal system of domination that has established itself culturally and socially as the ruling power and thereby shaped the redaction, range of influence and interpretation of its sources, one of which being the Bible (cf. Schüssler Fiorenza 1983 and 1994). The hermeneutical and methodological steps for the interpretation of source texts were developed from an analysis of the system of domination: 'experience that socially locates experience', 'domination, 'suspicion', 'assessment and evaluation', 're-imagination', 'reconstruction' and 'transformation and change' (Schüssler Fiorenza 1998: 76-77) are the elements of this feminist hermeneutical discourse according to Schüssler Fiorenza (Noller 1995: 1-23). Feminist hermeneutics takes place in the exchange between theory and praxis and in particular in the living community of the 'ecclesia' of women (Schüssler Fiorenza 1994: 51-61). Concepts such as

---

4. Compare with the first yearbook of the European Society of Women in Theological Research 1993 with regard to 'Feminist Theology in a European Context' (Esser and Schottroff [eds.] 1993).

relationship and experience are key motives for the interpretation of all significant systems in women's lives. Liberation is thus sought after and experienced in the 'ecclesia' of women. The goal is the liberation of all human beings from all kyriarchal systems of domination and their related intellectual structures and the development of valid, viable alternatives. The ultimate goal, as established by the early Jesus movement, is a liberated discipleship of equals. According to Schüssler Fiorenza, liberation is both origin and goal. Liberation is presented as a methodological process (kyriarchal analysis) as well as its imperative goal (discipleship of equals). The point of intersection of this ultimate faith experience with empirical reality is where the 'ecclesia' of women, then and now the first disciples in the Jesus movement, is located.

The many questions that were raised at the symposium with regard to Schüssler Fiorenza's hermeneutics stem from, in my opinion, this complex overlap between liberation as a ontological concept and the existing realities of the discipleship of equals. Can liberation, philosophically speaking, be defined through the christological image of a discipleship of equals[5] and can this serve as the paradigm for liberation? In other words, can one ontologically define what one historically and socially experiences?[6] The framework of these ideas can only be valid for Christians who describe liberation as the experience of freedom in Christ. But a christological understanding of freedom as the precondition for liberation poses major problems in dialogue with non-Christians. What are the criteria for dialogue with people of other opinions and beliefs? What do terms like 'discipleship of equals', 'liberation' and 'freedom' mean for proponents of other faith traditions, viewpoints or for those who have never experienced either the one or the other?

Freedom: The Fundamental Condition for Human Existence

If we now turn to the concept of freedom itself, then even the assumption that something like freedom exists, poses problems. For example, can it be assumed that freedom exists in the all-encompassing system of domination of patriarchy? If at all, one can only speak of liberation in the sense of a

5.   For critical inquiries, cf. also Noller 1995: 154-68.
6.   Dussel (1989: 73-74) introduces here the experience of the other, which he metaphysically understands as the revelation of the face of the other. The existing reality—that is, the suffering of the oppressed people—thus becomes an ontological place of liberation, and liberation becomes synonym to freedom.

responsible choice between two predetermined possibilities. But how do human beings make decisions and act under the assumption that they are free?[7] The most far-reaching concept is that freedom is a condition of being and the prerequisite for the possibility to decide and act. Statements about this assumption of such a category of freedom can, of course, only be made and experienced empirically.[8] Freedom is thus, for example, the prerequisite for shaping a responsible and other-oriented life.[9] Since freedom, understood in this manner, is not something within our power, then it is also something that is given to us as unconditional; it can neither be eliminated by human beings, nor is there a single, true form of realization that can be identified as 'freedom in itself'. The consequences for Schüssler Fiorenza's argument for a (Christian) discipleship of equals would be that it represents one possible form of experiencing freedom next to others. Then the question is raised as to how can it be examined with regard to its claims and its capacity for discourse. It is reasonable to conclude, therefore, that the question whether freedom and liberation are to be discussed empirically or ontologically is of central importance when attempting to determine the level of discourse with representatives from other cultures, traditions and contexts.

In principle, the future is open in every concept of freedom, for regardless of the nature of a (free) decision, its consequences cannot be foreseen (cf. Leder 1999: 217-25). The question arises, however, as to what the future opens to? Is it to a new quality of existence, which would consequently take on a different shape depending on context? An open future, a perception of differences and a qualified definition of truth are thus signs of freedom. Every form of freedom is one possible construction of reality among others. This rejection of a universal definition of freedom leads us back to contextual theology and the perception of others. The concept is contextualized, and this leads to the various real and specific forms of liberation and their analysis. This by no means relativizes freedom as a fundamental condition of human existence. Together with justice and responsibility it is one of the indispensable contemporary concepts with

---

7.   Also essential is the experience of how the existing reality shapes us as women or men and moreover how this occurs beyond the social construction of the body; cf. Nagl-Docekal 2000: 28-37.

8.   Cf., with regard to the concept of liberation, Pröpper 1991.

9.   Responsibility and social awareness are related to the concept of freedom in all theories of freedom.

regard to the definition of dignified human existence. This is expressed in the liberation theologies in Latin America, South Africa and Asia. They begin with an empirically analyzed reality that takes on a face in the lives of the suffering peoples. Liberation here, in contrast to the ontological concept of freedom as the ultimate condition of being, is defined in relation to praxis and a community of people as well as through the call to overcome injustice and oppression (Freire 1983; Fornet-Betancourt 1988: 31-38; Segundo 1995).

The Understanding of Freedom in a Western European Context

The concept of freedom assumes a different form in my context, for I live in one of the wealthiest countries in the world and enjoy all the rights and privileges as one of its citizens. This context is marked by urbanity, individualism and the advantages and disadvantages of democracy, widespread civil autonomy and capitalism. In general, freedom is understood here as self-determination, as 'the ability to realize opportunities' (Steinvorth 1994: 29). Ability thus becomes a possession in two senses. Animated by the desires of our affluent society and the gratification of consumerism, freedom is, first, associated with everything that increases desire, profit and the range of possibilities. And, second, the profit principle leads to the free choice of that which creates greater value. The various institutions of the state, organized religion, recreation, relationships and the economy have as their goal the service and promotion of these interests. Should an institution not satisfy these needs, then the possibility exists to openly reject this institution in one way or another. Withdrawal from the economic system which promises the greatest profit is the most difficult option. Western theology likes to speak of the compulsions of the free-market economy and the social state; it prefers to avoid reflection about the consequences of a liberation from this system of dependence.

The economic and social conditions of the Western world in interaction with the rather unilaterally defined principles of profit and pleasure have profound consequences for the understanding of freedom in the Western European context. Religion is involved just as much as all the other areas of life. Freedom is viewed as a means to an end: self-realization. The social, political and economic conditions that help determine will and action leading to or expressing freedom are seldom the focus of examination. This individualistic freedom *to* something is a completely different viewpoint from that which speaks of the freedom or liberation *from* something. The former emphasizes desire and its orientation toward a realization. Freedom of action emanates from the will to realize desire, and the subject as a human being or person has both at her/his disposal.[10] A retreat into one's private sphere is always possible should this not succeed. The realm of religion thereby has taken over an important function. The reading of the Bible in many women's groups and liturgical services, for example, is sensed as liberating when it provides assistance or comfort spiritually in one's personal life; the social or economic framework only plays a minor role. I by no means want to contest the fact that individual liberation can be experienced in this manner and freedom thus defined. Without experiencing liberation oneself, it is very difficult to acknowledge others' experience of it or to share it with others (Bechmann 1998). It is questionable, however, that this should suffice for a philosophical or theological understanding of freedom as a fundamental prerequisite of human existence.

The perspective of liberation from an intolerable condition or situation, on the other hand, focuses on the choice of existing possibilities that represent the first step in a freeing action; it proceeds from an existing reality and denotes the crossing of a border to something new. In this case concepts closely related to the philosophical concept of freedom, for example, responsibility and the ability to relate to others, and their significance for the contemporary world take on new meaning, not the least because they make room for the perception of others.

Liberation as Hermeneutical Learning from Others

All this poses many questions for biblical interpretation in a Western European context. How is this understanding of freedom to be placed in relation to the feminist hermeneutics of liberation? What is the significance of the fact that knowledge about the basis of Jewish–Christian tradition is decreasing for us while at the same time the groundwork for responsible interaction with human beings from other religions must be prepared? What is the social and religious framework in which women and men can acquire fundamental knowledge and experience about autonomy and relationships, freedom and responsibility, while also placing these in relation to religious traditions and the Bible?

10. Cf. Steinvorth 1994 for the development of the concept of freedom in modern philosophy.

I think that the first step must be to communicate basic knowledge about the various traditions of the meaning of human existence, not as authoritative systems but as models that can be embraced, argued and transformed. In relation to biblical hermeneutics this means that the praxis of reading the Bible should focus on fundamental statements from the Bible examined against the background of the freedom of diversity. Much can be learned in this respect from other contexts. The speakers and participants from Africa, Asia and Latin America at the symposium made this clear with regard to the role of narrative tradition. I, from my context, one that is characterized by analysis and abstract reflection (this article is no exception), have received many impulses from this approach. There is a time and a place to tell stories, to celebrate, to contemplate, as well as to analyze and to theorize. Stories deal with events that have been intensified into personal experiences.[11] They want to be told because they communicate fundamental insights about life and its contexts, because they provide information about human existence within a community. There are stories that reach back to fundamental events. The interpretation of such experiences stretch like a great arch over the ongoing history of a people. New interpretations arise in new situations, the present is given meaning by remembering, and the future is given a momentary form.[12] The story of the escape from the slavery in Egypt is one such impulse in the Hebrew Bible. By going beyond itself it became a model for freedom and liberation for the Jewish people and then also a fundamental message for others, for early Christians and much later for African American slaves in their quest for freedom. The narrative stories about biblical women likewise point beyond themselves; they, too, are models for how with the aid of tradition bridges can be built between contexts and can lead to new fundamental experiences of liberation.

11. Hermeneutics as a living act makes the interpreting person into a part of the 'production of meaning'. Text and interpreting person are placed on an equal exchange, or as Tamez 1998 expressed it, the lives of women are perceived themselves as sacred texts.

12. Croatto (1989: 65-68) coined the term 'kerygmatische Achsen' ('kerygmatic axes') that appear throughout the Hebrew Bible and the New Testament and which also can be discovered and communicated in a reading of the canon. The canon is thus open to the future, it can develop further because neither the reading which gives meaning nor the possibility for new fundamental events is closed or completed.

BIBLIOGRAPHY

Bechmann, Ulrike
1993   '"Unser Volk speisen, heilen und befreien"—Reflexionen zum Weltgebet-
stag der Frauen', in Esser and Schottroff (eds.) 1993: 111-28.
1998   'Reise ins Andere und finde dich selbst', Keynote Lecture of the 7th Conference of the European Society of Women in Theological Research
(Thessaloniki: Conference Publication): 65-83.

Croatto, J. Severino
1989   *Die Bibel gehört den Armen: Perspektiven einer befreiungstheologischen
Hermeneutik* (Ökumenische Existenz heute, 5; Munich: Chr. Kaiser Verlag).

Dubach, Alfred, and Roland J. Campiche (eds.)
1993   *Jede(r) ein Sonderfall? Religion in der Schweiz. Ergebnisse einer Repräsen-
tativbefragung* (Zürich: NZN Buchverlag; Basel: Friedrich Reinhardt).

Dussel, Enrique
1989   *Philosophie der Befreiung* (Hamburg: Argument).
1995   'Theologie der Befreiung und Marxismus', in Ellacuría and Sobrino (eds.)
1995: 99-130.

Ellacuría, Ignacio, and Jon Sobrino (eds.)
1995   *Mysterium Liberationis. Grundbegriffe der Theologie der Befreiung* (2 vols.;
Luzern: Edition Exodus).

Esser, Annette, and Luise Schottroff (eds.)
1993   *Feminist Theology in a European Context* (Yearbook of the European
Society of Women in Theological Research, 1; Kampen: Kok; Mainz:
Matthias Grünewald Verlag).

Fornet-Betancourt, Raúl
1988   *Philosophie und Theologie der Befreiung* (Frankfurt: Materialis Verlag).

Freire, Paulo
1983   *Pedagogy of the Oppressed* (New York: Continuum).

Kessler, Rainer
1999   *Micha* (Herders Theologischer Kommentar zum Alten Testament; Freiburg:
Herder).

Leder, Matthias
1999   *Was heisst es, eine Person zu sein?* (Paderborn: Mentis).

Nagl-Docekal, Herta
2000   *Feministische Philosophie. Ergebnisse, Probleme, Perspektiven* (Frankfurt:
Fischer Taschenbuch Verlag).

Noller, Annette
1995   *Feministische Hermeneutik. Wege einer neuen Schriftauslegung* (Neukirchen–Vluyn: Neukirchener Verlag).

Pröpper, Thomas
1991   'Freiheit', in Peter Eicher (ed.), *Neues Handbuch theologischer Grund-
begriffe* (new edn in 5 vols.; Munich: Kösel), II: 66-95.

Schottroff, Luise, and Marie-Theres Wacker (eds.)
1998   *Kompendium Feministische Bibelauslegung* (Gütersloh: Chr. Kaiser Verlag/
Gütersloher Verlagshaus).

Schüssler Fiorenza, Elisabeth

1983   *In Memory of Her: A Feminist Theological Reconstruction of Christian Origins* (New York: Crossroad).

1994   *Jesus—Miriam's Child, Sophia's Prophet: Critical Issues in Feminist Christology* (New York: Continuum).

1998   *Sharing her Word: Feminist Biblical Interpretation in Context* (Boston: Beacon Press).

Segundo, Juan Luis

1995   'Freiheit und Befreiung', in Ellacuría and Sobrino (eds.) 1995: 361-82.

Steinvorth, Ulrich

1994   *Freiheitstheorien in der Philosophie der Neuzeit* (Darmstadt: Wissenschaftliche Buchgesellschaft, 2nd edn [1987]).

Tamez, Elsa

1998   'Women's Lives as Sacred Text', in Kwok Pui-Lan and Elisabeth Schüssler Fiorenza (eds.), *Women's Sacred Scriptures* (London: SCM Press; Maryknoll, NY: Orbis Books) (= *Concilium* 34.3): 57-64.

THE BEAUTIFUL PRINCESS AND THE VILLAGE GIRLS:
THE POWER OF DIFFERENCE IN THE INTERCULTURAL RELATIONS
OF FEMINIST THEOLOGIANS

Heike Walz

'We need to celebrate our differences'—this was Stella Baltazar's counsel on the last day of the symposium in Ascona.[1] Differences between the participants became evident through the mutual challenge of describing one's specific hermeneutics with respect to the question of biblical interpretation. The symposium was special for me because it made a direct, personal perception of these differences possible. It may very well be that imaginary round table discussions of feminist theologies from different contexts have taken place, such as in the theological journal *Concilium*'s publication 'Feminist Theology in Different Contexts' (Schüssler Fiorenza 1996: 1). The actual encounter with women from so many different countries, however, was a particularly moving experience for me.

The question about the 'differences between women' also resounded in the story that Musa W. Dube from Botswana told in Ascona, a story that became a frequent topic of discussion during the course of the symposium.[2] Dube ended her story with the question 'But was the crime of patriarchy ever punished?', while also using the story to interpret the significance of the symposium: 'Why have we, the girls from the "global village", gathered together here in the heart of Europe in order to play the game "jumping the fire"?' The participants themselves asked 'How can we avoid allowing the worst to happen, killing the "other" because of her "otherness", in our encounters with one another?' And since encounters take place within systems of power and domination, Dube also raised the question if we are condemned to the patriarchal tactic of killing in order to survive.

---

1.   Cf. also Stella Baltazar's contribution to this publication.
2.   Cf. Musa W. Dube's story at the beginning of her contribution to this publication.

The story and the following discussions about it raised a number of questions for me that circle around the theme of 'difference'. What do feminist theologians actually mean when speaking of 'difference', 'otherness' or 'foreignness'? What differences came to light in Ascona and how did we women deal with them? How did we deal with the differences in power that exist between us, the differences between 'princesses' and 'village girls'? How do I as a Western European theologian perceive the differing viewpoints of theologians from other contexts? How can I responsibly deal with them—without appropriating them or remaining indifferent to them? Doesn't the danger exist of actually reinforcing the construct of 'we' and 'the others' by pointing out our differences? What role does the perception of differences play for common goals, solidarity and the liberation of women worldwide? Can common goals thereby be weakened or can the perception of differences actually promote solidarity among women, as paradoxical as that may sound? The general direction of these questions make it evident that my interest in the impulses that I received at the symposium with regard to the intercultural exchange between feminist theologians has been influenced by my own area of work, 'mission studies, ecumenism and intercultural current issues'.

My questions also are reflected in current feminist discussions, for questions about the differences between women and between the sexes have become increasingly important in ecumenical women's forums, in feminist theologies[3] and in feminist theories.[4]

The Term 'Difference' in Feminist Theological Thought

The term 'difference' has almost completely replaced the key term 'sisterhood' and can now be considered a category of feminist theological thought (Copeland 1996b: 141), especially if one considers the course of current discussions: despite a fundamental criticism of the androcentric and uni-

---

3.   Theological dictionaries characterize as 'feminist' those theologies that have theologically reflected upon the experiences of oppression and discrimination since the 1970s as well as successful liberation in the context of women and other discriminated/disadvantaged social groups and that have intended processes of change for women and men. The title 'feminist' includes a diversity of approaches and directions that are shaped by differing cultural, ethnic, geographical, social, religious and confessional contexts of women (Copeland 1996a).

4.   I employ the term 'feminist theoretical constructs' to include all feminist theories that have been developed in various disciplines, above all in philosophy and literature.

versal concept of 'wo/man' in society and the sciences, Western white feminists themselves are responsible for having developed a similarly universal concept of 'womanhood'. Since the mid-1980s, Black women, African American women and women from the Two-Thirds World have increasingly pointed out the differences between women throughout the world and have questioned the idea of a 'global sisterhood'. At the same time the question of the 'differences between the sexes' became increasingly important in gender studies.[5] Relationships between the sexes, that is, 'the relationship between women and men' as well as 'the relationship between women', became the focus of investigation (Meyer 1997: 134). And since the 1990s differences in the understanding of gender differences have become the focus of interest (Röttger and Paul 1999). The challenge facing feminist thought today is to examine the interrelationship between differences based on other conditions and of gender difference, which is interwoven into all differences. Discrimination based on sex, in the words of the Austrian philosopher Herta Nagl-Docekal, is 'often mixed together with discrimination based on other conditions, such as the affiliation with a certain ethnic, cultural, religious or economic group, or the color of one's skin, or one's sexual orientation' (Nagl-Docekal 2000: 12).[6] Elisabeth Schüssler Fiorenza coined the term 'kyriarchy' (Schüssler Fiorenza 1993: 116-17) for this in feminist theology. Nagl-Docekal warns of the danger that 'in the process of working out complex power structures...the specific problems of discrimination based on sex can be lost sight of' (Nagl-Docekal 2000: 12).

It can also be seen from the course of this treatment that feminist discussions are a child of their time. Terms such as 'distinction', 'difference' and 'the other' are 'key, post-modern terms' (Thürmer-Rohr 1999: 222). Post-modern thought dissociates itself from one-dimensional, universal-structured thought; differences are viewed positively. The terms mentioned here are often employed in various manners. What do feminist theologians

5. Gender studies 'analyze the hierarchical relationships between the sexes... Its primary assumption is that functions, rolls and characteristics that constitute masculinity or femininity do not arise causally because of biological differences between man and woman but are societal constructs and therefore can be changed' (Nünning [ed.] 1998: 185 [author's translation]).

6. In literary studies the thesis about the intermixture of gender differences with other differences has asserted itself, as Terry Eagleton expressed pithily, 'Through the influences of feminist and postcolonial theories *class, race* and *gender*...have become a sort of Holy Trinity in contemporary literary theory' (cited in Nünning [ed.] 1998: 261 [author's translation]).

actually mean when they speak of 'differences'? A study in itself would be necessary in order to clarify how these terms stand in relation to one another and when one term provides a more exact description of a situation.[7] Mary Shawn Copeland equates difference with 'a celebrative option for life in all its integrity, in all its distinctiveness' (Copeland 1996b: 143).[8] And Patricia Purtschert, a Swiss philosopher, speaks of the 'paradox of the other', suggesting 'to perceive the other as the same *and* as different' (Purtschert 1999: 9) The paradox here is that persons

> can relate to each other in two different and logically not compatible manners, namely, by speaking and dealing with each other they can perceive their likenesses, while at the same time they perceive themselves as different because their specific uniqueness cannot be captured in any standardized system of interpretation. (Purtschert 1999: 11)

I would also like to introduce the term 'foreigner' to the discussion. Within the framework of his 'interpretive mission studies' (Grünschloss 1998: 344), Theo Sundermeier, a mission scholar from Germany, understands 'the' foreigner as 'a person who comes from outside of one's own living area or country and who has been shaped by a different culture' (Sundermeier 1996: 12). Foreignness in a sociological sense is 'the result of a process of attribution in a relationship', between persons as well as between groups (Feldtkeller 1998: 342). Foreignness can be based on real differences, but its significance arises only during the process of self-identification—'whatever is not accepted or perceived as part of one's own self-image is foreign' (Feldtkeller 1998: 342). Foreignness can signify the antithesis to familiarity, but it can also describe the quality of a relationship between that which is different, which occurs not only in intercultural personal relationships. Foreignness is thus a relational term (Sundermeier 1996: 139), determined by situation and dependent on subjective perception. 'Tangible' differences do not have to correspond with the perception of foreignness. Something foreign can become familiar and thus lose its foreignness, while the differences continue to exist. These definitions cor-

---

7. My understanding of the term 'otherness' is guided by the following statement: 'The cultural consciousness reacts to a *clash of cultures* with descriptions of hetero- and auto-stereotypes…whose…artificial constructs are not perceived' (Nünning [ed.] 1998: 10 [author's translation]). What is meant in discussions about 'the others' should be examined more closely (cf. Purtschert 1999); when do women become 'the others' for each other?

8. Copeland distinguishes the use of the term 'difference' in feminist theology from the postmodern concept of 'différence'.

respond to one of my experiences in Ascona. When I wrote to one of the participants, Elżbieta Adamiak from Poland, that I was reflecting on the idea of encounters between 'foreign women' in Ascona, she wrote back and asked, 'Am I a foreigner to you?' And in fact, I sensed exactly the opposite. Soon after having met each other at the symposium we were conversing in a spirit of understanding and sensitivity, even though there were tangible differences (East and West, Catholic and Protestant, etc.) between us.

It is striking, however, that in philosophical literature one tends to speak of 'the other' and of 'differences', while mission scholars tend to speak of 'foreigners'.[9] But there are also many cases in which there are no clear lines of demarcation (Sundermeier 1996: 9). I discovered points of intersection with both arguments in the case of Theo Sundermeier. He has developed a process for the gradual understanding of 'something foreign' in his *Hermeneutik des Fremden* ('Hermeneutics of the Foreign') while also emphasizing the importance of a 'hermeneutics of differences' 'that learns to understand that which is different without appropriating it' (p. 13). I think that the conscious link between the categories of 'differences' and 'foreignness' could produce fruitful results. The concept of foreignness as a relational term leaves room for the dynamic processes that take place in the relationships between persons, thus giving the differences between persons new meaning.

On the other hand, feminist discussions have found little resonance in mission studies. Conversely, there have been a few individual ecumenical[10] as well as exegetical[11] studies about foreignness from the perspective of feminist theology, but a systematic study of the issue has not yet been made.[12] Farideh Akashe-Böhme, who was born in Iran and now lives in Germany, has pointed out how being a woman and being a foreigner can stand in relation to one another: women are foreigners to patriarchal civilization as well as to their own culture and thus experience a 'body that has become foreign through the impact of technology' (Akashe-Böhme 1993: 7). The idea of 'foreignness' in connection with questions of gender

9.   One reason for this is surely because terms such as 'foreign, foreignness and foreigner' play a roll in biblical texts, that is, in the Jewish–Christian tradition (Sundermeier 1996: 201-207).

10.   Cf. the literature about the Women's World Day of Prayer in Bechmann 1993.

11.   E.g. Maier 1995.

12.   There are a number of publications written by women ethnologists. See, among many others, Rohr 1995; WIDEE 1993, and particularly the articles by Christa Höllhumer and Elisabeth List therein.

thustakes on new facets. A connection of the 'hermeneutics of the foreign' with a 'hermeneutics of gender differences' is urgently needed.[13] It would also be an interesting undertaking to investigate the points of intersection and tension between the concepts of difference, gender difference and foreignness.

I shall limit myself in this article, however, to the question of 'difference(s)' between women and shall approach this theme from four perspectives. In the first section I will reflect on how the organization and staging of the symposium influenced the encounters between women in Ascona. What differences became evident and how did we deal with these differences? In the second section I will raise the question as to how I as a Western European woman theologian perceive the various viewpoints of women theologians from different parts of the world and how I can deal with them responsibly. I will introduce hermeneutic models for this that have been suggested by feminist theologians from my German-speaking context. The third section is dedicated to the question whether the emphasis of differences can stabilize the construct of a 'we' and 'the others'; I will glean from over feminist and postcolonial theories in this respect. In the last section I will attempt to determine what role the perception of differences can play for the common goals, solidarity and the liberation of women around the world. I will employ a narrative story as an introduction to the theme of differences and as a *leitmotif* through the whole. I was inspired in this respect by participants from the symposium, for example, from Africa and Latin America, where storytelling is a fundamental element of their culture.

Princesses and Village Girls in Ascona—'Tangible Others'?

I repeat Musa W. Dube's story here in a new reading:

> …one day the princess became angry again. Her brother the prince could participate at the king's conferences, sit with the king and his advisors at the same table and thus learn the kingdom's secrets. She felt shut out. But then she thought of the village girls. She quickly sent a messenger to the village. The messenger searched out the women's groups and brought them a message from the princess: 'Your majesty the princess lets it be known

13. Lienemann-Perrin 2000: 215. Gender differences and their influence on the perception of differences could have been a topic in Ascona, for it had not originally been planned as a women's conference. All male exegetes who were invited, however, declined participation.

that she is your sister. She suffers just like you do because of the supremacy of men at the king's court. We are all in the same situation.' The girls from the village were very pleased at first that the princess wanted to be their sister, but then the objection was raised: 'How can she be our sister? She enjoys the power of the royal family, eats every day from a silver platter, sleeps in a heavenly bed, and someday she will become queen! No, she doesn't really understand us, she sees us through her glasses. Has she ever visited us here in the village? Has she ever listened to what we have to say?'

In Ascona, however, the various differences between the participants did not end in hostility but in fruitful encounters. Women listened to each other, to how others interpreted the Bible. Silvia Schroer's report on the symposium gives an idea of the variety and kinds of differences present:

> An African American woman reads the Bible with the knowledge that her ancestors found strength and courage in the Bible during the time of slavery. A Christian Indian reads biblical texts in a culture that has not been primarily shaped by Christianity; she reads the Bible as one sacred book among others and thus remains in a continual inter-religious dialogue. A Hungarian or a Romanian woman reads the Bible with the knowledge that smuggling the Bible in her country during the communist dictatorship was just as dangerous as smuggling weapons, and that the precious books were confiscated and shredded in order to steal the people's religious roots and dignity. A Brazilian woman reads the Bible after twenty years of liberation theology and grass-roots work in the unending battle for the fundamental rights of her people. A secular Jewish woman reads the Bible as a historian with the knowledge that modern Israel would not exist without the existence of this religious book. A Christian Palestinian is torn between the liberating message of the biblical texts and the oppression and violence that the Bible and its interpretation set free in the Holy Land, especially for her people. A Swiss woman is confronted in reading the Bible with the legacy of the reformation and with dialectical theology. (Schroer 2001: 29)

The statement of one participant is telling: 'When I think of India now I do not see nameless faces, I see Paulina Chakkalakal's face before me'. Ascona made it possible for women from different continents to become 'tangible others'. Women did not speak *about* each other (like the village girls did about the princess) but *with* each other. This sounds like the realization of Seyla Benhabib's ethics of 'the tangible other'. Benhabib challenges the idea of a 'generalized other'; according to her it is much more important to concentrate 'on the specific individual' and to understand 'the needs of the other, her/his motives, goals or desires' (Benhabib 1995: 176). The symposium thus promoted a real and conscious listening for 'differences of viewpoint' (Copeland 1996b: 147).

I also discovered a hermeneutic principle as part of the staging of the symposium: a gathering of suppressed or excluded viewpoints and unquestioned assumptions in biblical exegesis. For example, Musa W. Dube's postcolonial feminist biblical interpretation challenged us with its thesis about the inherent imperialism in the Bible.[14] Nancy Cardoso Pereira from Brazil emphasized the legacy of oral culture; her hermeneutics juxtaposes biblical and folk stories with women's experiences of suppression and liberation in a dialogue of understanding and criticism. Moreover, the question was not excluded from the debate as to what 'feminist' exegesis represents and if a liberative (for women) interpretation of the Bible is even at the basis of a common hermeneutics for women theologians. A participant from Romania explained that 50 years of state-ordained atheism has left such deep scars in Eastern Europe that the question of the shriveling number of Christians has assumed first priority. Missionizing was therefore competing with the task of women's liberation for her.[15] I interpret the symposium thus as an attempt to speak the most *plurivoke* language possible with regard to feminist biblical interpretation.[16]

The symposium in Ascona thus followed, in the words of Mary Shawn Copeland, the genuine goal of feminist theology, 'to pluralize, to destabilize, to dismantle, to problematize any propensity to asphyxiate or suppress difference in critical theologies committed to the radical liberation of women' (Copeland 1996b: 142).

Finally, I also noticed the attempt to counterbalance differences based on existing disparities in power relationships by having two-thirds of the participants come from Two-Thirds World countries or Eastern Europe. A 'democratization of the microphone' also proved to be helpful.[17] There

14. More detailed information in Dube 2000: 168-84.

15. It remained open whether it is meaningful/useful to juxtapose mission(ary) and liberation.

16. Copeland 1996b: 142. The composition of the participants was very diverse insofar that the 40 women came from 20 different countries from all the continents and from various confessions (Protestant, Catholic, Orthodox). And the participation of a Jewish woman as well as of an atheist expanded the horizon beyond Christianity. Women from evangelical or charismatic groups or from Pentecostal churches were not represented. The common denominator among this great diversity was the interest for feminist biblical interpretation.

17. Following the presentation of the main speaker of the day—a US American, a Brazilian, an Afro-American and a woman from Botswana, respectively—other participants sat at the podium. Thus women from Asia, Eastern Europe, Western Europe, Israel, Palestine, etc., who did not have a chance to present their hermeneutics in a main

was thus no clear division between 'experts' and 'listeners', as is often the case at conferences; the participants alternated between the role of speaker and listener. The symposium as an encounter of women theologians from various contexts was thus based on a 'hermeneutics of differences' in which the following principles were important: mutual listening; the articulation of differences; conscious listening for differences of viewpoint; the encounter with participants as tangible others; the counterbalance of differences based on existing disparities in power relationships; the pluralizing consequence of the gathering (and/or revelation) of suppressed aspects in theology.

Feminist theologians, however, are not immune to the danger of 'shaping (or, at least, unconsciously assuming themselves to be shaping) the theoretical script and stage for the theologizing of "other" and different women in whose oppression they have historically participated and from which, even now, they continue to benefit' (Copeland 1996b: 147). This was likewise a topic among the participants in Ascona, who, despite the conscious efforts to counteract power contexts, discovered a 'lapse' in the programming of the symposium. They questioned the 'sandwich principle' with regard to how the conference was scheduled. That is, by having Elisabeth Schüssler Fiorenza (US) open the symposium discussion about biblical hermeneutics and by having Adele Reinhartz (Canada) and Marie-Theres Wacker (Germany) evaluate the proceedings of the conference at the end, a 'white sandwich' was created that was 'filled'[18] with main speakers from Brazil and Botswana and an African American from the US. The question was also raised, however, whether the European/North American categories of thought didn't actually form the 'system of coordinates' (Schroer 2001: 30) in which the other viewpoints were ordered. The challenge from Stella Baltazar (India) to act like Western academic theologians in the face of globalization likewise remained a lonely call. She would have preferred to see the conference not remain merely a theological exchange but to have culminated in concrete deeds in solidarity. I found the presence of theologians with non-Christian backgrounds very stimulating with respect to the disclosure of repressed aspects; other elements, on the other hand,

---

presentation were given the opportunity to introduce their contexts and viewpoints. Following the statements of the podium participants the microphone was passed through the plenum.

18. Marie-Theres Wacker on 7 July 2000; see also Adele Reinhartz and Marie-Theres Wacker's contribution to this publication.

remained repressed. For example, a number of theologians based their arguments on their denominational background, but a session dedicated to the discussion of denominational differences was neither on the program nor initiated by the participants.[19]

It became clear to me that the 'hermeneutics of differences' as employed here transformed differences into a positive force—even if tolerating different viewpoints sometimes was not without difficulty. Perhaps the realization lay hidden therein that the complete fullness of the biblical text is attainable only in intercultural encounters (Sundermeier 1990: 395).

I also realized something else: a 'hermeneutics of differences' is closely linked to how relationships are shaped. Denise Ackermann from South Africa goes so far as to call for an 'ethics of relationships that allows for the expression of "otherness" and being different' (Ackermann 2000: 189; see also pp. 199-204). A connection between a hermeneutics of differences and an ethics of relationships could provide interesting impulses, which I will take up in the next section.

The Hermeneutics of Change and the Hermeneutics of Opacity— Models for Feminist Theologians

I vary the story of the princess and the village girls once again:

> ...and everyone jumped over the fire again. When it was the princess's turn one of the girls pushed her, but one of the other girls grabbed her at the last second and called out: 'Are you crazy, throwing the princess into the fire? Who rules this kingdom? The princess? She has to wear pretty clothes all the time and always be friendly! Is it her fault that we are not rich and famous? Don't you see that you are throwing the wrong person into the fire?'—'Yes', the other girls murmured, 'You're right, but...'—'But what?'—'Shouldn't she have shown some sense of responsibility toward us?'

This reading of the story leads to my question as to how I as a Western European woman theologian can show responsibility toward the varying theological viewpoints of women theologians from other parts of the world without falling into one of the two 'traps' that have shaped the history of the Occident and its treatment of culturally foreign persons. The 'model of equality' negates foreignness and differences, while the 'model of variance' calls forth both fear and fascination with respect to that which is foreign (Sundermeier 1996: 72-77). Both models contain the danger of

---

19. Teresa Paul 1996 has proposed interesting thoughts in this respect.

rejecting, contesting or appropriating that which is foreign, or in the end remaining simply indifferent to it.[20]

The first model that takes a different path stems from Eske Wollrad (Germany), who, as a white, Western European theologian critically examined 'responsibility with respect to the challenge of womanistic theology' (Wollrad 1999: 27).[21] The reception of womanist theology by white, women theologians often has fallen into one of the above-mentioned 'traps': either they 'otherize'—that is, they construct 'certain persons to quintessential "others"...whose lives are apparently so exotic that they cannot be comprehended by whites' (p. 27)—or they tend to 'appropriate' insofar that 'the voices of black women represent only the echo of white voices' (p. 27).[22] Wollrad suggests a third model that I would like to call a 'hermeneutics of change'.[23] White theologians should employ the theological models of womanistic theologians on themselves. Just as feminist theologians have exposed 'man-hood' as an unquestioned basis for standard theological thought, womanist theologians challenge white women theologians to realize that being white has established itself as a hidden norm by which everything is measured. The goal would be that 'white feminist theologians "color" their conversations with God to such a degree that they resist white domination' (Wollrad 1999: 212). Their hermeneutics of change would thus call forth conscious changes in self-awareness through encounters with the methods of 'other' theologians.

In Wollrad's case the critical inquiry led to a change in viewpoint with regard to the interaction of gender with other differences. She refuses to elevate the category of gender to the absolute priority of feminist thought since gender and other differences do not relate to each other in an additive sense, as if 'race'[24] and 'class'[25] were additional burdens to sexism that do

20. Only the 'complementary model' offers points of departure for further development; it views foreign elements as a supplement and as a detour to one's self (Sundermeier 1996: 75-77).

21. African American theologians call their theology 'womanist' since it is rooted in the tradition, culture and heritage of Black women (Wollrad 1999: 15).

22. Wollrad thus comes to similar results as the missionary scholar Theo Sundermeier in his 'hermeneutics of the foreign'. 'Annexation/appropriation' equals the 'model of equality' and 'other/change' equals the 'model of variance' (Sundermeier 1996: 73-74).

23. Cf. Wollrad 1999 with regard to the following.

24. With regard to the term 'race', cf. Wollrad 1999: 24-26, or Nünning (ed.) 1998: 450-51.

25. With regard to the term 'class', cf. Nünning (ed.) 1998: 260-61.

not touch upon the quintessential quality of female existence. Instead of that one should proceed from the basis of different 'genders', women being constructed as many different 'sorts' independent from their 'race' and 'class' (Wollrad 1999: 207).

The second model stems from Manuela Kalsky, who has pleaded for a 'hermeneutics of opacity' which tolerates the imperceptibility of the other by 'leaving space between so that the relational differences can exist in their own right' (Kalsky 2000: 314). It is interesting to note that she adopted the term 'opacity'—that is, imperceptibility—from a religious scholar likewise of African American descent. From the viewpoint of colonized peoples, Charles H. Long employs the term 'opacity' to describe religious experiences of the oppressed for whom Western reason did not have any room (Long 1986). Bulgarian philosopher Luce Irigaray, who lives in France, employs the term *Zwischenraum* ('space') in her ethics of sexual differences and thereby emphasizes that the 'passion of amazement' can guard the differences between two differing subjects (Irigaray 1991: 46-70, 88-100). And I also refer here to Kalsky's allusion to Dutch theologian Annelies van Heijst, who 'takes the position of an ethics of lasting differences in which the other can never be completely recognized' (Kalsky 2000: 314). All of this emphasizes the importance of 'opacity' as an important component in the perception of differences. It is interesting to note that Kalsky also hints at a connection between hermeneutics and ethical responsibility, something which has become clearer to me: since my perception of a theologian from a different context involves the paradox of the other insofar as she eludes complete understanding and thus ultimately remains incomprehensible, this requires an ethical conduct on my part that allows this space between us (*Zwischenraum*) to continue to exist. The following brief overview of feminist and postcolonial theories[26] is related to this insofar that it deals with constructs of the other.

Differences and the Construct of a 'We' and 'the Others': *Highlights of Feminist and Postcolonial Theories*

Differences are made for specific purposes. When marginalized groups define their own differences, this can actually contribute to their liberation. Womanists, for example, point out the differing socio-political reality of

26. Postcolonial theories deal with the changing relations/interaction between (former) colonizers and (former) colonized peoples. 'Postcolonialism' is a term in dispute (Nünning [ed.] 1998: 437-38).

'black' and 'white' in order to reveal concealed forms of domination or discrepancies of power. People or groups in positions of power often refer to differences in order to use them as 'place indicators' within the society. Women often have been refused access to positions within society based on reference to their otherness.

Postcolonial and feminist thinkers have revealed systems of thought that employ differences based on the construct of a 'we' and 'the others' in order to create socio-political realities. I can mention two exemplary positions in this respect. Gayatri Chakravorty Spivak from India criticizes in her article 'Can the Subaltern Speak?' that post-structuralist thinkers such as Michel Foucault or Gilles Deleuze do not treat non-academic groups (non-homogenic, subaltern groups, especially women) as subjects. Instead of this they construct a homogenic group of subaltern subjects (e.g. 'workers' or 'Maoists') within which gender differences are twice made to disappear: 'In the context of colonial production, the subaltern has no history and cannot speak, the subaltern as female is even more deeply in shadow' (Spivak 1988: 287).

Judith Butler, the US American philosopher, counterbalances the difference between 'sex' as a biologically based difference between the sexes and 'gender' as a culturally constructed difference between the sexes in her study *Gender Trouble*. In fact, she considers the biological difference of sex also to be a construct of society employed to substantiate the construct of 'gender' (Butler 1990).

Both theoretical articles are based on the explosive premise that the identity of a socially homogeneous, more marginal group (e.g. 'workers' or 'women') will reveal itself as a fiction or the construct of a 'we' and 'the other' upon closer examination. The construct and generalization of 'the other' cannot do justice to the real existing similarities and differences. Who is making the differences and the generalizations and to what purpose?—that is the question.

Differences and Solidarity in the Intercultural Exchange between Feminist Theologians

What role does the perception of differences play for common goals, solidarity and the liberation of women worldwide? Can common goals thereby be weakened or can the perception of differences actually lead to more solidarity among women, as paradoxical as that may sound? I would be very pleased to hear the opinions of other participants from the symposium.

The possibilities that a continually developing 'sensibility of differences', as suggested by Kerstin Söderblom (1997: 255), can offer are obvious. The consideration of differences strengthens feminist discussion (Copeland 1996b: 142) and ultimately leads to the realization of the integrity and uniqueness of life's hallowed options. In view of the danger of tensions, disagreements and de-solidarization through a growing awareness of differences, the connection between a hermeneutics of differences with an ethics of relationships has become important to me—when its goal is to counteract the discrepancy of the access to power and resources, to keep the passion for the amazement about 'the other' alive and to lead ultimately to common action. Then I have hope that we will be able to celebrate our differences.

BIBLIOGRAPHY

Ackermann, Denise M.
    2000   'Ein Mensch wird ein Mensch durch andere Menschen—eine Ethik der Beziehung angesichts von Andersartigkeit und Anderssein', in Wilhelm Gräb *et. al.* (eds.), *Christentum und Spätmoderne. Ein internationaler Diskurs über Praktische Theologie und Ethik* (Stuttgart: W. Kohlhammer): 189-204.
Akashe-Böhme, Farideh
    1993   *Frausein, Fremdsein* (Frankfurt: Fischer Taschenbuch Verlag).
Bechmann, Ulrike
    1993   '"Unser Volk speisen, heilen und befreien"—Reflexionen zum Weltgebetstag der Frauen', in Annette Esser and Luise Schottroff (eds.), *Feminist Theology in a European Context* (Yearbook of the European Society of Women in Theological Research, 1; Kampen: Kok; Mainz: Matthias Grünewald Verlag): 111-28.
Benhabib, Seyla
    1995   *Selbst im Kontext. Kommunikative Ethik im Spannungsfeld von Feminismus, Kommunitarismus und Postmoderne* (Frankfurt: Suhrkamp).
Butler, Judith
    1991   *Das Unbehagen der Geschlechter* (Frankfurt: Edition Suhrkamp). (First published as *Gender Trouble: Feminism and the Subversion of Identity* [London: Routledge, 1990].)
Cahill, Lisa Sowle
    1996   *Sex, Gender, and Christian Ethics* (New Studies in Christian Ethics; Cambridge: Cambridge University Press).
Copeland, Mary Shawn
    1996a   'Theologies for the Liberation of Black, Yellow, Brown and Red Women', in Letty M. Russell and J. Shannon Clarkson (eds.), *Dictionary of Feminist Theologies* (Louisville, KY: Westminster/John Knox Press): 286-87.
    1996b   'Difference as a Category in Critical Theologies for the Liberation of Women', *Concilium* 32: 102-10.

Dube, Musa W.
2000   *Postcolonial Feminist Interpretation of the Bible* (St Louis: Chalice Press).
Feldtkeller, Andreas
1998   'Fremde. IV. Sozialgeschichtlich, soziologisch, sozialethisch', in *Die Relig-ion in Geschichte und Gegenwart* (Tübingen: J.C.B. Mohr [Paul Siebeck], 4th edn): 342-43.
Grünschloss, Andreas
1998   'Fremde. VI. Fremde/Fremdheit, missionstheologisch', in *Die Religion in Geschichte und Gegenwart* (Tübingen: J.C.B. Mohr [Paul Siebeck], 4th edn): 344-45.
Irigaray, Luce
1991   *Ethik der sexuellen Differenz* (Frankfurt: Suhrkamp).
Kalsky, Manuela
2000   *Christaphanien. Die Re-Vision der Christologie aus der Sicht von Frauen in unterschiedlichen Kulturen* (Gütersloh: Chr. Kaiser Verlag/Gütersloher Ver-lagshaus).
Lienemann-Perrin, Christine
2000   'Fremdverstehen in der ökumenischen Frauenbewegung', in Dieter Becker (ed.), *Mit dem Fremden leben. Perspektiven einer Theologie der Konvivenz. Theo Sundermeier zum 65. Geburtstag* (Erlangen: Erlanger Verlag für Mis-sion und Ökumene): 205-15.
Long, Charles H.
1986   *Significations: Signs, Symbols, and Images in the Interpretation of Religions* (Philadelphia: Fortress Press).
Maier, Christl
1995   *Die 'fremde' Frau in Proverbien 1–9. Eine exegetische und sozialgeschicht-liche Studie* (Freiburg: Universitätsverlag; Göttingen: Vandenhoeck & Ru-precht).
Meyer, Ursula I.
1997   *Einführung in die feministische Philosophie* (Munich: Deutscher Taschen-buch Verlag).
Nagl-Docekal, Herta
2000   *Feministische Philosophie. Ergebnisse, Probleme, Perspektiven* (Frankfurt: Fischer Taschenbuch Verlag).
Nünning, Ansgar (ed.)
1998   *Metzler Lexikon Literatur- und Kulturtheorie. Ansätze—Personen—Grund-begriffe* (Stuttgart: J.B. Metzler).
Paul, Teresa
1996   'Konfessionen. Bekenntnis und Biographie', in Ulrike Wagener and Andrea Günter (eds.), *What Does it Mean to be a Feminist Theologian Today?* (Yearbook of the European Society of Women in Theological Research, 4; Kampen: Kok; Mainz: Matthias Grünewald Verlag): 96-102.
Purtschert, Patricia
1999   'Selbst im Angesicht der Anderen. Von der Konstruktion zum Ereignis der Anderen—eine Relektüre von Kant und Freud' (unpublished Masters disser-tation, the Faculty of Philosophy and Arts, the University of Basel).

Rohr, Elisabeth
1995   'Die fremde Frau. Der weibliche Blick auf eine fremde Kultur', *Fach-frauen—Frauen im Fach* (Frankfurt: Institut für Kulturanthropologie und Europäische Ethnologie): 265-96.
Röttger, Kati, and Heike Paul (eds.)
1999   *Differenzen in der Geschlechterdifferenz—Differences within Gender Studies. Aktuelle Perspektiven der Geschlechterforschung* (Berlin: Erich Schmidt Verlag).
Schroer, Silvia
2001   'Feministische Exegese und Hermeneutik der Befreiung. Nachdenkliches zum internationalen Symposium auf dem Monte Verità', *Schlangenbrut* 19.72: 28-31.
Schüssler Fiorenza, Elisabeth
1993   *But she Said* (Boston: Beacon Press).
1996   'Feminist Theology in Different Contexts', *Concilium* 32: 1-2.
Söderblom, Kerstin
1997   'Differenzen—Gedanken zum Unterschied zwischen lesbisch-feministischen und feministischen Theologien', in Elisabeth Hartlieb and Charlotte Methuen (eds.), *Sources and Resources of Feminist Theologies* (Yearbook of the European Society of Women in Theological Research, 5; Kampen: Kok; Mainz: Grünewald Verlag): 239-56.
Spivak, Gayatri Chakravorty
1988   'Can the Subaltern Speak?', in Cary Nelson and Lawrence Grossberg (eds.), *Marxist Interpretation of Culture* (Basingstoke: Macmillan Education): 271-313.)
Sundermeier, Theo
1996   *Den Fremden verstehen. Eine praktische Hermeneutik* (Göttingen: Vandenhoeck & Ruprecht).
1990   'Begegnung mit dem Fremden, Plädoyer für eine verstehende Missionswissenschaft', *Evangelische Theologie* 50: 390-400
Thürmer-Rohr, Christina
1999   'Die unheilbare Pluralität der Welt—Von der Patriarchatskritik zur Totalitarismusforschung', in *idem*, *Vagabundinnen. Feministisch-theologische Essays* (Frankfurt: Fischer Taschenbuch Verlag, 2nd edn): 214-30.
WIDEE (Wissenschaftlerinnen in der Europäischen Ethnologie)
1993   *Nahe Fremde—fremde Nähe. Frauen forschen zu Ethnos, Kultur und Geschlecht* (Vienna: Wiener Frauenverlag).
Wollrad, Eske
1999   *Wildniserfahrung. Womanistische Herausforderung und eine Antwort aus weisser feministischer Perspektive* (Gütersloh: Chr. Kaiser Verlag/Gütersloher Verlagshaus).

Women and War in India
(A Historical Event from the Ninth Century
Recounted by Stella Baltazar, India)

I would like to take up Elisabeth Schüssler Fiorenza's concept of the hermeneutics of struggle with regard to my understanding of theological language. What is the meaning of struggle? What is the content of struggle? What are struggles for? What is the struggle of feminist theology and of feminist theologians?

Let me begin with an incident that happened in India in the ninth century. There was a war between two small kingdoms. One clan was stronger than the other, and the stronger clan had declared war on the weaker. Now the women of the weaker clan knew that if their men went to war they would be massacred. So the women got together and came to a decision and then told their men: 'You are not going to war this time. It will be our business to manage things at the war front. This war will be fought by us.' And the day declared for war came and all of these women went with all their little babies and cradles. They took their little babies and cradles and set up a line at the war front. They set their cradles side by side and lined up with their children in front of them. The other clan came with all of their arms and they were shocked and dumb-founded by what they saw: 'What is this?' They didn't come to fight women with children. And according to Yudha Dharma, the justice of war, we call it the dharma of war, you cannot attack people who are unarmed, so they did not fight the war. These men became ashamed of themselves and left in retreat, and so the war never took place. And even to this day, this event, the war of the Kongars, a war that was won by women, is celebrated at the Kongar Padai festival.

What are women struggling for? Our struggle is to recognize our own humanity, our own 'personhood', our own process of becoming. This is the first stage of the struggle. It is a struggle to widen our horizons and to move beyond ourselves to bring about richer and fuller lives for the rest as well. Therefore, I think the need to transform structures of oppression and injustice ought to be intrinsic to our struggle for feminist liberation. We women have to struggle together collectively for a new world of respect, recognition and humanity.

The Sun, the Woman and the Peacock
(A Story Told by Stella Baltazar, India)

In India we have thousands of myths. One of these is about the sun and a peacock. The female sun married the male peacock, and they were very happy flying in the heavens. One day the peacock looked down and saw a very beautiful yellow woman on earth, and he fell in love with her. And he wanted somehow to be with her. Then his wife the sun said to him: 'If you go down to earth you will never be able to come back. You will never be able to be with me again.' So the peacock thought for a while, but the temptation became too strong and he could no longer resist. So he flew down to meet the yellow woman, but when he arrived he saw that she was a mustard field and not a woman, and he felt absolutely cheated. And then he began to yearn and pine for his wife who was up in the heavens, the sun, but she could never come down and he could never go up again. And so, when the peacock is yearning and pining for his wife she will cover herself with clouds, for she does not want him to see her. But the peacock will spread its wings and it will rain, for the sun is also weeping. Her tears fell on his outspread wings, and that is why you see spots on the peacock's feathers.

This story from Meghalaya, a north-eastern state in India, provides some insight into male–female relationships in a matriarchal society. The story depicts the natural attraction of the sexes and is a call to claim responsibility for one's actions. I think it demonstrates that one needs to claim responsibility for what one would like to achieve. This story has always fascinated me because it is the woman who expresses her dissent and protests against her husband's actions, something which is not so common in the rest of India where patriarchy dominates. It encourages us to motivate women to protest, to stand their ground and to demonstrate their independence. I also am particularly fond of the story because it calls the woman the sun.

WHEN WOMEN UNITE!
CELEBRATE OUR DIFFERENCES AS THE CAUSE OF OUR UNITY

Stella Baltazar

Introduction

A teenage girl was grazing a few goats along the side of a path near a field. Suddenly the goats entered the irrigated field and began to eat the plants. The owner of the field belonged to the so-called upper caste and the girl was from the so-called untouchable caste. When the man saw the goats in his field he charged at the girl and began to beat her and even tore her blouse. When news of the incident reached the ears of the women in the village they were infuriated. They took the girl to the police station to register a charge against the owner of the field. In normal circumstances the harassment of a woman from the untouchable caste would be viewed as common and the prerogative of the upper caste. But since the women were organized and determined, they would no longer accept such atrocities as normal. They were not satisfied to merely register a charge but demanded that the man be brought to the police station and that he should ask for forgiveness from the girl for the wrong committed. The situation became tense when the man refused to come to the police station. The women refused to go away until the man was brought. In the end he had no other option except to come to the station. When he saw the women gathered together he did not know what he should do. He also did not have the courage to ask for pardon. So he decided to make a statement: 'I consider her like my daughter, so don't take it seriously'. When the women heard this they were even more infuriated and one of them asked him: 'If you consider her like your daughter, will you give your son in marriage to her?' Culturally this is the worst insult for an upper caste man to hear from a lower caste person. But because of the determination with which the women stood together he could not escape punishment. He had to ask pardon from the girl as well as pay a fine for the wrong committed.

Although this incident happened only about ten years ago, it was the very first time in this village that women joined together to protest an injustice. From my perspective, this was perhaps the Pentecost moment in the lives of these women. This form of resistance and struggle provides the ground for interpreting God's action in the lives of women.

The determined act of these women has a solid link with the events at Monte Verità. Women theologians from throughout the world gathered at Monte Verità to claim a common heritage as women, to affirm their place in the theological realm and to assert their human rights as indeed a sign of the presence of the Spirit in our world. This experience itself is the fertile ground of our theological inquiries into the Bible. Women venturing into the Bible and re-reading it from this perspective is an affirmation of their belief that they are created equal yet unique. With courage and conviction women need to unearth its hidden treasures as well as decry the domination it has exerted on them for centuries. This moment of assessment and appraisal gives energy to strengthen their bonds and celebrate their differences. Women's ways of interpreting the Bible might be different. Their ways of understanding its message might differ from context to context based on their experience. Yet, can anyone destroy the unity that women wish to promote among themselves and the rest of womankind in the world? Plurality is a fact of reality and the sure way to arrive at unity. And that is the strength of oneness. Different forces in the world are operating to divide and rule. Patriarchy was able to rule by keeping women divided and isolated from the beginning. It is time to affirm our unity across the continents and face the challenge of the modern forms of patriarchy, which manifest themselves in the monopolization of social and cultural life through economic and political power. Therefore, women need to be aware of these divisive forces and strengthen their convictions by promoting solidarity and networking.

This does not mean that uniqueness, individuality and the cause of the people are at stake or are to be given up. Women face multiple forms of oppression and marginalization in their respective situations. These issues need to be recognized, acknowledged and supported, even if some of them might be directed against one's own background. Feminist theology is not a monolith enterprise. It is the collective expression of the multiple experience of women's lives in which the hidden power of God can be discovered in their struggle. Arundhati Roy articulates this sentiment in a creative way as the experience of raw power: 'This alliance is what gives the movement its raw power, its intellectual rigor and its phenomenal tenacity...

[W]e were not just fighting against a dam. We were fighting for a philosophy. For a world view' (Roy 2001: 49).

Women's unity is founded in such a search for clarity in their diverse experiences of oppression and exploitation, a search for a worldview that recognizes the diversity of women's experiences in different contexts while yet arriving at a level of unity. It allows the seed to flourish in the native soil of people's cultures, in our religions and in our lives. This is indeed a great challenge for the Christian community, particularly for the official Church. As an Indian woman I claim this plurality as the wellspring of my theological quest in my situation. Living next to fellow beings who live and profess different faiths and convictions is indeed both challenging and enriching. My theological perspectives are shaped by the way human life, in particular women's life, is molded in the reality of our existence.

Women as the Bearers of Revelation and Liberation

God's revelation is to be found in the context of women's lives. It is God addressing women as persons who are precious, who are dignified, who are respected, who are desired, who are exploited, who are marginalized, who are violated, who are discriminated on the basis of race and/or caste, and as persons whose rights are denied. This *Anubhava*, or experience, is the ground from which Indian women grasp and articulate their experience of God's revelation. Therefore, revelation takes place not only within formal Church circles where biblical revelation is given great importance. In our context, revelation takes place in the living reality of the struggle for survival as well as transformation. Every moment of every day is marked by signs of God's coming into the lives of women; women bear the creative and procreative potential of God in their bodies and contribute to it in their shared lives. Yet woman's body bears the scars of suffering and struggle, it bears the pain of giving birth, it bears the uncontrollable outbreak of violence of men who misuse women as the scapegoat for their suppressed emotions of anger, frustration, failure and fear. Woman's body also bears the power of self-determination, of facing the challenge of life and of creative transformation in order to bring greater justice and equality to future generations.

It is in this context that I want to explore the fact that woman's body is the medium of God's revelation, irrespective of her religion, caste or race. Her body is the language of God. It speaks of the power within and the power without. This realization dawned on me when I was confronted by the attitude of a chauvinistic man who claimed that the power of yoga can only be felt by men and that women are not eligible by birth to attain the experience of such bliss. It was hard for me to recognize any truth in this assertion. If there is a God or a transcendent being worthy of the name, how could such a being be partial by granting favors to some and leaving the rest empty? It was abundantly clear that this is the way patriarchy solidifies its position. In all patriarchal religions, partial truths are put forward in the name of God. Women's position of subordination has been reinforced by this control. Patriarchy has been nurtured and supported by such religions.

On the contrary, the experience of yoga gave me energy. My mind, body and spirit found another journey in life, the journey to my inner core, a journey that made me get in touch with my inner self. It enabled me to accept life as a gift with its successes and failures. It made me experience wholeness and wellbeing. It led me to fight situations of injustice in silence, to resist in a non-violent manner. It led me to understand and endure that I am not going to solve all the problems. It raised a consciousness in me to claim the heritage of my ancestors and share in their wisdom and fountain of intuitive knowledge. Learning to silence the mind, moving from thoughts to knowing the origin of thoughts and becoming aware of the feelings that enable me to grow, as well as those that contribute to the dehumanization of my existence; all of these were a source of great enrichment for me. I was able to see the reality of myself with all its limitations as well as its immense possibilities. This body is the medium of God's eternal revelation in the context of the now. And when many bodies of women gather together they become the force for change and transformation. The sheer number of women gathering to stand up for the cause of righteousness itself is the sign of God's powerful presence in their midst.

When women in villages and slums experience similar realities and express similar sentiments it confirms the fact that God's revelation to women need not come only through men (patriarchal men). Women's empowering action is the concrete manifestation of God's action in history. Thus, feminist theology derives its roots from such a living reality, the medium of God's revelation and liberation. Theology has to do with faith; it is critical reflection on faith and life in the light of faith. The first step then is decolonizing theology.

Understanding Biblical Revelation from the Indian Context

The Bible is the book in which the redemptive action of God in history is to be discovered. God is redeeming women from the fear of male aristocracy and domination in the story of Pharaoh and the three women—Miriam, her mother and Pharaoh's daughter, who were involved in caring for the child Moses. Ruth freed herself from patriarchal injunctions and made the independent decision to remain with her mother-in-law.

I similarly feel the power of God animating and motivating us to move forward with courage to face the struggles against patriarchy, which manifests itself today in the form of economic boom and women's doom. Modern globalization has led politicians and the economically powerful to the summit of profit maximization through competition as well as through submission to the dictates of the most powerful nations. In the case of the protests against huge dams it has been the poor under the leadership of Medha Patkar and Arundhati Roy who have risen up against the most powerful multi-national corporations and supreme court verdicts. Of course, it is the common masses who have given strength and vigor to the movement. In such protest situations God's revelation takes place in a tangible manner in these women who have been fearless even in opposing government decrees in their unending struggle for life. The movement has gained popularity throughout the world because of its great courage even in the face of great opposition and difficulties. The texts of many lives are written in these experiences and the Bible must be read from the perspective of such experiences. In this context it becomes important to build solidarity with the peoples of exploited economies and with women from the First World. What would be the hermeneutics which inspires this resistance? How could women raise their voice of protest in the face of such exploitation? It is through the solidarity of action that this question can be answered.

Claiming Our Quest for Oneness in the Midst of Division

Standing on a platform based on diversity, the challenge is to look ahead into the future with optimism and hope. When Two-Thirds World women engage in theological endeavors it is inevitable that they need to grapple with the multiple realities of the divisions imposed upon them. Women have been divided on the basis of caste, religion, language, race and gender. Their choices have been limited even before they have been aware of their common humanity. Therefore women need to interpret their experi-ence of colonization and suppression so as to bring to one category all the moments of exploitation, be they from indigenous dominators or colonial masters. The expansionist mentality of Europe and America needs to be recalled, as does the way Western theology molded itself to the process of legitimizing the power of the colonial masters. Women's rights, in this paradigm, did not count as human rights.

It is in this light that we need to understand the experience of racism and its impact on women's lives. We have much to learn from our sisters from the different continents, particularly those who have their roots in color. Theology ought to articulate the manifold experiences of discrimination, subordination and marginalization. Could we articulate a hermeneutics of 'color' and a hermeneutics of 'caste and untouchability'?

Elizabeth Schüssler Fiorenza affirms:

> Consequently, a critical interpretation for liberation does not commence by beginning with the text and by placing the bible at the center of its attention. Rather it begins with a reflection on one's own experience and sociopolitical religious location. For such a reflection it utilizes a critical systemic analysis of those kyriarchal oppressive structures which shape our lives and which are inscribed in biblical texts and interpretations. When reading biblical texts, I have consistently argued, a critical feminist perspec-tive must focus on those wo/men who struggle at the bottom of the kyriarchal pyramid of domination and exploitation... Hence a feminist critical interpretation for liberation insists on the hermeneutical priority of feminist struggles in the process of interpretation. It does so not only in order to be able to disentangle the ideological (religious-theologial) prac-tices and functions of biblical texts for inculcating and legitimating the kyriarchal order but also in order to identify their potential for fostering justice and liberation. Biblical readings that do not prioritize wo/men's struggles against multiplicative oppressions but privilege the biblical text itself or malestream frameworks of interpretation cannot but be either recu-perative or deconstructive. (Schüssler Fiorenza 1998: 77-78)

In this affirmation Schüssler Fiorenza envisions a new space of conscious-ness for women, a consciousness of the situation as well as a process of struggle for dignity, authority and self-respect. She identifies the concept of 'struggle' as 'a key interpretative metaphor' for 'such a critical feminist approach' and locates the sites of this struggle—as I understand her—in the realms of striving for survival, biblical interpretation, the authority of scripture, language and theory (cf. Schüssler Fiorenza 1998: 80-88).

Identifying these sites of struggle holds the key for feminist hermeneutics. It makes it possible to look at one's situation with a feeling of solidarity with a common cause. Women are no longer isolated individuals but the network of human/woman concern.

Being Evangelized by Indigenous Wisdom

Religions other than Christianity have a very important dimension to offer to our understanding of God. In India, God-talk can have credibility only when the giver and the receiver are in a mutual relationship of recognition and respect. There can be no dialogue in a position of either superiority or of inferiority. We must be willing to hold our beliefs in abeyance for a while in order to listen to the inspirational values of other religions. They, too, hold the seeds of God's word and have the capacity to lead people towards the fullness of life. Therefore it is of great importance that persons are recognized and acknowledged and respected. This is the lesson Christian women learn from the incarnation.

In our traditional practice of Christianity we were taught that other religions are from the devil and we should shun every acceptance or recognition of them in any way because of their pagan origins. Today there is a much more tolerant attitude and an effort to build up positive feelings in order to take in the values embedded in these religions. Raimondo Panikkar gives some very interesting examples of recognizing our common roots and their great diversity. He compares different religions to the colors of the rainbow. Each color is a reflection of different religions. They help us recognize the unique dimension of the divine from different angles. There is no question of superiority or inferiority. All of them reveal in a special way something that is not to be found in other religions. In this sense we have much to learn from the wisdom of popular religions which have not yet been codified and still remain as oral traditions (cf. the literature by Raimondo Panikkar: 1978; 1979; 1981; 1995).

For example, the Urali tribals of South India share the practice of reconciliation. Anyone who has been wronged calls for a meeting of the village. With a minimum of ten members and the tribal headman the discussion can begin. Both parties are given the chance to explain their position. Arguments are allowed until the village is convinced that a wrong has been committed and by whom. Then the leader of the village imposes a fine in accordance with the gravity of the crime. After this the entire group that was present for the discussion has to be given a festive meal by the offender as a meal of reconciliation, fellowship and friendship. Sometimes such a process goes on until early in the morning of the next day. Participating in such a function was a great eye opener for me. The Urali's sense of community and communion with one another, their way of safeguarding the respect and dignity of each person as well as their acceptance of each other in spite of faults touched me deeply. We Indians have much to learn from our native people, their values and convictions of being related to each other in a close-knit fashion.

Religions can also be compared to different streams that merge into the same ocean. The goals of all religions have certain similarities. All of them try to give answers to our present-day ills and try to explain the meaning of pain, failure, salvation and the like. There is a search for ultimate meaning which is found in the merging of all religions.

Raimondo Panikkar also affirms that the experience of God is not the monopoly of any particular culture. It is like a lamp lit on a mountain top. Many persons undertake a journey in the direction of the light; their speed may differ and their paths may be very different, but their directions are clearly set towards the same light.

Feminist consciousness of the divine is rooted in the above conviction that no one can make a categorical or complete claim over the experience of God. All are searching and are discovering the truth for themselves. So also are women in search of the authentic experience of God. This experience is not just mysticism or contemplation alone. It is also the living struggle of women for freedom and liberation from oppressive forms of socio-cultural living. In this sense the 'site of struggle' suggested by Elisabeth Schüssler Fiorenza is the contextual reality and the hermeneutic principle of women in the Indian context. It is an experience of struggle for: (1) self-understanding; (2) analyzing the context; (3) affirming women's personal and social space; (4) asserting their rights as human rights; (5) empowering action towards transformation; (6) resisting forms of violence; (7) contributing to the building up of society in economic, social, political and cultural spheres.

In this experience the Bible will be a store-house and a fountain of wisdom. It will be rediscovered as the voice of the marginalized, particularly of women who are yearning for liberation.

BIBLIOGRAPHY

Panikkar, Raimundo
    1978   *The Intrareligious Dialogue* (New York: Paulist Press).
    1979   *Myth, Faith and Hermeneutics* (New York: Paulist Press).
    1981   *The Unknown Christ of Hinduism* (London: Darton, Longman & Todd).
    1995   *Invisible Harmony* (Minneapolis: Fortress Press, 2nd edn).
Roy, Arundhati
    2001   *Power Politics* (Kotayam, Kerala/India: D.C. Books).
Schüssler Fiorenza, Elisabeth
    1998   *Sharing her Word: Feminist Biblical Interpretation in Context* (Boston: Beacon Press).

THE BIBLICAL HERMENEUTICS OF LIBERATION FROM THE PERSPECTIVE OF ASIAN CHRISTIAN WOMEN: RECOVERING THE LIBERATION-TRADITION OF EARLY CHRISTIANITY IN KOREA

Kyung Sook Lee

During the symposium at Monte Verità it became clear to me that there is no single right way of interpreting the Bible. The Bible should be interpreted from each reader's unique context and individual viewpoint. I was impressed and shocked by this realization while at the same time very excited to hear a variety of voices from all the continents of the world. It was a good opportunity for me to hear the voices of women from Latin America, Eastern Europe, North America, Africa and Asia. The situations of these women are so different; their ways of reading the Bible are just as diverse.

What does it mean for me as an Asian biblical scholar to read the Bible? How can I read and interpret the Bible from the perspective of Asian women, especially from the context of poor, suffering, struggling Asian women? What is the context of Asian Christian women? In order to consider my own context as a Korean woman I must reflect briefly on the early history of our Church.

The Christian Church in Korea

In many countries in Asia the Christian gospel came as part of Western colonization and as a symbol of modernization. The Bible was regarded both as Western thought and colonial exploitation. Christianity was depicted as the superior religion; many intellectuals became Christians in part through their own choice and in part because of the strong influence of the missionaries. Asian people have very mixed feelings about Christianity. On the one hand, they respect the modernization that Christianity represents, while, on the other hand, they are troubled by Christianity because it conflicts with their own culture in many respects. Although Christianity was not brought to Korea primarily by Western colonizers but by Koreans themselves, our situation was nevertheless very similar to that of other Asian countries. The Bible was brought to Korea by a progressive young generation that desired social and cultural change. Korea had had a very strict feudal social system under the Chosun Dynasty (1396–1910), but the Japanese invasion and the interference of other foreign powers that started in the 1880s changed the situation. The feudal structure began to collapse as the new winds of modernization came to Korea, the 'Land of the Morning Calm'.

Until the dawn of modernization, Korean women were subject to harsh and heavy oppression. They were the oppressed (*minjung*) among the oppressed (*minjung*). They experienced at least a threefold oppression. They were oppressed, first, under Japanese colonialism; second, under the patriarchal social structure; and third, under the Confucian family structure. Women's inferiority to men was one of the principles of Korean ethics: they had no proper name, no right to receive education and thus no means to claim their humanity or to enjoy an independent life. Because of Christianity they began to believe that men and women were equal, at least before God. Men and women attended Christian worship and sang gospel songs together in church. It was through Christian baptism that Korean women received their own names. Christian baptism meant for Korean women liberation from their oppression. One baptized woman, Sadie Kim, said, 'The day I was baptized was the happiest day in my life. We, Chosun women, had lived under the oppression of men. For years we did not have a life of our own. Without the Christian gospel, Korean women's status could not have improved like this' (Lee 1997: 26). Baptism was the event through which Korean women were released from the bondage of oppression. Gender equality, women's education and the opportunity for women to remarry were offered at last by Christianity.

Morevoer, the period of the early development of Christianity in Korea coincided with the period of national duress caused by Japanese colonial rule. Korean Christian women had to respond also to the reality of the Japanese occupation. They had to participate in the reality of the national conflict and the anti-Japanese independence movement that strove to overthrow colonial domination. As a result, the traditions of women's liberation and women's participation in the national movement also were established as Christianity was introduced in Korea. Christians were a minority at the time, less than one per cent of the Korean population. But the Korean Christian women who experienced liberation attempted to spread their experiences in Korean society by organizing Christian women's groups and pursuing activities for the mission of the gospel and the women's enlightenment movement. 'Biblewomen' distributed the Bible to the Korean public. The Bible was not only regarded as a spiritual and religious book but also as a basic textbook for Koreans in the struggle against illiteracy and ignorance. In this respect, early Korean Christian women experienced firsthand the essence of the gospel.

However, the situation has changed totally since those times. With the industrialization of Korean society, the modern character of Christianity has contributed to the very rapid growth of the Korean Church since 1960. Unfortunately, the positive traditions linked with Christianity such as women's liberation and women's participation in social issues have almost completely disappeared along with the rapid growth of the Church. The percentage of Christians in the Korean population has risen higher and higher and is now up to 20-25 per cent, but their actual contribution to women's liberation and social change is very low. The Korean Churches have been strongly influenced by the Korean traditional religions, such as Shamanism, Buddhism and Confucianism. After having established their own power and financial basis, the Korean Churches have started to oppress women just like the other religions. Women are treated as a secondary, subsidiary class; they have been forced to be silent and obedient in support of the male leaders in the Church. They have been forced to sacrifice their individuality, their achievements and even their emotions in order to comply with others.

In this context the Bible was always used as a tool of oppression in Korea. Patriarchy is the dominant system in the Church. Women have become the victims of the Church. We are told that Jesus had to die for our sins and that we Christians should also die for others. Women in the Church are taught to sacrifice themselves until death for family, factory, society and the Church. Jesus' atoning death has been misused and misunderstood. The Church oppresses and exploits women in the Church in the name of the Bible. Here we need the 'hermeneutics of suspicion' or the 'hermeneutics of rejection' and the 'hermeneutics of remembrance'. In Korea, most women in the Church would like to distance themselves from such hermeneutical methods because they fear losing their identity as Christians should they criticize the Bible and the male Church leaders. They have been trained to be silent and obedient and are controlled by the male Church leaders. This 'brain-washing program' in the Church has led them astray in their own social lives. Sometimes they are even very aggressive in victimizing other women and protecting their male Church leaders. These women must be liberated from their prejudices, otherwise there can be no changes in the patriarchal system that has established itself in our Church and society.

Suggestions for Change in the Korean Church

There are small groups of women in the Korean Church who have been trying to focus on this issue. They have recognized that the Bible can have many different voices. The problem is to decide which voice to listen to. We have learned a lot from Western feminist theologians about this problem, but there is a gulf between the Western context and the Korean context. We have no proper model to follow and so we have to go forward on our own. Recognizing that the gospel has come down to us through the framework, rituals and symbols of the Jewish and Greco-Roman cultures and later through European and American cultures, we do not need to accept those Western elements as intrinsic to Christianity or our own beliefs. We must shed the imperialistic and colonial clothes that have been put on the Bible by Western interpretation. We must try to define our own identity and develop our own methodology of reading the Bible in order to use it as an instrument of liberation in Asian society. For example, we should examine the curricula of schools and theological seminaries in Asia, which are quite different from those in Europe and America. If we merely imitate the curricula of Western theological seminaries without any criticism, then the gap between theological seminaries and local churches will only widen; the knowledge gained in the seminaries will be of little assistance in the work of ministry.

I would like to suggest several areas that we should consider in order to achieve this. First, Asians must remember the early Christian tradition of liberating women and the poor. We should be clear about the reasons why we became Christians. Why did we accept Christianity as our religion? Many Korean women became Christian because Christianity had the power to liberate from the oppression of colonialism, sexism, racism and Western economic exploitation. To overcome these bonds Asians converted to Christianity and began to raise their own voices and fight against the colonizers and dictators. We must return to this liberation-tradition of our early Church. We need to listen to the voice of the voiceless, the poor, the lower classes and women. Bible-reading in marginalized communities has offered valuable insights in the interpretation of the social biography of the oppressed in the Bible. It is biblical hermeneutics from a socio-political perspective. Asians calls this '*minjung* theology' (Suh 1991) or 'doing theology'. At the present stage we Asians need to claim a postcolonial hermeneutics that includes a strong emphasis on the liberation of women.

Second, the context of Asia is not only socio-political but also cultural and religious. Asians have their own classics and literary tradition, a very unique, profound and precious tradition. Unfortunately, Asians in my generation have not had enough chance to learn our own culture. We had to learn English and Western culture and the Western methodology of reading the Bible before we began to learn about and appreciate our own culture. Our culture and heritage have the resources and treasures for the development of women's liberation; the traditional methodology for interpreting our classics and customs could help us to interpret the Bible today. For example, although Confucianism was transplanted from China into Korea and then transformed into a most inhumane and sexist norm that has served as the foundation for a severe oppression of women, we also know that Confucianism can be interpreted to support the liberation of women. It is a matter of hermeneutics: context comes first, then the text. It is fortuitous for us that we are living in a multi-religious society, because we can learn from the history of other religions and learn how to interpret the Bible in order to promote the liberation of women and the oppressed. The comparative studies of Christianity and other religions can enlarge our perspectives, showing that there are no neutral hermeneutics in reading religious texts like the Bible. Christianity itself is not fixed but flows hand in hand with changing interpretations of the Bible. We therefore must learn our classics and traditions very carefully. Given its abundant resources and treasures, Asia can contribute a great deal to Christianity. We need to be more generous. Let us look at another example. If we consider the Bible as just one of many resources available to experience spiritual transcendence, then we can borrow the concepts of transcendence from the 'nirvana' or 'anubhavam' of other religions. Personal piety and spiritual exercise in these religions can help us to understand Christian spirituality. We can enrich our hermeneutic approaches by integrating our Asian cultures into the hermeneutic struggles. We need hermeneutics of inclusion or hermeneutics of diversity in a non-biblical world of postcolonialism and of post-patriarchalism (Chung 1996). We can use 'dialogical imagination' as a new approach to biblical interpretation (Kwok 1997: 141).

Third, there should be many levels of hermeneutics in Asia. According to our knowledge and preferences we could develop many ways of interpreting the Bible. Many Asian scholars stress the primacy of oral transmission in the history of Asian religions. For them it is sufficient just to read the Bible, to recite, to memorize, to chant and to perform the Bible. It can be a good method to experience the mystery of the Bible (Park 1997: 131). It is also important for them to have a so-called 'story-telling' method (Kwok 1997: 149). But this would not be sufficient for others. They want to have a more analytical and critical method of reading. In this sense, I do not agree with the opinion that hermeneutics in Asia should not be academic. I think that if we give up being academic it is actually another way of limiting ourselves. For example, we can learn so much from the historical-critical method. We limit ourselves if we ignore it entirely. Of course, the academic method has its own limitations and we should not restrict ourselves to only this method, but it can still be very useful for explaining certain readings of the Bible, such as multi-faith situations. We need to develop many new ways of interpreting the Bible, but we do not need to reject all scholarly methodology. We need a hermeneutics of 'openness'.

Conclusion

The situation of Christian women in Asia is very diverse. It is not possible to make a generalization about the situation of all Asian Christian women, but I do hope that we can develop the proper hermeneutical tools for the liberation of Asian women. Hoping that, several questions come to mind:

1. Most Asian Christian women live in multi-religious societies in which they are always a minority. They are continually confronted by identity problems and fear that the use of the hermeneutics of suspicion or inclusion will lead to the loss of their identity. How can we approach them? How can we make our hermeneutic tools available to and popular among our Christian women?

2. There are many Christian women in Asia with much energy and power. However, their power and energy are often limited to caring for their own families or kitchen service in their churches. How can we change this? How can we awaken their interest in political and social issues like women's liberation, environmental problems and economic insecurity? If we are bridge-builders linking Christianity to the wider society, to what extent should

we be involved in economic and political issues? The globalization process and the new economy are particularly dangerous for poor women in Asia.

We have a very beautiful tradition of early Christianity in Korea. We should remember it and return to this spirit. Recovering this early Christian spirit is our aim and duty.

BIBLIOGRAPHY

Chung, Hyun Kyung
    1996   'Christian Witness amidst Asian Pluralism and the Search for Spirituality from an Asian Feminist Perspective', *Ewha Journal of Feminist Theology* 1: 27-37.
Kwok, Pui-lan
    1997   'Discovering the Bible in the Non-Biblical World', *Ewha Journal of Feminist Theology* 2: 141-58. (First published in *Semeia* 47 [1989]: 25-42.)
Lee, Duk-joo
    1997   'An Understanding of Early Korean Christian Women's History', *Ewha Journal of Feminist Theology* 2: 11-50.
Park, Kyung Mi
    1997   'A Response to "Bread/Rice of Wisdom: Biblical Interpretation for Liberation" by Prof. Elisabeth Schüssler Fiorenza', *Ewha Journal of Feminist Theology* 2: 131-32.
Suh, David Kwang-sun
    1991   *The Korean Minjung in Christ: The Christian Conference of Asia* (Hong Kong: Glang Vieng).

Yak-Hwee Tan

The international symposium on feminist exegesis and the hermeneutics of liberation held at Monte Verità in Ascona, Switzerland, in July 2000 united a number of feminist biblical scholars and theologians from around the world in order to discuss and reflect on the different ways in which one can approach biblical texts with a focus on liberation. The key speakers at the symposium presented a variety of challenging methods and strategies that can be used to read biblical text with a liberative purpose in mind. I was particularly struck by the fact that these speakers, as many stated themselves, are greatly influenced by their social location in their encounters with biblical texts. For this reason I would like to address the question of social location and its importance for feminist biblical interpretation and the hermeneutics of liberation, in particular with reference to Musa W. Dube's presentation, 'Jumping the Fire with Judith: Postcolonial Feminist Hermeneutics of Liberation'.[1] In so doing I will contend that postcolonial feminist hermeneutics is just one of many possible approaches that empowers biblical scholars to engage in a hermeneutics of liberation. This ultimately poses a great challenge to Asian women engaged in biblical studies and theology.

Musa W. Dube began her presentation with the story of *Utentelezand-lane*, a beautiful princess who was pushed into a blazing fire by girls from her village who were envious of her status as well as her beauty. The beautiful princess was killed and buried in the forest. However, she told her story by singing it from her grave and eventually the village girls were arrested. On the basis of the story of the beautiful princess and the village girls, Musa W. Dube advocates that postcolonial feminist hermeneutics of liberation is 'a search for a relationship of liberating interdependence

---

1. Cf. Musa W. Dube's contribution to the present volume.

between genders, races, nations, countries, cultures, economies and political establishments—at national and international levels'.[2] She argues that women from the Two-Thirds World encounter oppression not only in patriarchal structures but also in colonial structures. Postcolonial feminist hermeneutics thus seeks to unravel the relationship between patriarchy and imperialism, establish the effects upon women and define possible forms of resistance. To further support her argument, Musa W. Dube positions herself as a reader who is informed by her social location, by her colonial/ postcolonial experience. In this respect I could resonate with Musa W. Dube, likewise being conditioned by a colonial/postcolonial experience and hence my recourse to the hermeneutical lens of postcolonial criticism.

My Social Location

I view myself as a real flesh-and-blood reader who is positioned and conditioned by my colonial/postcolonial experience. Singapore's modern history has its roots in the British colonialism of the nineteenth and twentieth centuries.[3] Even though Singapore has achieved political independence from the British,[4] it, like its Asian neighbors, continues to experience a subtle form of colonization, namely, globalization in the guise of economic and technological development.[5] Unlike its neighboring countries, whose exports are agriculture-based and/or industry-based, Singapore has few natural resources. Seventy per cent of the goods exported from Singapore

---

2. Cf. Musa W. Dube's contribution in this book.

3. In the early decades of the nineteenth century, the struggle for the control of trade in the East Indies between the Dutch East India Company and the British East India Company led these two empires to search for a port of trade in the East. The Dutch took control of Batavia (present-day Djakarta); the British acquired Temasek (present-day Singapore) through a treaty with the local chieftains in 1819. Singapore became a flourishing port and attracted overseas workers, from India and China, for example, who brought their culture(s) and religion(s) with them. For a detailed study of the history of Singapore, see Turnball 1977; Chew and Lee (eds.) 1991.

4. In 1959 the British granted Singapore a degree of independence but maintained control of the defense forces and foreign policy. Singapore became a sovereign nation in 1965, two years later as part of an independent Malaysia.

5. Radelet and Sachs 1997. Radelet and Sachs give a brief discussion on the growth of Asia's economy and their optimistic view of Asia's re-emergence in the world economy in the light of the money crisis in Asia. For a thorough discussion of the factors for the robust growth of the Asian–Pacific economies over the last three decades and their future economic trends, see Das 1996.

are produced by multinational corporations, thus continuing the nation's dependence on foreign-owned companies. Singapore's economy is inter-dependent with the world economic system.[6] Colonialism still exists, but in an elusive form. It is more appropriate to speak of imperialism. Unlike colonialism, 'the implanting of settlements on distant territory', imperialism connotes a broader meaning, 'the practice, the theory, and the attitudes of a dominating metropolitan center ruling a distant territory' (Said 1993: 9). In other words, even though colonialism has largely ended, imperialism lingers in the 'general cultural sphere as well as in specific political, ideological, economic, and social practices' (Said 1993: 8). Globalization and imperialism go hand in hand. The corrosive effects of Western influence on Singaporeans that have come with economic modernization pose a threat to the traditional values of the people. The result is the people's awakening to their cultural and religious identity as a rejoinder against modernization, which is often associated with Westernization. Christianity, which is seen as a 'core element of "Western civilization"' (Brouwer, Gifford and Rose 1996: 2), is not excluded. Ironically, the modernization and economic growth on which political and social stability are based have also enabled societies such as the one in Singapore to 'have confidence in their heritage and to become culturally assertive' (Huntington 1996: 33), rejecting and challenging any imperialism that contradicts Asian values. I find the hermeneutical lens of postcolonial criticism particularly attractive and challenging in view of such political and socio-economic contexts, which brings me to the issue of social location.

Social Location: Postcolonial Feminist Hermeneutics

Is there only one approach to doing feminist biblical interpretation and the hermeneutics of liberation? My answer is 'No'. The assertion that the biblical texts can be interpreted in only one manner and that their meaning is univocal overlooks the fact that real flesh-and-blood readers are behind these biblical interpretations. In his article 'Cultural Studies and Contemporary Biblical Criticism: Ideological Criticism as Mode of Discourse',

---

6. Neher 1994: 143: Singapore is primarily an 'urban entrepot with virtually no agricultural base, Singapore stands alone, bereft of the resources and land of its neighbors', whose populations and land space are greater and larger. See also Peebles and Wilson 1996 for a study of the current economic structure of Singapore and its important institutions and their comparisons with other economies before its independence (from Malaysia) in 1965.

Fernando F. Segovia contends that cultural studies have focused the attention upon the real readers who can no longer be 'seen as…neutral or impartial but as inextricably positioned and engaged within their own different and complex social locations' (Segovia 2000: 47). Various factors such as sexual orientation, socio-economic and socio-political class, socio-educational and intellectual moorings and ideological stance constitute the identity of the real readers. In other words, the real readers are no longer viewed as disinterested readers but as informed by their contexts and perspectives when they examine and interpret the biblical texts. A critical analysis of the biblical texts and their interpretation thus also should include an analysis of the readers of these texts and their readings, of their presence in 'texts'. The focus upon real readers also suggests that the dichotomy between readers who are academic or ecclesiastical professionals and those who are ordinary members of Christian communities or lay people—that is, between readers who are highly informed and those who are not—is minimal. The biblical critic, though highly trained, is no longer placed in a privileged position. The average readers from Christian communities are also important and authentic. The reading strategies and interpretations of critics and average readers alike are shaped by their social locations. As aptly put by Segovia, 'the open admission of contextualization and perspective does serve, in the end, to relativize and hence subvert the highly privileged education and position of the critic' (Segovia 2000: 47-48). As such, it paves the way for different and multiple ways of doing biblical hermeneutics, one of which is postcolonial feminist biblical hermeneutics.

Postcolonial feminist hermeneutics, however, do not address solely the oppressive nature of patriarchy but, more importantly, seek to highlight the all-embracing, oppressive nature of imperialism, which encompasses patriarchy. In short, its emphasis is upon the 'imperialist patriarchy' that has divided the liberation practices of First World feminist intellectual hermeneutics and Two-Thirds World hermeneutics. Musa W. Dube clarifies the relationship of patriarchy and imperialism/colonialism; she does not equate patriarchy with imperialism/colonialism but sees them as overlapping.[7] Patriarchal systems are primarily male-centered institutions that marginalize women, men of lower socio-economic class, homosexual orientation or the young. On the other hand, imperialism is an overarching system in which a foreign, aggressive nation imposes its political, economic

---

7.   Again, cf. Musa W. Dube's contribution to the present volume.

and cultural system upon another nation. Postcolonial feminist herme-neutics have to contend with these dual systems. A brief study of the rela-tionship between postcolonialism and feminism will help to elucidate postcolonial feminist hermeneutics of liberation.

In her discussion of postcolonialism and feminism, Leela Gandhi high-lights areas of controversy which cause a division between feminism and postcolonialism. The first and most significant controversy is with regard to the dubious figure of the 'Third World woman'. The 'Third World woman' is seen as the victim *par excellence*—'the forgotten casualty of both imperial ideology, and native and foreign patriarchies' (Gandhi 1998: 83). However, the term 'Third World' needs some clarification. It suggests the binomial opposites of 'self' and 'other', whereby the 'other' is seen as a 'minor' zone of non-culture and underdevelopment. Gayatri Chakravorty Spivak suggests that the 'Third World woman' has been displaced to the margin in order to serve the center: 'When a cultural identity is thrust upon one because the center wants an identifiable margin, claims for marginality assure validation from the center' (Spivak 1993: 55).[8] As such, the cate-gory 'Third World woman' is colonialist, first, 'because its ethnocentric myopic disregards the enormous material and historical differences be-tween "real" third-world women; and second, because the composite "Othering" of the "third-world woman" becomes a self-consolidating pro-ject for Western feminism' (Gandhi 1998: 85). The colonialist stance is reinforced when the 'Third World woman' or 'native woman' is silenced and spoken for by academic liberalism.[9] Gayatri Chakravorty Spivak chal-lenges such representational systems. In her essay, 'Can the Subaltern Speak?', Spivak argues that the 'gendered subaltern' disappears because we never hear her speak about herself (Spivak 1988). Moreover, the femi-nist who has knowledge of the 'other' also has the power to represent the 'other'; she thus reveals herself to be a 'feminist imperialist'.

The relationship between feminism and postcolonialism shows that postcolonial feminist hermeneutics of liberation must take into considera-tion both issues of patriarchy and imperialism as well as how they affect

---

8.   See also Minh-ha 1989: 86. Similarly, Minh-ha asserts that the 'Third World Women Issue' only serves to advertise the uniqueness of the mediating First World woman.

9.   See Kristeva 1977. In her book, Kristeva, a French feminist, records her obser-vations of the crowds of silent Chinese women at Huxian Square and depicts them in a discourse based on these observations. These women are never heard in their own voices but rather as the subjects of Kristeva's investigation, who speaks in their place.

gender oppression of women. Postcolonial feminist hermeneutics of liberation seeks to unravel such imperialist underpinnings as well as engaging in oppositional and/or resistant readings, thereby reshaping the predominant readings of these texts. Biblical scholars (both from the First World and the Two-Thirds World) are thus confronted with the task of decolonizing readers by exposing their reading and exegetical practices to be underlain and corrupted with colonial attitudes (see Dube 1996).

In the conclusion to her paper, Musa W. Dube outlines her concerns, assumptions, proposals and practices in an attempt to articulate post-colonial feminist hermeneutics of liberation. She cautions us to be critical in our reading practices, that is, to recognize that biblical texts have been used to justify and advance patriarchy and imperialism, as well as to suggest the need for decolonization.[10] The reader who does not do so is suspected of collaborating in the subjugation of the 'other', culturally, economically and politically. According to my reading of Musa W. Dube's paper, the 'self' refers to the 'First World' whereas the 'other' refers to the 'Two-Thirds World'. However, these binomial opposites are not static; within the 'Two-Thirds World' are many other binomial opposites and these opposites are informed and conditioned by their social location(s). Let me illustrate this taking the Asian context as an example.

Feminist Biblical Interpretation: An Asian Woman's Perspective

Asia is a continent of paradoxes and plurality. It is a continent marked by a great disparity between the rich and the poor. It is a continent where the major world religions are found. It is a continent where some nations have been colonized (by powers such as Britain and France) while others have acted as colonizers. In light of these pluralities and complexities, the question as to how one does an Asian biblical feminist hermeneutics of liberation poses a great challenge. To insist that there is only one way of reading the biblical texts and that its meaning is univocal is colonialist; the question of the social location of real flesh-and-blood readers is an important determining factor. As much as my colonial/postcolonial experience draws me to Musa W. Dube's thoughts in her article on postcolonial feminist hermeneutics of liberation, other aspects of my social location have informed and conditioned my reading practices in light of Asian women's biblical hermeneutics.

---

10. Cf. Musa W. Dube's contribution in this book.

I am an Asian woman, but I am also a first-generation Chinese Christian who was raised in the Confucian tradition and received my primary and secondary education in a Presbyterian mission institution. I am an ordained minister in the Presbyterian Church in Singapore and have lived all my life in Singapore, a country that has enjoyed recent economic success. I am one of a privileged, elite minority of Asian women who have had the opportunity of a Western academic education. To insist that my reading of the biblical text is univocal would put me in the status of an 'imperialist feminist'. And I certainly would not suggest that my interpretation of the biblical text is a normative interpretation for Asian women; my education is an exception and the dimensions of my experience are very different from those of women from India, Pakistan and even the People's Republic of China. The importance of the *particular* context and perspective of Asian women with respect to biblical hermeneutics raises the question: How does one do a hermeneutics of liberation?

I see two possibilities. First, Asian women must rejoice and celebrate the many dimensions, whether political, socio-economic, religious or cultural, of their human existence that influence their approach to the biblical texts. And we must cherish and value other Asian women's perspectives and their inherent differences. In so doing, one affirms one's own human existence as well as a celebration of the multiple approaches of doing biblical studies and theology. Consequently, I envision a community of Asian women that is 'inclusive', including women from academia, the ecclesiastical tradition and communitarian-based Churches. The voices of all women will be heard, included and celebrated, and will thereby be liberating for all.

In conclusion, when embarking on the task of a feminist hermeneutics of liberation, one must seriously consider one's social location and personal perspective with respect to the multiplicity and plurality of readings based on the premise that any reading must be liberating for all humanity.

BIBLIOGRAPHY

Brouwer, Steve, Paul Gifford and Susan D. Rose
  1996   *Exporting the American Gospel: Global Christian Fundamentalism* (New York: Routledge).
Chew, Ernest C.T., and Edwin Lee (eds.)
  1991   *A History of Singapore* (Singapore: Oxford University Press).
Das, Dilip K.
  1996   *The Asia–Pacific Economy* (London: Macmillan).

Dube, Musa W.
    1996   'Reading for Decolonization', in L.E. Donaldson (ed.), *Postcolonialism and Scriptural Reading* (Semeia, 75; Atlanta: Scholars Press): 37-60.

Gandhi, Leela
    1998   *Postcolonial Theory: A Critical Introduction* (New York: Columbia University Press).

Huntington, Samuel
    1996   'The West: Unique, Not Universal', *Foreign Affairs* 75/6: 28-37.

Kristeva, Julia
    1977   *About Chinese Women* (trans. Anita Barrows; London: Marion Boyers).

Minh-ha, Trinh T.
    1989   *Woman, Native, Other* (Bloomington: Indiana University).

Neher, Clark D.
    1994   *Southeast Asia in the New International Era: Politics in Asia and the Pacific: Interdisciplinary Perspectives* (Boulder, CO: Westview Press, 2nd edn).

Peebles, Gavin, and Peter Wilson
    1996   *The Singapore Economy* (Cheltenham: Edward Elgar Publishing).

Radelet, Steven, and Jeffrey Sachs
    1997   'Asia's Re-Emergence', *Foreign Affairs* 76/6: 44-59.

Said, Edward W.
    1993   *Culture and Imperialism* (New York: Vintage Books).

Segovia, Fernando F.
    2000   'Cultural Studies and Contemporary Biblical Criticism: Ideological Criticism as Mode of Discourse', in Fernando F. Segovia (ed.), *Decolonizing Biblical Studies: A View from the Margins* (Maryknoll, NY: Orbis Books): 34-52.

Spivak, Gayatri Chakravorty
    1988   'Can the Subaltern Speak?', in Cary Nelson and Lawrence Grossberg (eds.), *Marxism and the Interpretations of Culture* (Basingstoke: Macmillan Education): 271-313.
    1993   *Outside in the Teaching Machine* (New York: Routledge).

Turnball, Constance Mary
    1977   *A History of Singapore 1819–1975* (Kuala Lumpur: Oxford University Press).

JOURNAL FOR THE STUDY OF THE OLD TESTAMENT
SUPPLEMENT SERIES